Exchange Rates under the
East Asian Dollar Standard

Exchange Rates under the East Asian Dollar Standard

Living with Conflicted Virtue

Ronald I. McKinnon

The MIT Press
Cambridge, Massachusetts
London, England

MIT Press books may be purchased at special quantity discounts for business or sales promotional use. For information, please e-mail ⟨special_sales@mitpress.mit.edu⟩ or write to Special Sales Department, The MIT Press, 5 Cambridge Center, Cambridge, MA 02142.

This book was set in Palatino on 3B2 by Asco Typesetters, Hong Kong.
Printed and bound in the United States of America.

Library of Congress Cataloging-in-Publication Data

McKinnon, Ronald I.
Exchange rates under the East Asian dollar standard : living with conflicted virtue /
Ronald I. McKinnon.
    p.   cm.
Includes bibliographical references and index.
ISBN 0-262-13451-9 (hc : alk. paper)
1. Foreign exchange rates—East Asia. 2. Monetary policy—East Asia. I. Title.
HG3976.5.M35   2005
332.4'56'095—dc22   2004057389

10 9 8 7 6 5 4 3 2 1

To my seven beloved granddaughters:
Katy, Aly, Savannah, Alexandra, Charlotte, Emily, and Natalie

Contents

Preface

This book could not have been written without the generous help and support of four younger colleagues, much more technically adept than I: Rishi Goyal of the International Monetary Fund, Kenichi Ohno of the National Graduate Institute of Policy Studies in Tokyo, Huw Pill of the Harvard Business School, and Günther Schnabl of Tübingen University. Each was a co-author and key impetus for one or more chapters, some of which also have been published as stand-alone articles in professional journals. Nevertheless, by splicing with some rewriting all the co-authored pieces together, and then adding my own individual chapters with editorial overviews at the beginning and end of the volume, the result is an integrated book on what I call the East Asian dollar standard.

The introduction shows that there is indeed an exchange rate dilemma involving all the countries of East Asia as the scale and pace of their economic integration has increased dramatically over the past two decades. Because this increasingly integrated community does not have its own money—there is no "Asian euro"—the U.S. dollar plays a somewhat anomalous role as the region's key currency. The peculiar nature of the foreign exchange risk facing both debtor and creditor countries under this East Asian dollar standard helps explain why the region remains so fragile financially.

This book is not about politics, nor is it critical of Asian politicians and their governments. In Japan, for example, politicians have been unfairly blamed for failing to take resolute action to clean up bad loans in the nation's banks, restructure the industrial system, and avoid ongoing deflation by following a sufficiently expansionary domestic monetary policy. Instead, I shall argue that economists—outside commentators on Japan from the United States but also within Japan itself—have failed to understand the foreign exchange origins of Japan's deflation.

Similarly, governments in the smaller East Asian economies are unfairly criticized by the International Monetary Fund and foreign pundits for softly pegging their currencies to the dollar, which, it is alleged, contributed to the great crisis of 1997–1998. Like Japan in the 1980s and 1990s, China in the new millennium is under foreign mercantile pressure—to which it may or may not succumb—to appreciate its currency against the dollar.

This book develops a conceptual framework to show where conventional economic thinking on these important exchange rate and financial issues has gone off the rails. Although highly empirical in analyzing interactions among East Asian economies, it is also about economic ideas—both when they are right, and when they are wrong.

I would like to thank Hong Qiao for her excellent research assistance in helping to put this book together, and Margaret McKinnon for her ever-helpful and painstaking editing. Fellowship support was provided by the Stanford Institute for International Studies, and additional financial support by the Stanford Center for International Development. The staff at the MIT Press, particularly Elizabeth Murry, Ruth Edelglass, and Deborah Cantor-Adams, have been both patient and helpful.

Exchange Rates under the
East Asian Dollar Standard

Introduction: The East Asian Exchange Rate Dilemma

The East Asian economies—China, Hong Kong, Indonesia, Japan, Korea, Malaysia, Philippines, Singapore, Taiwan, and Thailand—are the main empirical focus of this book. All have experienced periods of rapid growth by adapting remarkably fast to modern technologies in manufacturing. From Japan in the 1950s and 1960s to China's remarkable industrial growth from 1980 into the new millennium, rapid increases in exports have been the engine of their economic success. And this foreign trade dynamic is becoming more regional: the East Asian countries now trade as much with each other as they do with the rest of the world.

A decade ago, eminent development economists at the World Bank were so caught up with infectious enthusiasm for the unprecedented pace of technical advance, and for the increases in both physical and human capital in East Asia, that they put together a book called *The East Asian Miracle* (1993). It rapidly became the World Bank's best seller, with widespread sales both to general readers and to students of economic development in many countries throughout the world. Uncontroversially, it lauded the East Asian economies for following sound domestic monetary and fiscal policies, particularly in comparison to Latin American or African economies. Controversially (even then), it praised state-directed industrial policies whereby, the book suggested, astute and well-intentioned governments intervened to guide the flow of credit or foreign exchange into more socially preferred investments, often to promote export expansion.

Subsequently, two remarkable surprises exposed the financial vulnerability of these "miracle" economies beyond what an uncritical reader of the 1993 book would have dared to believe.

The first was the great East Asian crisis of 1997–1998 in countries that had built up high short-term foreign exchange indebtedness.

Starting with Thailand in May 1997 and followed by Indonesia, Korea, Malaysia, and Philippines, Asian countries experienced contagious attacks on their currencies, with deep devaluations, a spike in interest rates, and massive bankruptcies in domestic financial institutions and business enterprises. In the face of such financial trauma, output fell sharply, although since 1998 output in these economies has recovered and has begun to grow once more. But the consequences of governments' leaning on banks to make dubious loans to enterprises, with moral hazard in the banks themselves from accepting too much foreign exchange exposure and other risks, became uncomfortably clear. Not only did these previously debtor economies experience widespread bankruptcies in banks and industrial enterprises, but subsequent research showed that their overall rate of profit had been falling for some years: the seemingly dynamic Korean economy was the most notable example.

The second surprise might more accurately be called a nonevent or "silent spring." Despite Japan's being at the cutting edge of modern technology and being a huge international creditor, its decade-long failure to recover from the bursting of its asset bubbles in equity and land prices in 1990–1991—with ongoing deflation and a zero interest rate liquidity trap—has turned out to be the greatest mystery in modern macroeconomics. Less obviously, the smaller but equally wealthy and technically advanced East Asian creditor economies, such as Hong Kong, Singapore, and Taiwan, are no longer referred to as "tigers" and show slower growth, with signs of at least incipient deflation. Alone among East Asian economies, China's high growth continues unscathed by major macroeconomic or financial difficulties, but even here deflation led by appreciating exchange rates is an ever present threat in the longer term.

In this book I show that these seemingly disparate East Asian macroeconomic surprises were and are linked to foreign exchange risk arising out of the (necessary) use of an outside currency, the U.S. dollar, to denominate cross-country flows of goods and finance. Liquid dollar liabilities threaten debtor countries, and, less obviously, liquid dollar assets threaten creditors. The volatility, both actual and potential, of exchange rates and foreign capital flows affects both creditor and debtor countries adversely. Strangely, in its 1993 "miracle" book, the World Bank did not recognize dollar dominance and how the dollar standard worked in East Asia: the term *dollar standard* was not even mentioned. The details of managing financial risk—in the foreign exchanges, in interest rates, and in credit markets—were omitted. But the devil was, and is, in the financial details of these East Asian traumas. Before going into these details in succeeding chapters, I summarize how the dollar standard operates in East Asia.

1 The East Asian Dollar Standard: An Overview

Before the 1997–1998 crisis, the East Asian economies—except for Japan—informally pegged their currencies to the U.S. dollar (see chapter 1). These soft dollar pegs made these economies vulnerable to fluctuations of the yen against the dollar, and the yen's depreciation from mid-1995 into early 1998 worsened the great East Asian crisis (see chapter 2). To limit future exchange rate misalignments and "hot" money flows, the International Monetary Fund argues, East Asian currencies should float more freely. Alternatively, several authors have proposed increasing the weight of the yen in the currency baskets of the smaller East Asian economies. However, I argue that the East Asian dollar pegs are entirely rational from the perspective of each country, both to facilitate hedging by merchants and banks against exchange rate risk, and to help central banks anchor their domestic price levels.

Central bank behavior supports my position. By 2003 the high-frequency volatility of each country's dollar exchange rate had become not significantly different from its precrisis level, as measured on a day-to-day basis (see chapter 1). For month-to-month and lower-frequency changes in exchange rates, the currencies of the smaller East Asian countries still exhibit more drift against the dollar than they did before the crisis. However, if Japan could narrow the range of variation of the yen/dollar rate, and if China succeeds in maintaining its rate at 8.28 yuan/dollar, the precrisis dollar pegging of the smaller countries could be fully restored and macroeconomic stability in East Asia as whole would be greatly enhanced.

The Rise of Intraregional Trade in East Asia

The rationale for dollar pegging does not primarily arise because of strong trade ties between East Asia and the United States. Figure 1 shows the amazingly rapid increase in intra–East Asian trade over the last two decades. In 2002 about 50 percent of overall trade of these countries was with each other as China became an increasingly important trading partner; in 1980, before China's great opening to foreign

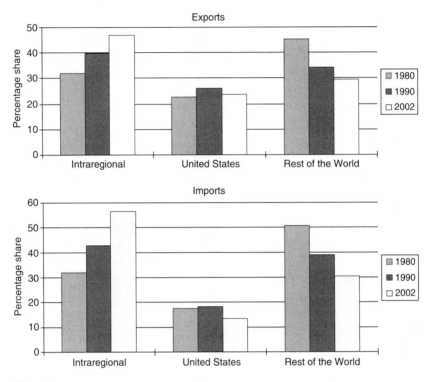

Figure 1
The Rise of Intraregional Trade in East Asia, 1980–2002. East Asia comprises China, Hong Kong, Indonesia, Japan, Korea, Malaysia, Philippines, Singapore, Taiwan, and Thailand

trade, intraregional trade was only 32 percent. Figure 1 also shows that in 2002 the United States received 23.1 percent of overall exports from East Asian economies and shipped only 14.4 percent of their imports. These American trade shares have remained fairly steady since 1980. By contrast, the share of East Asia's trade with the rest of the world is in sharp relative decline although, because of East Asia's high economic growth, not in absolute decline.

The Dollar as International Money
More important than direct trade with the United States is the currency of choice for invoicing East Asian trade and capital flows. Although Japan is as important a trading nation in East Asia as the United States is, almost all the intraregional trade is invoiced in U.S. dollars

except when that trade is directly with Japan. Korea is a typical example. As shown in table 1.1 of chapter 1, 85 percent of Korean exports and about 80 percent of imports are invoiced in U.S. dollars, with about 12.4 percent of imports (from Japan) invoiced in yen. Despite strong trade and investment ties with Japan, yen invoicing is surprisingly small in Korean trade. In Japan's trade with East Asia more generally, the dollar is more important than the yen as an invoice currency. And in trade between any other East Asian countries, say, Thailand trading with Malaysia, or China trading with Singapore, the dollar is used almost exclusively.

Original Sin
This voluntary use of the U.S. dollar in private East Asian trade, combined with incomplete domestic financial markets, helps explain why individual East Asian governments choose (not always successfully) to stabilize their exchange rates against the dollar. Most developing economies lack broad and deep bond markets in the domestic currency. Thus, they cannot *borrow* internationally in their own currencies—sometimes called the problem of *original sin* (Eichengreen and Hausmann 1999), and forward markets in foreign exchange remain expensive or poorly developed. Because their exporters and importers have trouble hedging against such exchange fluctuations, their governments often provide an informal (and imperfect) forward hedge for short-term transactions by trying to keep their spot dollar exchange rates fairly constant through time (see chapter 1).

In a debtor economy, however, the risks are compounded by private *net* holdings of short-term dollar liabilities—as in Indonesia, Korea, Malaysia, Philippines, and Thailand before the 1997–1998 crisis—which are intermediated through banks and other financial institutions. Although most lending by banks was denominated in their domestic currencies, these countries built up dollar liabilities that they could not, or did not want to (because of moral hazard), hedge.

Risk premiums in the domestic interest rates of debtor economies with original sin are typically much higher than on dollar assets of the same term to maturity, as in the East Asian crisis economies before 1997 (see figures 6.6–6.11 in chapter 6). Thus individual domestic firms and banks may be tempted to borrow in dollars without covering the exchange risk. And this tendency to overborrow in foreign exchange can be greatly aggravated if the banks themselves suffer from moral hazard, which arises naturally if there is formal or informal insurance protecting depositors should banks go broke. This overborrowing syndrome is analyzed in chapter 6 in what is sometimes called the third-generation model of banking and currency crises. As risky dollar debts pile up, domestic interest rates rise further, leading to more uncovered foreign borrowing: a vicious circle.

In any debtor economy with original sin, the financial fragility from the currency mismatch is compounded by a maturity mismatch: deposits are very short-term compared to loans or other banks assets. Then a currency attack forcing an immediate repayment of short-term dollar debts to foreigners could precipitate, and did precipitate, devaluations. The value of the banks' liabilities shot up relative to their assets so as to cause massive domestic bankruptcies. So, clearly, soft pegging should be accompanied by rigorous regulations to prevent banks from taking net open positions in foreign exchange.

From Debtors to Creditors

In the new millennium, however, most East Asian economies are becoming dollar creditors. For two decades or more, Japan, Singapore, and Taiwan have run with current account surpluses. China has had small current account surpluses since 1995. Economies that were formerly in crisis, such as Korea, Malaysia, and Thailand, have recovered strongly since 1997–1998 and are running large current account surpluses and rapidly transforming themselves from international debtors into creditors. However, instead of building up claims on foreigners denominated in their domestic monies, most of the foreign claims, either private or official exchange reserves, are highly liquid dollar assets.

Conflicted Virtue

Any international creditor country that cannot *lend* in its own currency cumulates a currency mismatch that I call the syndrome of *conflicted virtue*. Countries that are "virtuous" by reason of having a high saving rate (unlike the United States) tend to run surpluses in the current account of their international balance of payments; that is, they lend to foreigners by acquiring dollar claims on them. For empirical estimates of the cumulated stocks of these liquid dollar assets, see chapter 4 for the case of Japan and chapter 5 for China. But with the passage of time, two things happen:

• As the *stock* of dollar claims cumulates, domestic holders of dollar assets worry more that a self-sustaining run *into* the domestic currency will force an appreciation.

• Foreigners start complaining that the country's ongoing *flow* of trade surpluses is unfair and results from having an undervalued currency.

Of course, these two effects interact. The greater the foreign mercantile pressure to appreciate the domestic currency, the greater the concern of the domestic holders of dollar assets. As runs into the domestic currency out of dollars begin, the government is conflicted because appreciation could induce deflation ending with a zero-interest liquidity trap, particularly if the domestic price level was already stable. But foreigners may threaten trade sanctions if the creditor country does not allow its currency to appreciate. Thus we have the syndrome of conflicted virtue for creditor economies, which is the mirror image or twin of the problem of original sin for debtor economies.

In creditor economies unhedged individual or institutional holders of dollar assets are at risk should the domestic currency appreciate. For example, Japanese insurance companies, whose liabilities to annuity holders are in yen but who hold a substantial share of their assets in higher-yield U.S. dollar bonds, could be bankrupted should the yen appreciate against the dollar. Thus, as an economy's dollar assets accumulate, holders of them become more fearful that a run out of dollars into the domestic currency would force an appreciation. When the world price level measured in U.S. dollars is itself quite stable and the domestic currency actually appreciates, the government would worry about its exporters' sudden loss of mercantile competitiveness followed by a domestic deflationary spiral.

Because of Japan's large size by the 1980s, its rapid growth in industrial exports, coupled with large current account surpluses, marked it as a prime mercantile competitor of both the United States and the Western European bloc of industrial economies. From the 1970s into the mid-1990s "Japan bashing" continually recurred, with U.S. threats of trade sanctions on the one hand and demands for the yen to appreciate on the other. Chapter 3 shows how repeated yen appreciations from the 1980s to 1995 contributed to Japan's deflationary slump in the 1990s, a slump from which it has yet to recover. Even in the absence of persistent yen appreciation since 1995, continued fluctuations in the yen/dollar exchange rate created a negative risk premium in interest rates on yen assets (see chapter 4). Japanese interest rates are compressed toward zero, the so-called liquidity trap, which renders monetary policy impotent and new bank lending unprofitable. So Japan was an early victim of conflicted virtue, although when chapters 3 and 4 on Japan were written, I had not yet coined that term.

In the new millennium, China's astonishingly rapid export growth —with proportionately smaller current account surpluses measured multilaterally but with a very large bilateral surplus with the United States (see chapter 5)—attracts the attention of foreign mercantile competitors, governments, and pundits, who clamor for the renminbi to be appreciated. Will China eventually go down the same deflationary road as Japan?

The problem is not confined to China. Almost all the East Asian economies, with their high saving and trade surpluses, now suffer from conflicted virtue to greater or lesser degrees (see chapter 8).

Soft Dollar Pegs

Because dollar dominance in East Asia creates financial fragility in debtor economies with original sin and in creditor economies with conflicted virtue, the imperfect solution is for each East Asian government to keep its dollar exchange rate as stable as it can. This then reduces risk seen either by unhedged dollar debtors or by unhedged dollar creditors *within* the economy in question. Hence the resort to the soft, or informal, dollar pegging we observe in noncrisis periods (see chapter 1).

To be sure, some governments would like to give full assurance that the domestic exchange rate is never going to change. But no government dares commit itself to an absolutely fixed exchange rate when its neighbors, who are close trading partners, have not done so. The spillover effects from other countries' changing their exchange rates are too great for any country to risk becoming completely inflexible in responding. (In the late 1990s, Argentina's decade-long fixed dollar exchange rate was undermined when Brazil and Chile allowed large depreciations of their currencies.) So, short of adopting a full-fledged system of regional dollar parities, a difficult exercise in collective action although a potentially great public good for East Asia, soft pegging is the result.

Of course, the collective macroeconomic consequences of all East Asian governments' opting individually to peg to the U.S. dollar, if only softly, enlarges the effective zone of stable dollar prices far beyond each country's direct trade with the United States. Thus, each national central bank can lean more heavily on its own stable dollar exchange rate to anchor its domestic price level. This in turn helps its neighbors, with whom it is closely connected in trade, to stabilize their own price levels: a virtuous circle for a change.

Using the dollar as the key currency for stabilizing relative exchange rates within East Asia is tenable as long as the U.S. Federal Reserve Bank keeps the international purchasing power of the dollar fairly constant, as it has over the last decade or so. Perhaps in the very distant future, the dollar's role as the central anchor currency in East Asia could be replaced by the creation of an "Asian euro," which could float freely against the dollar like its European counterpart. Until then, East Asian countries should cooperate to keep their exchange rates stable against the dollar—perhaps coalescing around China's benchmark rate of 8.28 yuan/dollar—and thus stable against each other.

2 Objectives

This book aims to provide guidelines for, and confidence to, policymakers for achieving collective exchange rate security among the East Asian economies. It also provides insights into how financial institutions, particularly banks, might be better regulated to avoid risk and to support this objective. In certain circumstances capital controls may be necessary to supplement prudential regulations over banks. But beyond limiting microeconomic risks facing debtors or creditors, East Asia is also an optimum currency area over which stable exchange rates with a common monetary policy can lead to greater macroeconomic stability (see chapter 7). Collectively stable exchange rates can help national central banks more securely anchor their national price levels and smooth business cycle fluctuations; at the same time, they encourage greater diversification of private asset holdings across countries.

Theoretical Agenda
Out of necessity, therefore, I have a deeper theoretical agenda that conflicts with traditional theory favoring flexible exchange rates. Looking at countries just one at a time, with the rest of the world being a faceless sink, traditional theory has it that a flexible exchange rate is an efficient device for controlling the current account of the balance of payments to match exogenous capital flows. When capital flows in, as

in China currently, the traditional prescription is for appreciation to create a matching trade deficit. When capital flows out, as in Thailand and other crisis economies in 1997, the traditional prescription is a devaluation to help create a trade surplus.

In an earlier book, *Dollar and Yen: Resolving Economic Conflict between the United States and Japan* (1997), Kenichi Ohno and I showed theoretically why exchange rate changes by themselves need have no predictable effect on net trade (im)balances between countries. We illustrated the point by showing that Japan's long experience with an appreciating yen from 360 yen per dollar in early 1971 to just 80 yen to the dollar in early 1995 left Japan with an even larger trade surplus (scaled for GNP growth) in 1995 than in 1971, and in a deflationary slump with interest rates approaching zero. We also showed that balancing international competitiveness between high- and low-productivity-growth economies can proceed more satisfactorily when nominal exchange rates are fixed, as between high-growth Japan and the United States in the 1950s and 1960s, when the yen was fixed at 360 to the dollar under the old Bretton Woods system of dollar parities. In the new millennium this exchange rate lesson has an obvious parallel for the rest of the world's adjusting to China's relatively rapid economic growth.

While building on McKinnon and Ohno (1997), the analytical structure of this book differs further from traditional theorizing on exchange rates in three additional respects.

First, this book looks at countries that are part of a natural trading region, as is East Asia, and focuses on the exchange rate spillover effects from one country to another. Mutual exchange rate stability is the quintessential public good. Because of neighborhood effects, national decisions to fix or float should not be made independently. Indeed, a collective fix, among countries highly integrated in trade and with the requisite internal fiscal and monetary controls in place, is much preferred to individual floats. This point was well recognized by the designers of the old Bretton Woods parity regime in 1944, but their successors governing today's official International Monetary Fund policy, with its emphasis on exchange rate flexibility, act as if they have become oblivious to it.

Second, traditional theory focuses on trade flows and how exchange rate changes might affect those flows, as did McKinnon and Ohno (1997). This book focuses on cross-border financial claims—whether assets or liabilities—and the destabilizing effects of *potential*, as well as actual, exchange rate changes on international portfolio preferences.

When future exchange rates are unknown, an efficient international capital market cannot exist because certain key risks cannot be hedged. These risks are particularly pronounced when some countries are large net debtors and others are large net creditors. This duality in exchange risk between debtors and creditors is essential for understanding the East Asian exchange rate dilemma.

Third, this book explores the operation of monetary and exchange rate policies within a natural trading region when the key trading currency for the region comes from outside the region. Although Japan is extremely important in East Asian trade and capital flows, the U.S. dollar is the region's key currency. For the indefinite future, securing East Asian exchange rates—China, Hong Kong, and Malaysia already have hard pegs to the dollar—must necessarily be based, if somewhat anomalously, on the dollar. Thus theorizing must be concerned with the financial fragility in East Asian countries from having their currencies on the dollar's periphery, and also with the consequent softening of budget constraints in the United States itself.

Chapters 1 through 7 explain the rationale and need for greater exchange rate security among the ever more integrated East Asian economies. The ongoing efforts of each government to stabilize, even if only partially, its own dollar exchange rate is a step in the right direction. So are individual efforts to forge new institutional rules to curtail banks and other domestic financial institutions from assuming too much credit or foreign exchange risk.

Chapter 8 further suggests how the dollar standard in East Asia could be rationalized through collective action by national governments in a region where conflicted virtue is becoming more of a problem. It also discusses the role of the United States as the center country. How do American monetary and fiscal policies affect what is going on in its East Asian periphery?

A Positive Outlook
Fortunately, most if not all East Asian countries have the fiscal potential for securing domestic macroeconomic and exchange rate stability. With the possible exception of Indonesia and perhaps Philippines, each has sufficient taxing capability or a large enough domestic banking system to support its government's finances without inflating. True, their governments can fail to properly regulate banks and control money supplies. Their domestic macroeconomic equilibriums can still be upset by exchange rate changes on the part of their neighbors or

by a common regional business cycle. But, unlike in most countries in Latin America and Africa, domestic financial instability is not endemic.

Although the U.S. dollar remains the region's key currency, East Asian governments could collectively decide on greater regional monetary harmonization with stable exchange rates and domestic price levels. *Could* is not the same as *will*, of course. But unless the economic pros and cons are spelled out, the political *will* will always be lacking.

Stanford, California
October 2004

1

The East Asian Dollar Standard, Fear of Floating, and Original Sin

with Günther Schnabl

Well before the 1997–1998 Asian economic crisis, eight East Asian economies (Hong Kong, Indonesia, Korea, Malaysia, Philippines, Singapore, Taiwan, and Thailand) had pegged their exchange rates to the U.S. dollar. Although these countries used a variety of exchange rate systems, their common peg to the dollar provided an informal common monetary standard that enhanced macroeconomic stability in the region. China joined the system in 1994, when it unified its foreign exchange market and adopted a stable peg to the dollar. (Only Japan was a "pure" floater, with wide fluctuations in the yen/dollar exchange rate.)

With the advent of the crisis, the common East Asian monetary standard fell apart. Although China and Hong Kong retained their dollar pegs, the debtor countries (Indonesia, Korea, Malaysia, Philippines, and Thailand) were forced to float, that is, to let their currencies fall precipitately when they were attacked. Even the creditor countries that were not attacked, Taiwan and Singapore, engineered moderate depreciations. And Japan, as the outlier, let the yen float downward substantially over 1997 through mid-1998 and thus worsened the crisis for the other East Asian economies (see chapter 2).

However, in this chapter we show that the dollar's predominant weight in East Asian currency baskets has returned to its precrisis levels. By 2004 the day-to-day volatility of each country's exchange rate against the dollar has again become negligible. In addition, most governments are rapidly accumulating a fund of official dollar reserves, which portends that this exchange rate stabilization will extend over months or quarters. Contrary to the prevailing doctrines

Adapted from Ronald I. McKinnon and Günther Schnabl, "The East Asian Dollar Standard, Fear of Floating, and Original Sin," *Review of Development Economics* 8 (August 2004).

of the International Monetary Fund (IMF), the U.S. Treasury, and many pundits in the private sector, we argue that this fear of floating is entirely rational from the perspective of each country. In addition, their joint pegging to the U.S. dollar has macroeconomic benefits for the East Asian dollar bloc as a whole, although Japan remains an important outlier.

1.1   More Exchange Rate Flexibility in East Asia?

The lesson the IMF and many other commentators drew from the currency attacks on the debtor economies is that the pre-1997 system of soft dollar pegs was itself at fault. Before 1997, because of high risk premiums, the interest rates in the East Asian debtor economies were much higher than on dollar or yen assets. Thus, in order to make loans in, say, Thai baht, Thai banks were tempted to accept low-interest dollar (or yen) deposits instead of relatively high-interest baht deposits. And this temptation to risk foreign exchange exposure was all the greater because the baht/dollar exchange rate was (softly) fixed. So, this critique runs, if the exchange rates of the debtor economies had been fluctuating more randomly, the Thai (or Korean, or Indonesian, or Malaysian, or Philippine) banks would see greater risk and be less prone to short-term overborrowing in foreign exchange in the first place. Further, by introducing more flexibility in exchange rates ex ante, the critics of soft dollar pegging contend that large discrete depreciations become less likely ex post, i.e., after some political or economic disturbance provokes an attack.

This line of reasoning against restoring soft dollar pegs has been so persuasive that academic commentators and international agencies fear a return to the pre-1997 regime. Postcrisis the IMF has warned of "an important danger ... in slipping back into de facto pegging of exchange rates against the U.S. dollar" (Mussa et al. 2000, 33). For emerging markets open to international capital flows, Stanley Fischer (2001) has argued, soft pegs are not sustainable. Postcrisis Fischer sees most emerging markets moving toward more flexible exchange rates. Indeed, he sees movement toward a bipolar world where a few emerging markets such as Hong Kong adopt hard pegs while all others move toward greater exchange rate flexibility:

In the last decade, there has been a hollowing out of the middle of the distribution of exchange rate regimes in a bipolar direction, with the share of both hard pegs and floating gaining at the expense of soft pegs. This is true not only for economies active in international capital markets, but among all countries. A look ahead suggests this trend will continue, certainly among the emerging market countries. The main reason for this change, among countries with open capital accounts, is that soft pegs are crisis-prone and not viable over long periods. (22)

Similarly, based on monthly observations, Hernández and Montiel (2003) find that Indonesia, Korea, Philippines, Singapore, Taiwan, and Thailand have more flexible (but not purely flexible) exchange rates than in the precrisis period.

The IMF position in favor of more exchange rate flexibility in East Asia is reflected in its official classification of East Asian exchange rate arrangements. East Asian countries that had *not* adopted clearly visible pegs (China, Hong Kong, and Malaysia) are classified as managed or independent floaters. Going one step further, the IMF sometimes pressures countries to announce an internal monetary standard, such as inflation targeting, as a substitute for relying on the exchange rate as their nominal anchor.

Against this by now conventional wisdom, we argue in favor of dollar pegging, at least for East Asia. Indeed, we argue that the IMF's worst fears could well be realized: low-frequency dollar pegging (as in Malaysia) will follow the path of high-frequency pegging, and exchange rate volatility will diminish. The informal East Asian dollar standard could be accidentally resurrected by national central banks acting independently. Our analysis has both an empirical and a theoretical dimension.

First, we rationalize why developing countries with incomplete domestic financial markets use (soft) dollar pegging to mitigate short-term domestic payments risk on the one hand, while providing a useful nominal anchor for national monetary policies on the other. What underlying theories could explain soft dollar pegging as optimizing behavior?

Second, we show empirically that, Japan aside, the East Asian dollar standard is reestablishing itself in the postcrisis period. But to get a balanced view of the extent of this reformation, we distinguish high-frequency (day-to-day or week-to-week) dollar pegging from low-frequency (month-to-month or quarter-to-quarter) dollar pegging. The return to soft dollar pegging is most evident at high frequencies of observation.

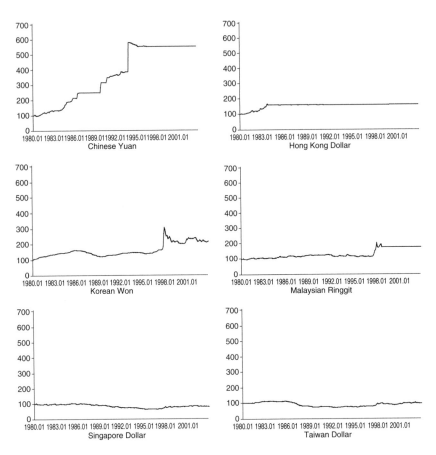

Figure 1.1
East Asian Exchange Rate Pegs against U.S. Dollar, January 1980–December 2003 (Monthly). Index January 1980 = 100; note different scale for Indonesia. (International Monetary Fund, *International Financial Statistics*; Central Bank of China)

1.2   Low-Frequency Dollar Pegging and the Common Nominal Anchor

To clarify the rationale for the return to the precrisis exchange rate arrangements, let us discuss low-frequency dollar pegging first. Based on monthly observations from 1980 to 2003, figure 1.1 shows that all East Asian countries except Japan stabilized the dollar values of their currencies up to the 1997–1998 crisis and, with the major exception of Indonesia, could be returning to such pegging in the near future. With base 100, the various country panels in figure 1.1 use the same vertical

Figure 1.1
(continued)

scale for dollar exchange rates (except for Indonesia) so that the observer can more easily compare proportional changes.

Before 1997, East Asian countries used a variety of exchange rate systems ranging from a currency board hard peg in Hong Kong to a sliding or crawling peg in Indonesia. Although these pegs were often not openly admitted or were disguised as currency baskets, the common adherence to the dollar is easy to recognize. After a series of official devaluations before 1994, China has since maintained a hard, if informal, peg of 8.28 yuan/dollar and a unified foreign exchange market.[1] Malaysia introduced a fixed exchange rate of 3.8 ringgit/dollar in September 1998.

Table 1.1
Invoice Currencies in Korean Trade, 1980–2002 (percent)

	Exports (Receipts)					Imports (Payments)				
	US$	¥	DM	£	Other	US$	¥	DM	£	Other
1980	96.1	1.2	2.0	0.4	0.3	93.2	3.7	1.7	0.5	0.9
1985	94.7	3.7	0.6	0.3	0.7	82.4	12.3	2.0	0.5	2.8
1990	88.0	7.8	2.1	0.5	1.7	79.1	12.7	4.1	0.9	3.4
1995	88.1	6.5	2.4	0.8	2.2	79.4	12.7	3.8	0.7	3.4
2000	84.8	5.4	1.8	0.7	7.3	80.4	12.4	1.9	0.8	4.4
2002	86.8	5.2	5.8	0.8	1.4	80.6	12.1	5.4	0.6	1.3

Source: Bank of Korea, Monthly Statistical Bulletin.
Notes: Trade in services is not included; DM represents the euro starting from 2000.

Trade Invoicing

The rationale for low-frequency dollar pegging does not primarily arise because of strong trade ties with the United States. The United States accounts for only about 23 percent of overall exports of the smaller East Asian economies and for only 14 percent of their imports. Instead, we focus on the fact that most of East Asian commodity trade is invoiced in U.S. dollars.

To show the predominance of dollar invoicing in East Asia, table 1.1 displays Korea's invoicing practices from 1980 to 2002. In 2002, 80.6 percent of Korean imports were invoiced in U.S. dollars, and the proportion of dollar invoicing of Korean exports was even higher, at 86.8 percent—similar to the proportions observed in the preceding two decades. Because the other countries, with smaller economies, are less industrialized than Korea, their currencies are even less likely to be used in foreign trade, with the proportion of dollar invoicing being correspondingly greater.

In striking contrast, yen invoicing in Korean trade is surprisingly small. Table 1.1 shows that in 2002 only 5.2 percent of Korean exports and only 12.1 percent of Korean imports were invoiced in yen. This is surprising because Japan is at least as important a trading partner with Korea as the United States is, and direct investment by Japan in Korea has been much higher. Table 1.1 also shows that the use of European currencies is negligible.

The use of the yen in invoicing intra-Asian trade is of special interest because the economic linkages with Japan are particularly strong. From table 1.2, which summarizes how different currencies are used in

Table 1.2
Invoice Currencies in Japanese Trade, 1980–2002 (percent)

Exports

	World			U.S.			Asia			EU		
	US$	¥	Other	US$	¥	Other	US$	¥	Other	US$	¥	Other
1980	66.3	28.9	4.8									
1987	55.2	33.4	11.4	84.9	15.0	0.1	56.5	41.1	2.4	8.2	44.0	47.8
1990	48.8	37.5	13.7	83.7	16.2	0.1	48.1	48.9	3.0	6.4	42.1	51.5
1995[a]	52.5	36.0	11.5	82.9	17.0	0.1	53.4	44.3	2.3	12.2	34.9	52.9
2000[a]	52.4	36.1	11.5	86.7	13.2	0.1	50.0	48.2	1.8	13.0	33.5	53.5
2002[a]	48.0	38.4	13.6	86.4	13.4	0.2	44.7	53.3	2.0	11.2	27.4	54.4

Imports

	World			U.S.			Asia			EU		
	US$	¥	Other	US$	¥	Other	US$	¥	Other	US$	¥	Other
1980	93.1	2.4	4.5									
1987	81.7	10.6	7.7	90.6	9.2	0.2	87.6	11.5	0.9	19.5	27.3	53.2
1990	75.5	14.6	9.9	88.2	11.6	0.2	78.8	19.4	1.8	16.3	26.9	56.8
1995[a]	70.2	22.7	7.1	78.4	21.5	0.1	71.9	26.2	1.9	16.1	44.8	39.1
2000[a]	70.7	23.5	5.8	78.7	20.8	0.5	74.0	24.8	1.2	17.5	49.7	32.8
2002[a]	68.7	24.6	6.7	80.2	19.3	0.5	71.0	27.8	1.2	13.2	49.4	32.0

Sources: Sato (1999); MITI, Yushutsu (Yu'nyû) Kessai Tsûka-date Dôkô Chôsa; and Ministry of Finance, Bôeki Torihiki Tsûka-betsu Hiritsu.
Note: Asia = 19 to 22 Asian countries.
a. September.

overall Japanese trade, we draw two conclusions. First, in contrast to the practice in other industrial countries, the U.S. dollar, not the domestic currency, dominates. In 2002, 48 percent of Japan's worldwide exports and 68.7 percent of its aggregate imports were invoiced in dollars, and only 38.4 percent of world exports and 24.6 percent of imports were invoiced in yen.

Second, although Japan's currency is a bit more important in trade with Asian neighbors, the differences are surprisingly small. In 2002, 53.3 percent of Japan's exports to Asia and 27.8 percent of its imports from Asia were invoiced in yen. By comparison, 44.7 percent of Japanese exports to Asia and 71 percent of its imports from Asia were invoiced in U.S. dollars.

Although Japan is the world's second largest industrial economy, the dollar is more widely used in Japanese trade with East Asia than is the yen. As Sato (1999, 574) puts it, the East Asian countries are unlikely to use the yen in their foreign trade except when that trade is with Japan. The U.S. dollar predominates in invoicing East Asian trade in general and intra–East Asian trade in particular, for instance, when Thailand trades with Malaysia. Thus, despite lively discussions as in Kwan (2001) about the possibility of a yen zone in East Asia, the revealed invoicing preferences of Asian importers and exporters indicate the contrary: the area has been, and is, a strong dollar zone from which the dollar shows no signs of being displaced. This dollar invoicing helps explain why the smaller East Asian economies, including China, are so anxious to peg to the dollar at both low and high frequencies.

The Macroeconomic Rationale for Low-Frequency Pegging

Using a much larger data set going beyond East Asia, Guillermo Calvo and Carmen Reinhart (2002) showed what they called fear of floating in developing countries on a worldwide scale. Although a small number of former European colonies and Eastern European transitional economies peg to the euro, the rest of the developing world pegs softly to the U.S. dollar. From monthly data, they showed that exchange rates in developing countries were much less volatile—and interest rates and exchange reserves much more volatile—than in the industrial countries.

Their rationale for the low-frequency (month-to-month, quarter-to-quarter) pegging they observed is nicely summarized by Reinhart (2000):

The root causes of the marked reluctance of emerging markets to float their exchange rates are multiple. When circumstances are favorable (i.e., there are capital inflows, positive terms of trade shocks, etc.) many emerging markets are reluctant to allow the nominal (and real) exchange rate to appreciate.... When circumstances are adverse, the fear of a collapse in the exchange rate comes from pervasive liability dollarization. Devaluations are associated with recessions and inflation, and not export-led growth. (69)

Calvo and Reinhart's argument explaining fear of floating has two related aspects, both macroeconomic in nature. First, in the absence of capital controls, volatile capital flows could sharply affect nominal exchange rates and, because the domestic price level is relatively sticky, lead to large changes in a country's real exchange rate. Its international competitiveness could fluctuate sharply from one month to the next.

Second, the common low-frequency peg to the dollar helps anchor any one country's price level because such a high proportion of world trade is invoiced in dollars. In noncrisis periods, price increases in the traded goods sector are pinned down. The upward drift of prices in nontradable services is muted because of substitution relationships.[2]

How successful was the dollar anchor in East Asia? Figures 1.1 and 1.2 show the close link between exchange rate stability and price stability for tradable goods (wholesale prices). From 1980 to 1997 the country panels in figure 1.2 show that only the wholesale price indexes of Indonesia and Philippines rose significantly. Both countries had allowed their currencies to depreciate continually against the dollar, albeit in a controlled fashion. In contrast, the wholesale prices of the smaller East Asian countries that did not depreciate, or depreciated very little, are grouped around the wholesale price index of the United States. Before 1997, Singapore had allowed its currency to float gently upward against the dollar and thus had slightly less wholesale price inflation than did the United States. Thanks to this collective pegging to the U.S. dollar, the developing countries of East Asia had low or moderate inflation.

This common dollar anchor was more robust because all East Asian countries except Japan were on it. Then international commodity arbitrage within the whole East Asian dollar zone, and not just with the United States, could better pin down the domestic price level of any one participating country. Indeed, in the great 1997–1998 crisis, when Indonesia, Korea, Malaysia, Philippines, and Thailand were suddenly forced to devalue and curtailed imports while trying to stimulate exports, this forced a deflation in the *dollar* prices of goods traded in

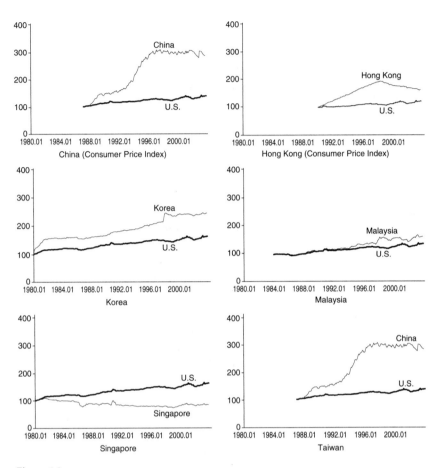

Figure 1.2
Wholesale Price Indexes of East Asian Countries, January 1980–December 2003 (Monthly). Indonesia, except petrol; Hong Kong, January 1990 = 100; Malaysia, January 1984 = 100; China, January 1987 = 100. (International Monetary Fund, *International Financial Statistics*; Central Bank of China)

the region (McKinnon 2001a). Thus China and Hong Kong, which did not devalue, experienced significant deflation in their domestic prices.

Pre-1997 exchange rate targeting was consistent with fiscal discipline and the absence of excessive monetary expansion. As stressed by the World Bank's report (1993) on the East Asian "miracle" and by the IMF in the aftermath of the Asian crisis, government budgets in the East Asian economies, except for Japan's and perhaps China's, had been virtually balanced. Before the crisis these East Asian countries had low budget deficits or were even running budget surpluses. Infla-

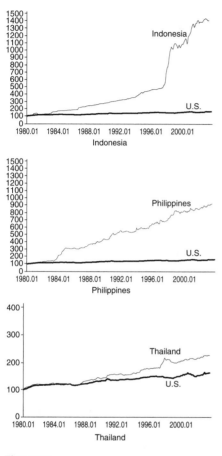

Figure 1.2
(continued)

tion was moderate. Their budget deficits were low even by the standards of industrialized countries.[3] Instead of currency overvaluation in the usual sense arising from uncontrolled domestic inflation, the currency attacks in the five crisis economies were mainly provoked by an undue buildup of short-term dollar indebtedness over 1994–1996 (see chapter 6), followed by the "extraneous" sharp depreciation of the yen in 1997–1998 (see chapter 2).

1.3   High-Frequency Dollar Pegging and Original Sin

The argument for anchoring the domestic price level is all well and good for low-frequency exchange rate pegging on a quarterly or yearly basis. However, this nominal anchor argument cannot be used to rationalize high-frequency pegging on a daily or weekly basis, where continual changes have little or no effect on domestic prices. Instead we hypothesize that high-frequency pegging reflects the fact that the capital markets of emerging markets are incomplete and facilities for hedging against exchange risk are inadequate, as per the doctrine of original sin put forward by Barry Eichengreen and Ricardo Hausmann (1999):

"Original sin" ... is a situation in which the domestic currency cannot be used to borrow abroad or to borrow long term, even domestically. In the presence of this incompleteness, financial fragility is unavoidable because all domestic investments will have either a currency mismatch (projects that generate pesos will be financed with dollars) or a maturity mismatch (long-term projects will be financed by short-term loans).

Critically, these mismatches exist not because banks and firms lack the prudence to hedge their exposures. The problem rather is that a country whose external liabilities are necessarily denominated in foreign exchange is by definition unable to hedge. Assuming that there will be someone on the other side of the market for foreign currency hedges is equivalent to assuming that the country can borrow abroad in its own currency. Similarly, the problem is not that firms lack the foresight to match the maturity structure of their assets and liabilities; it is that they find it impossible to do so. The incompleteness of financial markets is thus at the root of financial fragility. (3)

This incompleteness in domestic financial markets can also apply to creditor countries that cannot lend internationally in their own currencies—the problem of conflicted virtue (see chapters 4, 5, and 8). In this chapter, however, we follow Eichengreen and Hausmann and focus on the hedging problem in underdeveloped debtor economies.

In developing countries, in what sense are financial markets incomplete? First, a fixed-interest bond market is typically absent. The reasons are many. On the private side, domestic firms tend to be small, without well-developed accounting systems, and cannot issue bonds in their own names. Firms with longer-term projects cannot issue fixed-interest bonds or mortgages for finance at comparable terms to maturity. Instead, they must roll over short-term bank loans or, at best, borrow at medium term with variable interest rates tied to short rates.

Even on the government side, developing countries may have shaky financial histories—inflation and interest rate volatility coupled with exchange controls—that inhibit potential buyers of government bonds from making medium- or long-term commitments. Insofar as a market in government bonds exists into the medium term, interest rates are typically adjusted to reflect some very short-term rate. An ostensible one-year bond might have its interest rate tied to that on overnight Treasuries.

Second, most developing countries lack an active forward market in foreign exchange against the dollar or any other currency. While a missing domestic bond market is obviously bad for domestic capital markets, why should it affect forward transacting by risk-averse traders wanting to hedge their open positions in foreign exchange? Potential market makers such as banks cannot easily cover transactions involving selling the domestic currency forward for, say, dollars because they can't hold a convenient array of interest-bearing domestic bonds liquid at different terms to maturity. Indeed, domestic interest rates (vis-à-vis foreign) are not available for determining what the proper premium on forward dollars should be.

In contrast, forward exchange transacting between any two industrial countries can thrive because each has a well-developed domestic bond market denominated in its domestic currency. Long-term forward markets, with a well-defined forward premium equal to the interest differential between the two national bond markets at each term to maturity, can thrive at much lower cost.

The Microeconomic Rationale for High-Frequency Pegging

Absent an efficient forward market in foreign exchange, risk-averse importers and exporters cannot conveniently hedge. Nor can banks easily cover open positions in foreign exchange.

Suppose first that the private sector of an underdeveloped economy were *not* a net debtor to the rest of the world and its imports and exports were more or less balanced. Then domestic importers could possibly buy dollars forward from domestic exporters at shorter terms to maturity, although such matching would be difficult (high transaction costs) because the domestic forward market for foreign exchange lacks liquidity. Absent liquid domestic money market instruments at all terms to maturity, banks, which typically act as agents for domestic importers and exporters in the forward exchange markets, could not easily cover themselves.

Now suppose that the private sector is a net short-term debtor, largely in dollars, to the rest of the world. Then, notwithstanding the country's government having positive official dollar reserves, the hedging problem for private traders is compounded. Collectively, domestic debtors with future foreign exchange obligations should buy dollars forward to cover themselves. But foreigners collectively are unwilling to sell dollars forward net because they cannot find liquid interest-bearing assets in domestic currency, that is, bonds, to hold in the interim. There's an inevitable currency mismatch: economic agents with net foreign exchange (dollar) exposure, usually very short term, cannot hedge even if they want to.

What are the implications for official foreign exchange policy? To offset the nonexistent private market in forward exchange, the government is induced to provide an informal hedge by keeping the exchange rate stable in the short to medium term. Private banks and enterprises can then repay their short-term foreign currency debts, which are largely denominated in U.S. dollars, with minimal exchange rate risk. If a country's financial markets are condemned by original sin, its regulatory authorities have strong incentives to undertake high-frequency exchange rate pegging in order to mitigate payments risk (McKinnon 2001a). The emerging market countries in East Asia are no exception.

Alternatively, the same argument about the missing domestic bond market could be used to justify official intervention to create a "market" in forward exchange. Presuming that the government has plentiful dollar reserves, it could risk selling dollars forward to individual importers or to financial institutions, which have forward exchange exposure. Even if the government has the best of intentions, however, this leaves open the question of what the appropriate forward premiums on dollars should be for these various individualized contracts. Worse, a government could easily use such contracts to subsidize its friends in the private sector. All around the world, patronage scandals erupt when governments try to simulate forward markets. In June 1997, at the outset of the East Asian crisis, it was suddenly discovered that the central bank of Thailand had sold forward most of the country's foreign exchange reserves to finance companies and other "deserving" Thai businessmen. Similarly, late in 1997, the new incoming Korean government found that the Bank of Korea had committed much of its official dollar reserves to the overseas subsidiaries of Korean commercial banks.

So, a more neutral and more visible second-best strategy (the first-best being to create a domestic bond market) for reducing foreign exchange risk is for the government to keep the exchange rate from moving much on a day-to-day or week-to-week basis. At higher frequencies of observation than those considered by Calvo and Reinhart (2002), there is fear of floating. Except for the small economies in Eastern Europe attached to the euro, the U.S. dollar is the natural currency to which to peg. It is the principal invoice and vehicle currency in East Asia and elsewhere in the developing world. And East Asian countries do peg softly to the dollar at high frequencies.

But pegging to the dollar to limit exchange risk still leaves open two big problems in risk management. The first is the question of extraneous exchange rate fluctuations between the dollar and other major currencies. The second is moral hazard in the sense that economic agents, whether domestic banks or firms, prefer to gamble rather than to hedge their bets in the foreign exchanges.

Extraneous Exchange Rate Risk and Double Hedging

The first problem is that of extraneous exchange rate changes between major currencies, as in East Asia when the yen fluctuates against the dollar. For example, table 1.1 showed that a small but significant proportion (12 to 13 percent) of Korean imports are invoiced in yen. Suppose that in the short and medium terms these yen prices are sticky. Similarly, all dollar prices that Korean importers (or exporters) face are sticky and invariant to fluctuations in the yen/dollar rate. Thus, if the won is pegged to the dollar, Korean importers of yen-invoiced goods are at risk when the yen/dollar rate fluctuates.

Suppose a Korean importer is obligated to pay 100 yen in 60 days. Then any random appreciation of the yen against the dollar within the 60-day interval will increase the won cost of servicing that debt. If the won prices for which the importer can sell his Japanese goods in Korea are sticky, then he could buy forward 100 yen *for dollars* in order to hedge the transaction. Because both Japan and the United States have well-developed bond markets, a well-defined and highly liquid forward interbank market between yen and dollars is cheap to use. Thus, the Korean importer, using his bank as agent, can buy forward all the yen he needs for dollars. And with the won kept predictably stable against the dollar in the spot markets, he can use spot won to buy the dollars 60 days hence when his yen payment is due.

So, we have a theory of the optimal, albeit second-best, *double hedge* against currency risk. The bulk of the goods traded by any East Asian emerging market economy are priced to market (sticky-priced) in dollars. For these goods, the government's soft pegging against the dollar in the short and medium terms is an informal hedge against exchange risk, which compensates for the absence of a forward market between the domestic currency and dollars. However, for that subset of imports or exports invoiced in yen, euros, sterling, or some other major currency that fluctuates widely against the dollar, supplementary hedging in the well-developed forward markets between dollars and that major currency is also necessary. This strategy of reducing exchange risk by double hedging, starting with a peg to just one major international currency, dominates the trade-weighted currency basket approach involving a developing country's pegging to several major international currencies with different weights.

Moral Hazard

So far, we have presumed that merchants and banks are well behaved: they want to hedge against currency risk. But we know that deposit insurance for banks and other bailout provisions for some firms create moral hazard that makes at least some of them willing to gamble at the government's expense. In particular, banks might actively increase their net foreign exchange exposure as well as making domestic loans with a high risk of default. (Moral hazard associated with both default and currency risk is spelled out in more analytical detail in chapter 6.) Thus governments in developing countries typically try, albeit imperfectly, to constrain banks from taking open positions in foreign exchange, and these ordinary prudential regulations are sometimes supplemented with some form of capital control.

We have just shown that, under original sin, governments want to peg (softly) to the dollar to allow legitimately risk-averse firms and banks to informally hedge their forward exchange exposure. But didn't this soft pegging encourage badly behaved banks to overborrow by accepting dollar or yen deposits with very low interest rates to make loans at much higher interest rates in the domestic currency? After all, much of the genesis of the 1997–1998 East Asian crisis came from banks' overexposing themselves in dollars or yen.

Although very contentious, there are two offsetting considerations. First, the IMF contends that soft pegging took away much of the immediate risk from borrowing in dollars because "bad" banks did not have to worry about near-term exchange rate fluctuations (Fischer 1999). Thus, in this conventional view, for any given interest differential, the moral hazard would have been better contained had the currencies of each of the Asian countries floated more freely against the dollar. Against this, however, is the view that the risk premium in domestic interest rates is a direct function of how stable the domestic money is relative to the central currency, the U.S. dollar. Thus if the domestic exchange rate against the dollar varies erratically in a free float, domestic interest rates will be higher and so will the margin of temptation to overborrow in foreign exchange (see chapter 6).

In summary, one cannot say a priori whether soft pegging worsens the moral hazard in badly regulated banks to overborrow. But for well-behaved banks and merchants, those that are properly risk-averse, soft pegging to the dollar reduces forward exchange risks.

Capital Controls versus Limits on Net Foreign Exchange Exposure by Banks

Governments typically try to contain moral hazard in banks by various kinds of regulations. What then are implications of such regulations for optimal exchange rate policy?

The government could impose strict capital controls to ensure that private banks don't hold or owe foreign currencies. This would drive the banks out of the profitable business of accepting low-interest foreign exchange deposits to finance higher-yield loans in domestic currency. The inflow of short-term capital and associated dollar indebtedness would be restricted, which could well be what a prudent government prefers. However, full-scale capital controls on taking any *gross* positions in foreign exchange have the unfortunate side effect of limiting double hedging. Domestic importers and exporters cannot then hedge their extraneous foreign exchange risk because their banks could not take forward positions in markets among major currencies.

Government regulatory agencies could still prohibit banks (and possibly other financial institutions) from taking *net* open positions in foreign exchange; this would be less draconian than full-scale capital controls. In this case, banks could still do covered interest arbitrage and thus provide forward exchange cover for their retail customers. For example, if a Thai importer wanted to hedge extraneous exchange rate risk by buying yen with dollars 90 days forward, the Thai bank could sell the necessary forward yen to the importer. But the Thai bank would be required to cover itself immediately by buying yen for dollars spot or forward, most likely in the international interbank market for foreign exchange.

Similarly, preventing banks from having net foreign exchange exposure need not hinder some development of the domestic bond market with a rudimentary forward exchange market between the domestic currency and the dollar. Even if the forward market were not (yet) very liquid, the banks could still sell dollars forward to importers and match this by buying dollars forward from exporters, provided the country's private sector was not a large net dollar debtor. But domestic banks would still be prevented from being international financial intermediaries, that is, borrowing in foreign currencies to lend in the domestic one. For the economy overall this would forestall a buildup of net short-term foreign currency indebtedness like that preceding the 1997–1998 Asian crisis.

The Impossibility of Freely Floating Exchange Rates?

When governments impose tough prudential regulations against banks' taking foreign exchange risks, can exchange rates float freely? With either general capital controls or prudential regulations against net foreign exchange exposure by banks in place, we hypothesize, governments have little choice but to peg their exchange rates, perhaps only softly from one day to the next. Why?

The interbank spot and forward exchange markets are at the center of foreign exchange trading the world over. In any country, its banks normally have direct access to this international market and are the dealers who match buy and sell orders for the domestic currency. Absent any government intervention, these dealers must continually take open positions for or against the domestic currency in order to "make" the foreign exchange market. In textbooks on international finance, banks are the natural stabilizing speculators when there is confidence in the domestic currency. In a well-behaved market expectations about short-term movements in exchange rates are naturally regressive. That is, when the domestic currency depreciates, market makers believe that it will eventually rebound, and vice versa. Then a reasonably smooth bank-based float is feasible.

Now suppose that domestic commercial banks are not allowed to take open positions in foreign exchange. Moreover, in the presence of original sin, there is no liquid market in domestic bonds. *Foreign banks are then unwilling to take open positions in the domestic currency.* Thus, with a tightly regulated domestic banking system or capital controls, a satisfactory free float is impossible. With no natural market makers in the system, the exchange rate would move so erratically as to be intolerable. In most developing countries governments recognize this problem, at least implicitly. Day to day, the central bank then makes the market often by simply pegging, softly and informally, the domestic currency to the dollar.

In summary, governments in developing countries usually have two complementary reasons for keeping their exchange rates stable on a high-frequency basis:

• Without a well-organized market in forward exchange (original sin), the government wants to provide an informal forward hedge for importers and exporters.

• Fear of overborrowing leads many prudent governments to limit net foreign exchange exposure by domestic banks—in the extreme, by using capital controls. These regulatory restraints then prevent the banks from being active dealers to stabilize the exchange rate.

In industrial countries these problems are not so acute. Because of a well-developed domestic market in forward exchange, their banks need not be so tightly regulated to prevent foreign exchange exposure. In part because of the active forward exchange market, the problem of containing moral hazard in banks is less—a virtuous circle. So the industrial countries can more easily tolerate a free float. But first consider the exchange rate practices of developing countries in East Asia.

1.4   The Postcrisis Return to High-Frequency Pegging: A Formal Empirical Test

Our empirical analysis of high-frequency dollar pegging in East Asia proceeds in two stages. First, we test whether the developing countries of East Asia really did, in noncrisis periods, key on the dollar more than on the yen or euro and whether basket pegging, where all three currencies are given some weight, was the norm. Was this keying permanently interrupted by the crisis of 1997–1998? Second, we test for any changes in the volatility of these dollar pegs in the postcrisis period compared to the precrisis period.

With Japan being such an important trader and an even more important source of capital in East Asia, many authors since the crisis have proposed pegging to a broader currency basket (Rajan 2002). For instance, Kawai and Akiyama (2000) and Kawai (2002) propose increasing the weight of the Japanese yen in the East Asian currency baskets. Williamson (2000) recommends a 33 percent weight of the Japanese yen.

The Composition of Currency Baskets

Using the regression model developed by Frankel and Wei (1994), we show that the smaller East Asian countries have more or less ignored these recommendations. Instead they have clandestinely returned to high-frequency dollar pegging on a day-to-day basis.

Before the crisis a few East Asian currencies were de jure pegged to a basket of major currencies, but typically the weights assigned to various currencies in the official basket were not announced. To detect the weights of various currencies, Frankel and Wei use an outside currency—the Swiss franc—as a numéraire for measuring exchange rate volatility for any East Asian country (except Japan). These volatilities could then be partitioned among movements in major currencies against the Swiss franc. For example, if changes in the Korean won against the Swiss franc are largely explained by the changes in the U.S. dollar against the Swiss franc, we can conclude that the Korean won is virtually pegged to the U.S. dollar. Alternatively, it could be pegged to the Japanese yen or the German mark.

To show this, we regress the exchange rates of each of the nine East Asian currencies (EA) on the U.S. dollar ($), the Japanese yen (Y), and the German mark (M)[4] with the Swiss franc (SF) as numéraire.[5] Equation 1.1 is the regression model.

$$e_t^{EASF} = \alpha_1 + \alpha_2 e_t^{\$SF} + \alpha_3 e_t^{YSF} + \alpha_4 e_t^{MSF} + u_t \tag{1.1}$$

The multivariate OLS regression[6] is based on first differences of logarithms in these exchange rates. The residuals are controlled for heteroscedasticity, which can be assumed to be strong during the crisis and the postcrisis period. The daily data are compiled from Datastream. According to Frankel and Wei, the α coefficients represent the weights of the respective currencies in the currency basket. If the East Asian currency is closely fixed to one of the major currencies appearing on the right-hand side of equation 1.1, the corresponding α coefficient will be close to unity. If a coefficient is close to zero, we presume no exchange rate stabilization against that particular currency.

As in McKinnon (2001a), we run the regression for three periods: precrisis, crisis, and postcrisis.[7] The precrisis period (869 observations) is from February 1994, when China unified its foreign exchange market, to May 1997. We specify the crisis period (415 observations) to start in June 1997, when the peg of the Thai baht came under strong pressure and was abandoned, and end in December 1998, when the

Table 1.3
Pegging on a High-Frequency Basis, Precrisis (2/01/94–5/30/97)

	Constant α_1	US$ α_2	Yen α_3	DM α_4	R^2
Chinese yuan	−0.00	1.01[a]	−0.01	−0.02	0.97
	(−1.15)	(158.63)	(−1.48)	(−1.70)	
Hong Kong dollar	0.00	1.00[a]	0.00	−0.01	1.00
	(0.30)	(454.79)	(0.25)	(−1.36)	
Indonesian rupiah	0.00	1.00[a]	−0.01	0.01	0.97
	(3.19)	(144.93)	(−0.92)	(0.85)	
Korean won	0.00	0.97[a]	0.06[a]	0.01	0.93
	(1.42)	(66.27)	(3.31)	(0.29)	
Malaysian ringgit	−0.00	0.88[a]	0.09[a]	0.01	0.90
	(−1.48)	(54.80)	(5.30)	(0.45)	
Philippine peso	−0.00	0.97[a]	0.02	−0.01	0.86
	(−0.34)	(43.34)	(0.74)	(−0.45)	
Singapore dollar	−0.00	0.82[a]	0.14[a]	0.08[a]	0.86
	(−1.32)	(34.37)	(4.83)	(2.97)	
New Taiwan dollar	0.00	0.98[a]	0.03[b]	−0.01	0.93
	(0.84)	(57.30)	(1.38)	(−0.54)	
Thai baht	−0.00	0.92[a]	0.08[a]	−0.01	0.95
	(−0.61)	(81.25)	(5.17)	(−0.35)	

Source: Datastream.
Notes: Daily data; *t*-statistics in parentheses; 869 observations; white heteroscedasticity-consistent standard errors and covariance.
a. Significant at the 1% level.
b. Significant at the 5% level.

currency attacks had ended. The postcrisis period (1,304 observations) starts in January 1999 and goes up to December 2003.

Precrisis: February 1994 to May 1997   Table 1.3 reports the regression results for the precrisis period and shows the tight peg around the U.S. dollar. The α_2 coefficients in equation 1.1 are all close to unity and reveal the strong efforts by Asian governments to keep the currencies stable against the dollar on a day-to-day basis. The α_2 coefficients range from 0.82 for the Singapore dollar up to 1.0 for the Chinese yuan, Hong Kong dollar, and Indonesian rupiah. The correlation coefficients (R^2) being close to unity indicates that fluctuations of the East Asian exchange rate against the Swiss franc can be almost fully explained by fluctuations of the U.S. dollar against the Swiss franc.

More specifically, the α_2 coefficients of the Chinese yuan, the Hong Kong dollar, and the Indonesian rupiah are 1.0. Precrisis, Indonesia let its currency crawl smoothly downward at 4–5 percent per year, but nevertheless it kept the rupiah virtually fixed to the U.S. dollar on a day-to-day basis. China and Hong Kong maintained their fixed pegs to the dollar with no downward crawl. The α_2 coefficients of the Korean won, the Philippine peso, and the Taiwan dollar are very close to 1 with lower but still large t-statistics. For the Thai baht and the Malaysian ringgit, the α_2 coefficients are still close to 0.9 with some small weight on the yen as measured by α_3.

Singapore pegged less closely to dollar. Its α_2 was still 0.82 and highly significant statistically, but some small weight was given to the yen and the mark. Indeed, on a lower-frequency basis, before 1997 the Singapore dollar drifted smoothly upward against the U.S. dollar at about 1–2 percent per year. Singapore's somewhat different behavior is quite consistent with its being a creditor country with longer-term domestic capital markets. With a less fragile domestic financial system, the authorities were less concerned with pegging to the dollar and could give more weight to other currencies such as the yen.

In contrast to the high weights of the dollar, as table 1.3 shows, the α_3 coefficients for the yen and the α_4 coefficients for the mark are small or close to zero. Small weights can be observed for the Japanese yen for Korea, Malaysia, Singapore, Taiwan, and Thailand, but in general the weights are low, ranging from 0.03 (new Taiwan dollar) to 0.14 (Singapore dollar).

Crisis: June 1997 to December 1998 During this period, attempts to stabilize East Asian currencies against the U.S. dollar broke down. Large capital outflows and high volatility in the foreign exchange markets defeated any official stabilization efforts. As shown in figure 1.1, from 1994 only China and Hong Kong continued with unwavering dollar pegs. All other countries abandoned their pegs at low as well as high frequencies.

For high-frequency observations, table 1.4 shows the estimations of equation 1.1 for the crisis period. For α_2, the significantly smaller t-values for all countries except China and Hong Kong represent higher standard errors and thus higher volatility in the exchange rate against the dollar. The goodness-of-fit for these regressions falls completely apart: R^2 fell sharply.

The decline in R^2 is particularly marked for the rupiah, won, ringgit, peso, and baht. Noncrisis Singapore and Taiwan coped with the crisis by lowering the weight of the U.S. dollar and increasing the weight

Table 1.4
Pegging on a High-Frequency Basis, Crisis (6/01/97–12/31/98)

	Constant α_1	US$ α_2	Yen α_3	DM α_4	R^2
Chinese yuan	−0.00	0.99[a]	0.00	0.01	0.99
	(−0.39)	(165.56)	(0.68)	(1.45)	
Hong Kong dollar	0.00	1.00[a]	0.01[b]	0.00	0.99
	(0.01)	(194.07)	(1.99)	(0.11)	
Indonesian rupiah	0.00	0.48	0.64[b]	−0.16	0.03
	(1.12)	(1.01)	(2.36)	(−0.28)	
Korean won	0.00	1.22[a]	0.05[a]	0.05	0.13
	(0.62)	(7.05)	(0.59)	(0.58)	
Malaysian ringgit	0.00	0.70[a]	0.33[a]	0.11	0.20
	(1.39)	(5.19)	(3.95)	(0.62)	
Philippine peso	0.00	0.75[a]	0.25[a]	0.27	0.24
	(1.42)	(5.24)	(4.51)	(1.25)	
Singapore dollar	0.00	0.69[a]	0.33[a]	0.02	0.49
	(1.01)	(10.16)	(6.53)	(0.18)	
New Taiwan dollar	0.00	0.87[a]	0.08[b]	0.11	0.59
	(1.24)	(15.19)	(2.91)	(1.69)	
Thai baht	0.00	0.64[a]	0.32[a]	0.21	0.15
	(1.04)	(4.45)	(3.81)	(1.10)	

Source: Datastream.

Notes: Daily data; *t*-statistics in parentheses; 415 observations; white heteroscedasticity-consistent standard errors and covariance.

a. Significant at the 1% level.
b. Significant at the 5% level.

of the Japanese yen, which itself had depreciated sharply. Except for China and Hong Kong, the weight of the yen (the α_3 coefficients) increased during the crisis.

Clearly, by refusing to devalue in the great crisis, China and Hong Kong helped contain the inadvertently beggar-thy-neighbor devaluations in Indonesia, Korea, Malaysia, Philippines, and Thailand. Indeed, Malaysia's pegging of the ringgit in September 1998, albeit at a depreciated level, also helped contain contagious exchange rate changes in the region.

Postcrisis: January 1999 to December 2003   Since the crisis, however, dollar pegging—at least when measured on a high-frequency, day-to-day basis—has made a remarkable return. As shown in table 1.5, the α_2 coefficients for all countries again have returned toward the high values of the precrisis period. Except for Indonesia and to some extent Philippines, the goodness-of-fit as measured by R^2 for each country's

Table 1.5
Pegging on a High-Frequency Basis, Postcrisis (1/01/99–12/31/03)

	Constant α_1	US\$ α_2	Yen α_3	DM α_4	R^2
Chinese yuan	0.00	1.00[a]	−0.00	−0.01	0.99
	(0.00)	(228.69)	(−0.07)	(−1.36)	
Hong Kong dollar	0.00	1.00[a]	0.00[b]	0.00	1.00
	(0.13)	(545.81)	(2.20)	(0.49)	
Indonesian rupiah	0.00	0.95[a]	0.21[a]	−0.01	0.32
	(0.15)	(15.31)	(4.03)	(0.00)	
Korean won	−0.00	0.85[a]	0.18[a]	−0.00	0.74
	(−0.01)	(37.44)	(9.72)	(−0.01)	
Malaysian ringgit	−0.00	1.00[a]	0.00[b]	0.00	1.00
	(−0.07)	(979.34)	(35.98)	(0.01)	
Philippine peso	0.00[c]	0.93[a]	0.10[a]	−0.01	0.64
	(1.85)	(32.41)	(4.05)	(−0.45)	
Singapore dollar	0.00	0.75[a]	0.20[a]	0.05[a]	0.80
	(0.38)	(41.66)	(13.40)	(1.93)	
New Taiwan dollar	0.00	0.94[a]	0.03[c]	0.02	0.92
	(0.76)	(84.61)	(3.14)	(0.92)	
Thai baht	0.00	0.78[a]	0.18[a]	0.02[b]	0.77
	(0.97)	(39.30)	(11.06)	(0.64)	

Source: Datastream.
Notes: Daily data; *t*-statistics in parentheses; 1,304 observations; white heteroscedasticity-consistent standard errors and covariance.
a. Significant at the 1% level.
b. Significant at the 5% level.
c. Significant at the 10% level.

regression equation again becomes tight. The smaller East Asian countries have largely returned to the precrisis practice of informal dollar pegging.

True, as argued by Kawai (2002), the Japanese yen seems to have assumed a certain postcrisis role in some currency baskets, particularly those of Indonesia, Thailand, Korea, and Singapore, but the yen weights remain low in comparison to those of the U.S. dollar. Small values for the goodness-of-fit of the regressions for the Indonesian rupiah and the Philippine peso indicate, however, that both countries have been less successful in stabilizing their currencies after the Asian currency crisis. In particular, Indonesian foreign exchange policy and domestic inflation remain out of control.

A formal statistical test of the postcrisis return to dollar pegging at high frequencies supports this view. To detect if the weights of dollar and yen in the East Asian currency baskets have changed significantly

Table 1.6
Wald Test for Change of U.S. Dollar Weights in East Asian Currency Baskets

	Weight Precrisis (2/01/94–5/30/97)	Weight Postcrisis (1/01/99–12/31/03)	Wald Test Probabilities
Indonesian rupiah	0.99	0.94	0.78
Korean won	0.97	0.85	0.12
Philippine peso	0.97	0.93	0.39
Singapore dollar	0.82	0.75	0.02
New Taiwan dollar	0.98	0.94	0.05
Thai baht	0.92	0.78	0.02

Source: Datastream.

in the postcrisis period, we perform the Wald test for all currencies except the Chinese yuan, the Hong Kong dollar, and the Malaysian ringgit, which are now firmly pegged to the dollar for any frequency of observation. The Wald test is performed based on the comprehensive model described in note 7. This allows us to test if the coefficients (weights) of the U.S. dollar and yen have changed postcrisis in comparison to the precrisis period within one consistent framework.[8]

We proceed in two steps. First, the null hypothesis is that the coefficient for the dollar weight α_2 is the same precrisis and postcrisis. If the probability of the Wald test is low (say, smaller than 5 percent), we reject the null hypothesis. Otherwise we accept the null hypothesis that the weights of the U.S. dollar in the East Asian currency baskets have not changed. Table 1.6 reports the results. The null hypothesis is that the α_2 coefficient of the dollar weight for each country is the same before and after the crisis. At the 5 percent level of significance, we can reject the null hypothesis only for Singapore and Thailand. Postcrisis, only these two countries seem to be giving the yen more weight in their currency baskets, but still at a much lower level than that given to the dollar.

In a second step, we test if the yen weights in the East Asian currency baskets have changed (table 1.7). Some authors such as Kawai (2002) and Ogawa and Ito (2002) have argued that the East Asian countries should increase the weights of the Japanese yen in their currency baskets to avoid economic turmoil in times of yen depreciation. To test if the East Asian countries have followed this proposition, the null hypothesis is that the weights of the yen are the same precrisis and postcrisis.

Table 1.7
Wald Test for Change of Yen Weights in East Asian Currency Baskets

	Weight Precrisis (2/01/94– 5/30/97)	Weight Postcrisis (1/01/99– 12/31/03)	Wald Test Probabilities
Indonesian rupiah	−0.01	0.21	0.20
Korean won	0.06	0.18	0.09
Philippine peso	0.01	0.09	0.14
Singapore dollar	0.14	0.20	0.05
New Taiwan dollar	0.03	0.02	0.99
Thai baht	0.08	0.18	0.08

Source: Datastream.

In this complementary test, we cannot reject the null hypothesis for Singapore at the 5 percent level. But at the 10 percent level, there is evidence for changed yen weights in the Indonesian, Korean, and Thai currency baskets. In Korea the weight of the yen seems to have increased from about 6 to about 18 percent, in Indonesia from 0 to 21 percent, and in the Thailand from about 8 to about 18 percent. Both tests indicate that Indonesia, Korea, and Thailand have increased the weights of the Japanese yen in their currency baskets to some extent, but the U.S. dollar remains the dominant anchor currency.

Using rolling regressions, the country panels in figure 1.3 summarize the dollar's weight in each East Asian currency basket during the 1990s. Based on daily data, the rolling 130-day α_2 coefficient is plotted for each of the East Asian countries (except Japan). A window of 130 days corresponds to an observation period of six months (five observations per week). The first window starts on January 1, 1990, and ends on June 29, 1990. The α_2 coefficient is calculated for the first period. Then the window is shifted by one day, and the α_2 coefficient is calculated again, up to December 2003. A value of unity stands for a 100 percent weight of the respective currency in the respective currency basket. If the coefficient rises above 1, the estimation process is unstable.

Figure 1.3 shows the time path of the dollar weights in the East Asian currency baskets. China and Hong Kong have a very stable dollar weight of unity for the whole observation period. For the other countries in the precrisis period, the dollar weights are also close to unity but slightly more volatile. However, during the crisis period, the exchange rate stabilization broke down in Indonesia, Korea, Malaysia,

Philippines, and Thailand. For these economies figure 1.3 shows an increase in volatility or sharp declines of their α_2 coefficients. Also Singapore lowers the dollar's weight in its currency basket during the crisis.

After the crisis, as figure 1.3 shows, countries have evolved differently. The stabilization process seems still out of control in Indonesia. Malaysia has increased the dollar's weight to 100 percent. In Korea, Philippines, Singapore, Taiwan, and Thailand the trend is somewhat uncertain. For Korea, Thailand, and Singapore the weights of the dollar in the currency baskets seem to decline, as we concluded from the Wald tests reported previously. For Taiwan and Philippines the weights are more stable and roughly the same as in the precrisis period.

In general we observe that the postcrisis weights of the dollar and yen in the currency baskets of Korea, Philippines, Taiwan, and Thailand seem more flexible (volatile) than in the precrisis period but that the dollar continues to predominate.

Reducing Daily Exchange Rate Volatility against the Dollar

However, knowing the dollar's α_2 coefficients and the yen's α_3 coefficients from equation 1.1 is not the whole story on exchange rate volatility. In principle, the dollar could get the highest relative weight (Frankel and Wei 1994) in the currency basket without the absolute day-to-day volatility of any one East Asian currency against the dollar's returning to its precrisis level.

Thus, a more direct, but complementary, test is necessary. We measure volatility as the percentage daily change of the national currency against the dollar (first log differences) from January 1990 through December 2003. The y-axes in the country panels in figure 1.4 have the same scale of ± 8 percent against the dollar for all currencies.

To understand what is high and what is low volatility, we need a standard of comparison. Calvo and Reinhart (2002) suggest that the only truly floating exchange rates are those of mature industrial countries, such the United States, Japan, Germany, or Switzerland. Because these countries have mature, long-term domestic capital markets, their governments have little incentive for day-to-day exchange rate stabilization. Figure 1.4 compares the daily dollar volatilities of the East Asian countries to those of Germany, Japan, and Switzerland.[9]

As shown in figure 1.4, the daily volatility of the dollar exchange rates of Germany, Japan, and Switzerland is indeed an order of magnitude higher than those of East Asian countries in the noncrisis periods.

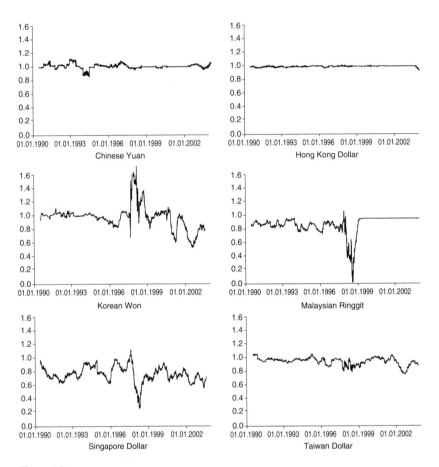

Figure 1.3
U.S. Dollar's Weight in East Asian Currency Baskets, 130-Trading-Day Rolling Regressions for α_2, 1990–2003 (Daily). Index $1 = 100$. An α_2 coefficient close to unity shows strong dollar pegging. (Datastream)

Not only is the daily exchange volatility of these industrial countries very high, but it does not change significantly over time. In contrast, the volatility of the East Asian currencies is generally much lower but with greater variability over time.

Specifically, the hard pegs of China and Hong Kong exhibit extremely low day-to-day volatility as well as a high stability over time. Discretionary changes in the Chinese yuan in the early 1990s occurred before the introduction of the hard peg in February 1994. Since then, the yuan has been even more stable on a day-to-day basis than has the Hong Kong dollar.

Figure 1.3
(continued)

For all the other East Asian economies, we observe a changing pattern of daily volatility over time. Up to 1997–1998 high-frequency volatility was low except in the Philippines, which experienced higher volatility in the first half of the 1990s, although not as high as in the industrial countries. During the Asian crisis, turmoil in the capital and currency markets is reflected in much greater day-to-day volatility, which is most striking for Indonesia, Korea, Malaysia, Philippines, and Thailand.

For the postcrisis period we observe a more heterogeneous pattern. First, Singapore and Taiwan, not as strongly affected by the crisis, returned rather fast to the precrisis pattern. Note that both countries

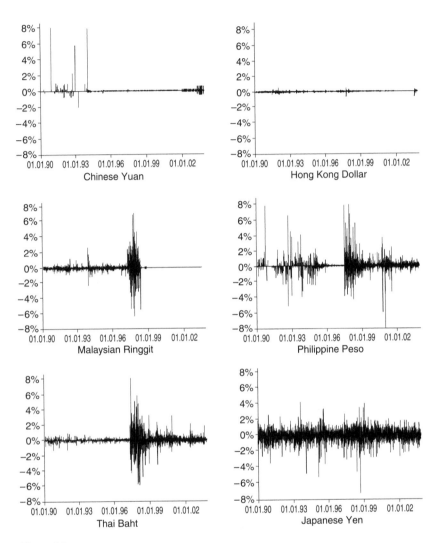

Figure 1.4
Exchange Rate Volatility against U.S. Dollar of Selected Crisis and Noncrisis Currencies, 1990–2003 (Daily). "Volatility" is daily percentage changes against dollar. (Datastream)

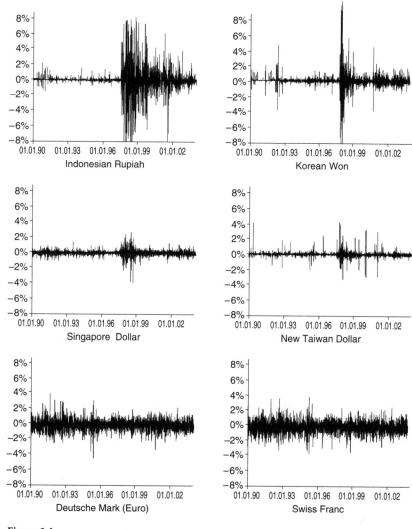

Figure 1.4
(continued)

Table 1.8
Standard Deviations of Daily Exchange Rate Fluctuations against the U.S. Dollar

	Precrisis (2/01/94– 5/30/97)	Crisis (6/01/97– 12/31/98)	Postcrisis (1/01/99– 12/31/03)	2003
Chinese yuan	0.03	0.01	0.00	0.00
Hong Kong dollar	0.02	0.03	0.00	0.00
Indonesian rupiah	0.17	4.43	1.15	0.42
Korean won	0.22	2.35	0.44	0.51
Malaysian ringgit	0.25	1.53	0.01	0.00
Philippine peso	0.37	1.31	0.53	0.27
Singapore dollar	0.20	0.75	0.27	0.36
New Taiwan dollar	0.19	0.50	0.21	0.15
Thai baht	0.21	1.55	0.39	0.26
Japanese yen	0.67	1.00	0.64	0.53
Deutsche mark	0.60	0.58	0.66	0.63
Swiss franc	0.69	0.66	0.71	0.72

Source: Datastream.
Note: Percent changes.

were creditor countries and so could more easily control their exchange rates. Second, Malaysia has adopted capital controls and a hard peg to the dollar, so its exchange rate volatility has declined to zero.

Third, Korea and Thailand have significantly reduced exchange rate volatility, but it seems still to be slightly higher than before the crisis. The larger weight of the yen in the Thai and Korean currency baskets inhibits a complete return to the precrisis level of dollar pegging. Finally, although Indonesia and the Philippines have been quite successful in reducing the day-to-day volatility of their exchange rates compared to during the crisis, volatility is still much higher than before.

The evidence given in figure 1.4 is supported by table 1.8, which reports the standard deviations of daily exchange rate fluctuations against the U.S. dollar. In the precrisis period the standard deviations of the day-to-day exchange rate volatility of all East Asian currencies are much smaller than the standard deviations of the so-called free floaters (Japan, Germany, and Switzerland), which are the comparison set. The standard deviations of the hard pegs (China and Hong Kong) are close to zero during and after the crisis. For Indonesia, Korea, Malaysia, Philippines, and Thailand the standard deviations in table

1.8 increase massively during the crisis period, with Singapore and Taiwan increasing less. In contrast, exchange rate variability against the Japanese yen is high, similar to that of the industrial countries.

Since the crisis, the standard deviations against the dollar of all affected countries have declined again (table 1.8). Except for Malaysia, this exchange rate volatility of the crisis economies for the whole postcrisis period (1999–2003) is still larger than before the crisis. However, the volatility was relatively higher at the beginning of the postcrisis period in 1999 than more recently in 2003.

To underline this last point, suppose the postcrisis period includes only daily observations in the year 2003. Then the right-hand column in table 1.8 shows that many East Asian currencies, such as the Philippine peso, the Taiwan dollar, and to some extent the Thai baht, are now less or about equally volatile against the dollar than they were before the crisis. In 2003 only Indonesia and Korea had still a significantly higher standard deviation. All East Asian countries except Indonesia seem to have more or less returned to the precrisis level of high-frequency pegging.

1.5   The Case against Basket Exchange Rate Pegging

A major reason for the Asian crisis was the deep devaluation of the yen in 1997–1998 (see chapter 2). When the smaller East Asian economies peg to the dollar, they become collectively more vulnerable to fluctuations between the dollar and yen. When the yen is high against the dollar, their exports—and inflows of foreign direct investment from Japan—boom. When the yen depreciates, their international competitiveness falls, sometimes precipitously, as in 1997–1998.

In the aftermath of the Asian crisis many authors, including Williamson (2000), Kawai (2002), and Ogawa and Ito (2002), have proposed increasing the weight of the Japanese yen in the East Asian currency baskets. Because Japan and the smaller East Asian economies are closely linked in trade, they contend that a larger weight of the Japanese yen in the currency baskets of the smaller East Asian economies would reduce variance in trade flows. Japan in particular would like to reduce variance in its own international competitiveness from fluctuations in the yen/dollar rate by having its increasingly important East Asian neighbors give more weight to the yen in setting their exchange rates. For instance, Williamson proposes to give a weight of one-third each to the dollar, the yen, and the euro.

However, we have tried to show that unilateral pegs to the dollar might well be preferred to the currency basket approach, certainly from the perspective of the smaller East Asian economies. First, because the dollar invoicing of trade throughout the whole East Asian region is so prevalent, collective pegging to the dollar provides a quite strong nominal anchor for the national price levels of the smaller countries—albeit in noncrisis periods. Of course, the success of this nominal anchor depends heavily on the stability of the U.S. price level and U.S. monetary policy. But in recent years, U.S. prices have been quite stable while Japan has experienced deflationary pressure. Those advocating basket pegging are more concerned with minimizing the variance in a country's *real* effective exchange rate than with stabilizing its domestic *nominal* price level. Indeed, a commitment to stabilize real effective exchange rates leaves the nominal price level indeterminate.

Second, at a microeconomic level, pegging to just one major international currency helps individual merchants and bankers better hedge their own foreign exchange risks. Because of the missing bond and forward exchange markets in developing countries, governments provide an informal hedge by keeping the domestic currency stable against the dominant currency, the U.S. dollar in East Asia. This then exposes merchants to "extraneous" fluctuations of the yen against the dollar which, however, they can partially hedge by making use of the well-developed forward market between yen and dollars. If a Korean importer of Japanese products needs to pay 100 yen in 60 days, he can buy yen 60 days forward for dollars and then trade won for dollars in 60 days at a presumed unchanged (soft peg of the won against the dollar) exchange rate—what we call double hedging.

However, under a basket peg, the spot exchange rate of the dollar against the won in 60 days would be more uncertain. Because the dollar is the natural intervention currency that governments use, the Korean authorities would be obligated to keep changing the won/dollar rate as the dollar fluctuates against the yen and the euro. This then would confuse the Korean merchant's hedging strategy, particularly if the weights of the major currencies in the basket were somewhat uncertain, and the timing of official changes in the won/dollar rate in order to track the yen was also uncertain. In effect, people who argue that basket pegging would reduce risk are only looking at movements in spot exchange rates as if merchants could not hedge. That is, they are not accounting for the forward hedging strategies that almost all merchants use.

Finally, picking the appropriate official weights in a currency basket is problematic. A simple trade-weighted basket would not reflect the dollar's overwhelming predominance as a currency of invoice, where external dollar prices of goods and services are sticky and don't vary much with changes in the yen/dollar rate. Nor would it reflect the currency of denomination of outstanding foreign currency debts (Slavov 2002).

All in all, the best exchange rate strategy for any small East Asian economy may be the simple "corner solution" of pegging just to the dollar—as is the normal current practice by East Asian governments. However, we do not deny that large fluctuations in the yen/dollar exchange rate create serious problems of risk management for the East Asian dollar peggers (see chapter 2), and even bigger problems for Japan itself (see chapters 3 and 4). But the straightforward solution to this East Asian exchange rate dilemma is for Japan to peg the yen to the U.S. dollar in a convincing fashion, which may require American cooperation, as discussed in McKinnon and Ohno (1997), rather than beseeching nine or so other East Asian countries to give more weight to the yen by introducing basket pegging.

1.6 Conclusion: An Eventual Return to Low-Frequency Pegging?

With the benefit of hindsight, the postcrisis return to high-frequency dollar pegging (see table 1.8 and figures 1.3 and 1.4) is hardly surprising. For emerging markets in East Asia and elsewhere suffering from incomplete capital markets (original sin), high-frequency dollar pegging is an important tool for hedging foreign exchange risk and stabilizing exchange rates. But could this clandestine return to high-frequency pegging augur an eventual return to low-frequency pegging as well?

Many East Asian countries seem to be allowing more exchange rate variability at lower frequencies in the postcrisis period. In support of the finding of Hernández and Montiel (2003), figure 1.1 shows more dollar exchange rate drift after than before the crisis on a month-to-month basis. For Indonesia, Korea, Philippines, Singapore, Taiwan, and Thailand, monthly exchange fluctuations are greater than before, although those for China, Hong Kong, and Malaysia remain (close to) zero.

A more formal analysis of low-frequency exchange rate stabilization against the dollar is given by table 1.9, which allows us to compare the

Table 1.9
Standard Deviations of Monthly Exchange Rate Fluctuations against the U.S. Dollar

	Precrisis (2/01/94– 5/30/97)	Crisis (6/01/97– 12/31/98)	Postcrisis (1/01/99– 12/31/03)
Chinese yuan	0.25	0.03	0.00
Hong Kong dollar	0.08	0.07	0.04
Indonesian rupiah	0.26	26.54	5.28
Korean won	1.01	11.53	1.96
Malaysian ringgit	1.06	6.69	0.00
Philippine peso	1.19	5.25	1.71
Singapore dollar	0.76	2.88	1.20
New Taiwan dollar	1.01	2.63	1.37
Thai baht	0.43	8.88	1.62
Japanese yen	3.66	3.64	2.43
Deutsche mark	2.20	2.33	2.57
Swiss franc	2.62	2.60	2.55

Source: International Monetary Fund, *International Financial Statistics.*
Note: Percent changes.

standard deviations of monthly exchange rate fluctuations against the dollar in the precrisis and postcrisis periods. We observe that for all East Asian countries except the hard peg countries China, Hong Kong, and Malaysia the monthly exchange rate variability against the dollar is still significantly higher than in the precrisis period but much less than during the crisis itself.

An alternative approach for showing exchange rate smoothing at low frequencies in the East Asian postcrisis era is to use the euro's fluctuations against the U.S. dollar as the benchmark. As is largely true in practice, we assume that the European Central Bank, behaving as a free floater, leaves the dollar/euro rate to market forces. We partition the data into two subperiods: 1999–2001, when the dollar appreciated generally against the euro, and 2002 to December 2003, when the dollar generally depreciated against the euro.

Figure 1.5 plots the cumulative depreciation of the euro and all East Asian currencies for the period of dollar appreciation. All East Asian currencies except the Philippine peso but including the Japanese yen depreciated less than the euro against the dollar. Since the beginning of 2002, when the dollar started depreciating, the picture is reversed: figure 1.6 shows that all East Asian currencies appreciated considerably less than did the euro. At the same time, with the exception of

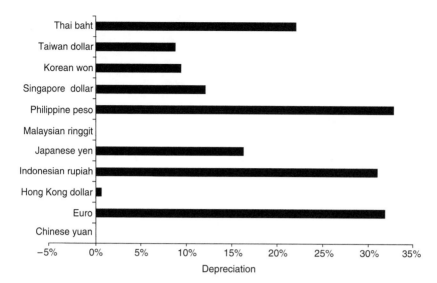

Figure 1.5
Exchange Rate Changes against U.S. Dollar, January 1, 1999–December 31, 2001.
(Datastream)

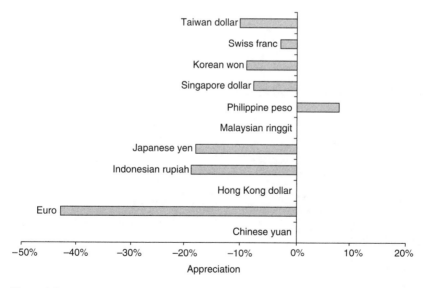

Figure 1.6
Exchange Rate Changes against U.S. Dollar, January 1, 2002–December 31, 2003.
(Datastream)

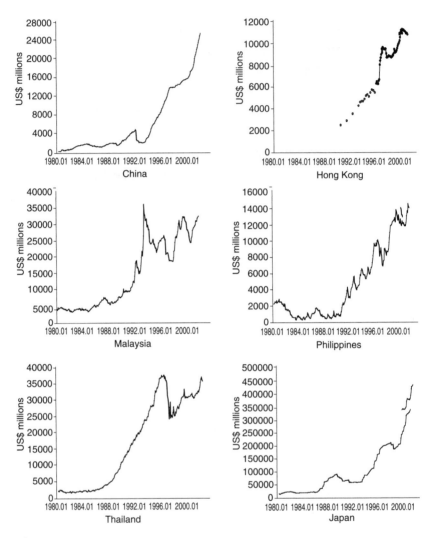

Figure 1.7
Official Foreign Exchange Reserves of Crisis and Noncrisis Countries, 1980–2003 (Monthly). Note different scales on y-axes. (International Monetary Fund, *International Financial Statistics*)

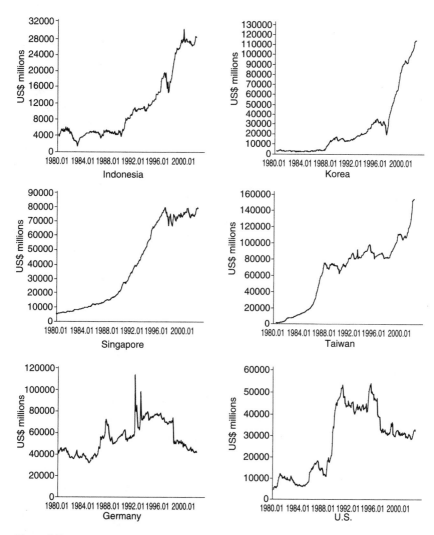

Figure 1.7
(continued)

Indonesia, the smaller East Asian economies appreciated less than did Japan's, thereby also safeguarding their competitiveness against Japan.

In resisting this exchange market pressure for currency appreciation, each East Asian central bank intervened heavily to buy dollars. As shown in figure 1.7, the official foreign reserves in East Asian countries have increased surprisingly fast in China, Hong Kong, Indonesia, Korea, Malaysia, Philippines, Taiwan, Thailand, and particularly Japan. Indeed, in 2003 the Japanese government intervened truly massively: official reserves rose by $222 billion, which is greater than Japan's current account surplus of $132 billion. (For a more comprehensive analysis of the enormous buildup of East Asian current account surpluses and official reserve accumulation, see chapter 8.).

Over the long run, sustaining exchange rate stability in East Asia at low frequencies will mainly depend on the region's two largest economies, China and Japan. So far, China has taken the lead by firmly keeping its exchange rate at 8.28 yuan/dollar since 1994 despite domestic pressure and foreign advice to depreciate in the 1997–1998 crisis and foreign pressure to appreciate in 2002–2003. Although fluctuations in the yen/dollar rate have been much more of a disturbing influence, particularly the deep depreciation of the yen that aggravated the crisis, the postcrisis signs show Japan to be somewhat more determined to stabilize the yen/dollar rate, if not as successfully as China. Chapters 3 and 4 on Japan and chapter 5 on China analyze the exchange rate dilemmas facing each of these dominant East Asian economies.

To be sure, more formal "parity" commitments to peg the yuan and yen to the dollar would encourage the smaller East Asian countries to similarly peg their dollar exchange rates—thus creating a zone of greater monetary and exchange rate stability for the increasingly integrated East Asian economy. However, even if Japan returns to being a dangerous outlier with wide fluctuations in the yen/dollar rate, having the other East Asian countries stabilize their dollar exchange rates collectively seems more rational than the IMF's cumulative institutional wisdom of pushing for greater exchange rate flexibility with no well-defined constraint on how any one country's rate affects its neighbors.

2

Synchronized Business Cycles in East Asia and Fluctuations in the Yen/Dollar Exchange Rate

with Günther Schnabl

Should the Japanese yen be depreciated to revive the country's economy? Since the bursting of the stock and land market bubbles in 1990–1991, the Japanese economy has fallen into its deepest postwar recession. Because fiscal policy and monetary policy are at their limits in combating recession and deflation, a possible solution through foreign exchange policy has gained wide attention. (True, in 2004, the Japanese economy is weakly recovering on the back of the China boom. But the exchange rate argument remains well worth examining.)

For instance, McCallum (2000) proposes to stimulate Japanese output through unsterilized foreign exchange intervention. Meltzer (1999) states that yen devaluation by unsterilized foreign currency purchases would restore Japan's competitive position in the world economy and thus support a sustained recovery. Svensson (2000) presumes to have found a "foolproof way of escaping from the liquidity trap" by combining an inflation target with a real yen depreciation. The International Monetary Fund (2001, 33–34) has urged the Bank of Japan "to use all instruments at its disposal to combat deflation," that is, to further expand money supply and to depreciate the yen.

In late 2002 several Japanese officials, hoping that a weaker yen would boost the country's ailing economy, stepped up efforts to talk the yen lower. Financial Services Minister Takenaka expressed his country's desire for a weaker yen. Similarly, Finance Minister Shiokawa repeatedly stated that the yen is overvalued (*Financial Times*, December 9, 2002).

However, Okina (1999, 179) of the Bank of Japan rejects the demands for a weaker yen. Large-scale purchases of foreign currency by the

Adapted from Ronald I. McKinnon and Günther Schnabl, "Synchronized Business Cycles in East Asia, and Fluctuations in the Yen/Dollar Exchange Rate," *The World Economy* 26 (August 2003): 1067–1088.

Japanese authorities with the aim of depreciating the yen could provoke opposition from its major trading partners and be criticized as a beggar-thy-neighbor policy. Japan's small East Asian neighbor countries vehemently oppose a weaker yen (*The Economist* 2002).

The proponents of a significant yen depreciation doubt that it would hurt Japan's neighboring economies. Bernanke (2000, 161) argues that the beggar-thy-neighbor argument against competitive devaluation had its origins in the Great Depression and does not apply to contemporary Japan and East Asia. According to Meltzer (1999, 189–190) a yen devaluation has no strong negative impacts on Japan's trading partners, particularly if the positive impact of a Japanese recovery is counted: "In my view—and supported by the experience of the past decade—devaluation would be a cheaper, and I believe, faster way to restore prosperity to Japan and its neighbors."

Svensson (2000) and the International Monetary Fund (2000, 28–30; 2001, 28–29) assume that the negative effect that a yen depreciation might cause in East Asia's smaller countries would be more than offset by more Japanese imports from the region. In an IMF working paper, Callen and McKibbin (2001) apply a macroeconomic G-cubed Asia-Pacific model with international trade and capital flows to explore how yen depreciation affects the smaller East Asian economies. They contend that Japanese monetary expansion coupled with yen depreciation would have minimal effects on the rest of Asia.

In this chapter, however, we contend that the opposite is true. Updating a model pioneered by C. H. Kwan (2001), we show that the current and lagged effects of a yen depreciation on output in the smaller East Asian economies have been strongly negative. Within plausible ranges of income growth in Japan or movements in the yen/U.S. dollar exchange rate, the positive impulse of more regional imports from Japan should Japanese income growth increase is swamped by the negative effect of substantial yen depreciation. Indeed, for the past two decades, fluctuations in the yen/dollar rate have generated a synchronized business cycle in the smaller East Asian economies.

2.1 Growing Economic Integration and Synchronized Business Cycles in East Asia

Since the early 1980s, East Asian countries outside Japan chose a development strategy based on international trade and sound macroeco-

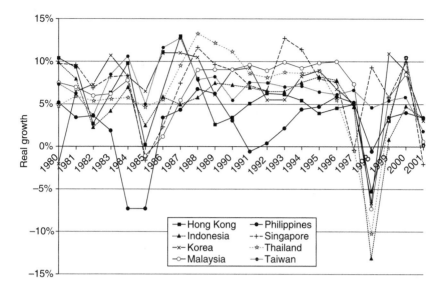

Figure 2.1
Synchronized Business Cycles in East Asia (EA$_1$), 1980–2001 (Yearly). EA$_1$ comprises Hong Kong, Indonesia, Korea, Malaysia, Philippines, Singapore, Taiwan, Thailand. (International Monetary Fund, *International Financial Statistics*; Central Bank of China)

nomic policies. Their subsequent rapid export-led economic growth with fiscal balance and relative price-level stability led to what the World Bank (1993) called the "The East Asian Miracle."

Less well known is that these high-growth economies have experienced a synchronized business cycle. Figure 2.1 suggests, as is shown later by econometric estimations, that since 1980 the real GDPs of the smaller East Asian economies have fluctuated in parallel. In particular, growth rates of Hong Kong, Indonesia, Korea, Malaysia, Taiwan, and Thailand have been highly correlated. These countries are the core of the East Asian business cycle, to which the Philippines and Singapore are more loosely attached.

For ease of notation, we denote the bloc of the eight smaller East Asian countries—Hong Kong, Korea, Singapore, Taiwan, Indonesia, Malaysia, the Philippines, and Thailand—by EA$_1$. Then EA$_2$ is EA$_1$ plus China, and EA$_3$ is EA$_2$ plus Japan.

Output synchronization in the EA$_1$ countries springs from several related factors. First, their regional proximity and growing direct trade linkages have strengthened economic interdependence. More indirectly, they have been export competitors in third markets such as the

Table 2.1
Intra-Asian Trade, 1980–2002 (percent)

	Exports			Imports		
	EA$_3$	EA$_2$	EA$_1$	EA$_3$	EA$_2$	EA$_1$
EA$_1$						
1980			18.9			15.3
1990			22.2			19.6
2002			28.9			27.2
EA$_2$						
1980		21.7			18.2	
1990		32.0			30.1	
2002		37.9			45.3	
EA$_3$						
1980	32.0			31.8		
1990	39.6			42.9		
2002	46.8			56.4		

Source: International Monetary Fund, *Direction-of-Trade Statistics.*
Notes:
EA$_1$ = Hong Kong, Indonesia, Korea, Malaysia, Philippines, Singapore, Taiwan, Thailand.
EA$_2$ = EA$_1$ + China.
EA$_3$ = EA$_2$ + Japan.

United States and Japan. Second, they follow similar exchange rate, monetary, and fiscal policies. Third, the EA$_1$ countries are directly or indirectly affected by exogenous fluctuations in the yen/dollar exchange rate, our primary focus in this chapter.

International trade has been the driving force behind the so-called miracle growth with rapid industrialization. Initially, the East Asian economies relied heavily on exports to, and imports from, the United States, Japan, and other industrial countries. In the last two decades, however, intra–East Asian trade became relatively more important (Urata 2001). From 1980 to 2002, as table 2.1 shows, exports to other EA$_1$ countries rose from 18.9 percent to 28.9 percent of overall EA$_1$ exports. The share of imports from other EA$_1$ countries increased from 15.3 percent to 27.2 percent. If China is included, the share of intraregional trade increases further: EA$_2$ exports to other EA$_2$ countries increased from 21.7 percent in 1980 to 37.9 percent in 2002. If Japan is included, intra–East Asian trade increased from 32 percent in 1980 to 56.4 percent in 2002.

Table 2.2
East Asian Trade with China, Japan, U.S., and ROW, 1980–2002 (percent)

	Exports				Imports			
	China	Japan	U.S.	ROW	China	Japan	U.S.	ROW
EA$_1$								
1980	1.5	19.2	23.1	37.3	4.7	23.8	17.1	39.1
1990	6.4	14.4	24.9	32.0	9.4	23.0	16.1	31.9
2002	13.8	9.5	18.9	28.8	16.2	15.3	13.5	27.8
EA$_2$								
1980		19.6	20.9	37.6		24.2	17.4	40.2
1990		14.4	22.5	31.1		21.9	15.6	32.4
2002		10.9	21.9	29.4		15.5	12.3	26.9
EA$_3$								
1980			22.6	45.4			17.4	50.8
1990			26.2	34.2			18.1	39.0
2002			23.7	29.4			13.5	30.2

Source: International Monetary Fund, *Direction-of-Trade Statistics.*
Notes:
EA$_1$ = Hong Kong, Indonesia, Korea, Malaysia, Philippines, Singapore, Taiwan, Thailand.
EA$_2$ = EA$_1$ + China.
EA$_3$ = EA$_2$ + Japan.
ROW = Rest of the world.

In contrast, East Asian trade with industrial countries other than the United States has declined comparatively. Table 2.2 shows the share of EA$_3$ exports to the rest of the world (ROW)[1] as a percentage of overall exports declined from 45.4 percent in 1980 to 29.4 percent in 2002. The share of imports from ROW declined from 50.8 percent in 1980 to 30.2 percent in 2002.

Instead of relying on exports to and imports from the industrial countries as the sole driving force behind their rising incomes, the smaller East Asian countries have developed their own economic dynamics. While there is no doubt that the intensification of intra-Asian trade and the synchronization of the business cycles are closely intertwined, the causality is unclear. Do closer trade linkages contribute to a common business cycle, or are there common external shocks, or both?

Theoretically, rising trade between two countries can result in greater or weaker synchronization of aggregate demand fluctuations (Frankel and Rose 1998). If two countries engage in Heckscher-Ohlin or Ricardian type trade, they become more specialized in certain economic sectors or industries. Thus their business cycles tend to be more idiosyncratic. As trade in dissimilar products between two countries increases, with one country specializing in the production of, say, cars and the other specializing in the production of palm oil, both countries will react differently to industry-specific exogenous shocks. Business cycles will also differ.

Suppose, however, that intraindustry trade predominates, as in electrical equipment and semiconductors. Because one country both imports this equipment from, and exports it to, the other, exogenous shocks will affect both in the same way. Business cycles will be synchronous. A sudden decline in the demand for computers would slow economic growth in both countries.

Because both types of trade patterns can be observed, the impact of strengthened trade linkages on the common business cycle is ambiguous. First, the newly industrialized club of Hong Kong, Korea, Singapore, and Taiwan, of which China is an increasingly important member, has highly developed and capital-intensive industries where intraindustry trade could be important. Second, the ASEAN core countries of Indonesia, Malaysia, Philippines, and Thailand focus more on agricultural products, raw materials, and labor-intensive products, where intraindustry trade is less important. Between the two groups, (horizontal) interindustry trade as well as (vertical) intraindustry trade within the East Asian production system are possible.

The upshot is that industry-specific random shocks are unlikely to generate the highly synchronized business cycles shown in figure 2.1. Instead we must look for macroeconomic shocks that affect aggregate demand and broad industrial competitiveness across the board in East Asia outside of Japan. Thus we focus on fluctuations in the yen/dollar exchange rate.

2.2 Fluctuations in the Yen/Dollar Exchange Rate: The Loose Cannon

Central to our argument in chapter 1 is the fact that all East Asian countries except Japan tend to stabilize their exchange rate against the U.S. dollar in noncrisis periods. Before 1997–1998 all smaller East Asian countries pegged to the U.S. currency, more on a high-frequency day-to-day or week-to-week basis but with some drift at lower frequencies of observation. McKinnon (2000; 2001a) called this mutual exchange rate stabilization the East Asian dollar standard.

Contrary to the IMF's urging, by 2002 the East Asian countries other than Japan were returning or had returned to their precrisis practices of pegging to the dollar (see chapter 1). Indeed, China, Hong Kong, and Malaysia now appear to be firmly pegged to the dollar at all frequencies of observation, although Indonesia remains an out-of-control outlier. The other East Asian countries except Japan pursue looser, but still rather tight, pegs to the dollar on a high-frequency basis. Because the dollar is the dominant currency for invoicing intraregional trade and denominating international capital flows, the smaller East Asian economies peg to the dollar to reduce payments risk and to anchor their domestic price levels. But this leaves them vulnerable to changes in the yen/dollar exchange rate.

Because of their export orientation and their relatively small size, the EA_1 economies are already very open. In 2001 trade (exports + imports) as a percentage of GDP ranged from 74 percent in Indonesia to 277 percent in Hong Kong, reflecting the latter's status as the center of entrepôt trade with the Chinese mainland. Although international trade has been, and will be, a critical factor in their economic success, it also increases their collective vulnerability to foreign shocks. And fluctuations in the yen/dollar exchange rate have been the most important of these shocks.

Alone among East Asian countries, Japan has chosen or been forced to accept (McKinnon and Ohno 1997) a situation where its currency varies widely against the U.S. dollar. Since early 1971, figure 2.2 shows, the yen has appreciated from its Bretton Woods parity of 360 yen/dollar to around 106 yen/dollar in early 2003. Although the trend of continual yen appreciation seemingly ended in 1995, fluctuations in the yen/dollar exchange rate have not abated in the last decade. Figure 2.2 also shows the large variations in the yen/dollar exchange rate since 1990.

By keeping their exchange rates stable against the U.S. dollar, the smaller East Asian economies must cope with extraneous fluctuations of the dollar against the yen. To illustrate the magnitude of this problem over the past decade, figure 2.3 shows the large fluctuations of the yen against the Hong Kong dollar, which has remained firmly pegged to the U.S. dollar since the early 1980s. The upper panels in figure 2.3 show the gradual swings in the absolute level of the Hong Kong dollar's exchange rate against U.S. dollar and yen; the lower panels show the monthly percentage exchange rate fluctuations. Clearly in both terms—absolute swings and relative changes—the yen/U.S. dollar

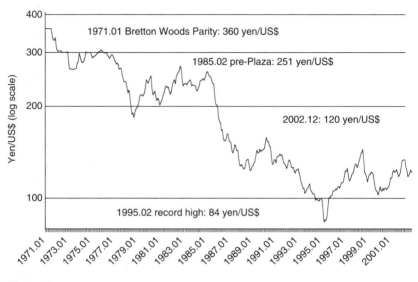

Figure 2.2
Yen/U.S. Dollar Exchange Rate, 1971–2002 (Monthly). (International Monetary Fund, *International Financial Statistics*)

exchange rate is a volatile outlier for Hong Kong in particular and for the East Asian exchange rate system as a whole. This imbalance has important consequences.

The yen/dollar exchange rate affects collective EA_1 output in two ways: trade and foreign direct investment (Kwan 2001). The first is a real exchange rate or international competitiveness effect. Yen/dollar fluctuations impact Japan's international competitiveness both against the United States and against all the other East Asian countries, which peg to the dollar. While yen appreciation stimulates EA_1 exports to Japan and to the rest of the world, yen depreciation impairs the international competitiveness of the EA_1 economies. When the yen depreciates, EA_1 imports and competition from Japanese goods increase while their exports decline.

Figure 2.4 shows that the exports of the smaller East Asian countries have fluctuated with the yen/dollar exchange rate. When the yen appreciated, such as following the Plaza Agreement (September 1985), EA_1 exports strongly expanded. In contrast, yen depreciation after 1995 slowed East Asian export expansion significantly. And the sharp yen depreciation of 1996–1998 (figure 2.2) greatly worsened the crisis in other East Asian economies in 1997–1998. The change in overall

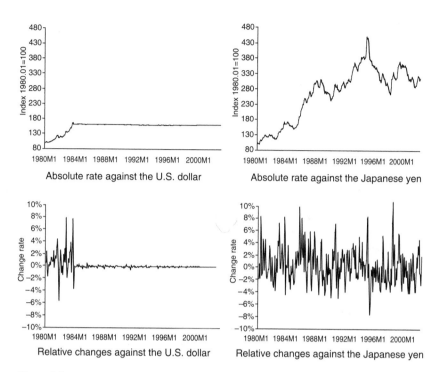

Figure 2.3
Hong Kong Dollar against U.S. Dollar and Yen, 1980–2002 (Monthly). (International Monetary Fund, *International Financial Statistics*)

EA$_1$ exports can be subdivided into a Japan, an intra-Asian, and a third-market effect. Although not plotted here, all three effects move in parallel with respect to changes in the yen/dollar exchange rate.

The second transmission channel is Japanese foreign direct investment (FDI) into the rest of East Asia. FDI is highly correlated with the yen/dollar exchange rate. FDI accelerates when the yen appreciates (figure 2.5) because production and investment in Japan itself become relatively more expensive. When the yen is high and appreciating, the influx of Japanese long-term capital and know-how boosts domestic gross fixed investment in EA$_1$ and stimulates output, and vice versa when the yen is low.

The exchange-driven nature of Japanese FDI was particularly pronounced in the early 1990s. When the yen rose from 145 per dollar in 1990 to less than 80 per dollar in 1995, Japanese FDI to EA$_1$ increased fast (figure 2.5). Japanese multinationals and even small and medium

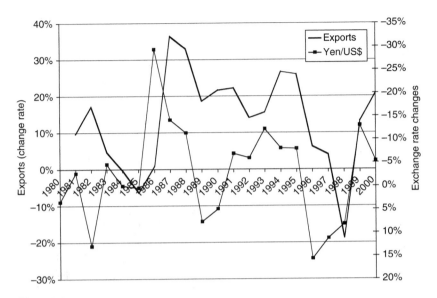

Figure 2.4
East Asia (EA₁) Exports and the Yen/U.S. Dollar Exchange Rate, 1980–2001 (Yearly).
EA₁ comprises Hong Kong, Indonesia, Korea, Malaysia, Philippines, Singapore, Taiwan,
Thailand. (International Monetary Fund, *International Financial Statistics*)

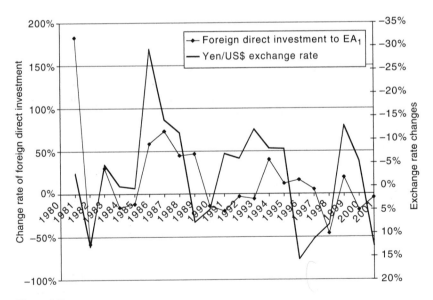

Figure 2.5
Japan's Foreign Direct Investment to East Asia (EA₁) and the Yen/U.S. Dollar Exchange
Rate, 1980–2001 (Fiscal Years). (Japanese Ministry of Finance; International Monetary
Fund, *International Financial Statistics*)

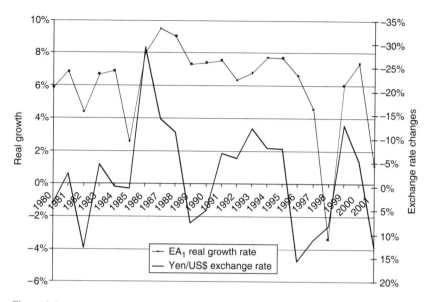

Figure 2.6
East Asia (EA$_1$) Business Cycle and the Yen/U.S. Dollar Exchange Rate, 1980–2001 (Yearly). EA$_1$ comprises Hong Kong, Indonesia, Korea, Malaysia, Philippines, Singapore, Taiwan, Thailand. (International Monetary Fund, *International Financial Statistics*; Central Bank of China)

enterprises shifted unprofitable parts of the production process to the low-wage and generally lower-cost East Asian countries. In Japan this rationalization process was perceived as hollowing out (*kûdôka*) of the Japanese economy, while it provided an additional growth stimulus to its smaller neighbors.

Froot and Stein (1991) give another explanation for the dependence of FDI on exchange rates. The exchange rate affects FDI (and thus domestic investment) more when firms are capital-constrained. Because of asymmetric information, the profits of an FDI acquisition of real estate or production facilities are much more difficult to know for outsiders than is the case for portfolio investment.[2] Thus, the more internal financing (wealth) a firm can bring into an FDI project, the lower the total costs will be. An appreciation of the domestic currency increases the relative net worth of the domestic enterprise for investing abroad, and the domestic investor can bid more aggressively for foreign assets. The FDI out of the home country increases.

Figure 2.6 shows that the economies of the EA$_1$ countries[3] tend to grow faster when the yen is appreciating, and vice versa. But lags are so involved that the full effects cannot be discerned graphically. Thus to show the pervasive impact, both collectively and individually, of fluctuations in the yen/dollar exchange rate on income growth in the other East Asian countries, a more formal regression analysis is necessary.

2.3   The Impact of Yen/Dollar Fluctuations on Regional Output

Econometrically, we estimate the impact of yen/dollar fluctuations on output in the East Asian region outside of Japan. Consider first the econometric model of Kwan (2001, 38–41). For the period 1982–1997, Kwan regressed the real growth rate of EA_2 (the EA_1 countries plus China) on yearly changes in the yen/U.S. dollar exchange rate $(e^{Y\$})$ and on real growth in the United States (y^{US}). Kwan's multivariate distributed lag model of economic interdependency in East Asia is described thus:

$$y_t^{EA_2} = \beta_1 + \beta_2 y_t^{US} + \beta_3 e_t^{Y\$} + \beta_4 e_{t-1}^{Y\$} + u_t \tag{2.1}$$

Table 2.3 reports our reestimated coefficients of Kwan's model. As Kwan did, we used yearly data because quarterly data on real GDP

Table 2.3
Kwan Model of Fluctuations in East Asian Output (EA_2), 1982–2001

U.S. GDP Growth	Yen/US$ Exchange Rate		Adj. R^2	Durbin-Watson
	Current	One-Year Lag		
0.31			0.03	1.12
(1.25)				
	−0.11[a]		0.29	1.49
	(−2.97)			
	−0.09[b]	−0.08[b]	0.42	1.42
	(−2.67)	(−2.19)		
0.18	−0.10[b]		0.28	1.40
(0.83)	(−2.70)			
0.19	−0.08[b]	−0.08[b]	0.41	1.43
(1.01)	(−2.38)	(−2.23)		

Sources: International Monetary Fund, *International Financial Statistics*; Central Bank of China.
Notes: The dependent variable is annual output growth in EA_2; regression coefficients correspond to elasticities; *t*-values in parentheses.
a. Significant at the 1% level.
b. Significant at the 5% level.

are not available for most East Asian countries for the whole observation period. All regressions are run with yearly rates of change (first differences) to avoid problems caused by nonstationarity.[4] Table 2.3 shows a strong inverse correlation between the yen/dollar exchange rate and growth in EA_2, as Kwan found. For every 1 percent increase in the yen/dollar rate both current and lagged one year, real growth in EA_2 falls about 0.17 percent.[5]

To further investigate the transmission of business cycles in East Asia, we modified Kwan's model in four respects. First, we introduced the impact of Japanese output fluctuations on the other East Asian countries as an additional exogenous variable.[6] Second, we disaggregated Kwan's model down to the individual country level to test whether fluctuations in the yen/dollar exchange rate have a different impact on output across Asian countries. Third, we isolated the important role of China within the East Asian macro system. Fourth, we identified the cyclic spillover effects from the EA_1 countries as a whole to individual members.

The estimations are performed in three steps. In step 1 we estimate only the interactive output effects in East Asia, from which exchange rate effects are excluded. The impact of changes in output in the United States, China, Japan, and $REA1_j$ (the EA_1 countries other than the jth one being considered) on output of the single East Asian country j is estimated. In step 2 we estimate the impact of the yen/dollar exchange rate on output in the East Asian countries collectively and individually, both including and excluding the crisis years of 1997–1998. In step 3 we draw conclusions from the combined interpretation of steps 1 and 2.

Measuring Output Fluctuations
We show how output fluctuations in the large countries—Japan, China, and the United States—influence output in the smaller East Asian economies. Let y_{Japan}, y_{China}, y_{US}, and y_{REA1j} be annual growth in real output in Japan, China, the United States, and the rest of EA_1 (EA_1 except country j, which is the dependent variable), respectively. We then regress the economic growth of country j on these variables. We don't use any lagged exogenous variables because they did not yield any significant results in previous tests. The tested equation is

$$y_j = \beta_1 + \beta_2 y_{US} + \beta_3 y_{Japan} + \beta_4 y_{China} + \beta_5 y_{REA1j} + u_t \tag{2.2}$$

Table 2.4
Mutual Determinants of East Asian Output, 1980–2001

j	U.S. (β_2)	Japan (β_3)	China (β_4)	REA1$_j$ (β_5)	Adj. R^2 (R^2)
Hong Kong	0.16	0.90[a]	0.18		0.04
	(0.34)	(1.86)	(0.61)		(0.18)
	0.07		0.11	1.04[c]	0.45
	(0.21)		(0.49)	(4.38)	(0.53)
Indonesia	−0.44	1.22[b]	0.23		0.15
	(−0.90)	(2.47)	(0.78)		(0.27)
	−0.60		0.13	1.16[c]	0.50
	(−1.61)		(0.56)	(4.85)	(0.58)
Korea	0.27	0.97[b]	0.17		0.08
	(0.57)	(2.01)	(0.58)		(0.21)
	0.25		0.10	0.84[c]	0.26
	(0.58)		(0.38)	(3.03)	(0.36)
Malaysia	−0.16	0.84	0.08		−0.01
	(−0.31)	(1.63)	(0.24)		(0.13)
	−0.29		−0.01	1.19[c]	0.57
	(−0.87)		(−0.03)	(5.50)	(0.63)
Philippines	−0.19	0.06	−0.57[b]		0.20
	(−0.50)	(0.15)	(−2.43)		(0.31)
	−0.25		−0.60[b]	0.40[a]	0.31
	(−0.71)		(−2.78)	(1.80)	(0.42)

Because economic growth in Japan and in REA1$_j$ are interdependent, the assumption of independence between the exogenous variables is violated. To cope with this multicollinearity problem we estimate a first regression with Japan as the exogenous variable and leaving REA1$_j$ out. In a second regression we drop Japan, using REA1$_j$ as the exogenous variable.

The regression results are reported in table 2.4, where the effect of fluctuations in each of these larger countries on the individual smaller ones is shown. There are four main findings. First, the business cycles in China and the United States have no measurable impact on the output fluctuations of the smaller East Asian countries.[7] All coefficients for the United States (β_2) and China (β_4) in equation 2.2 are insignificant.[8] Only Taiwan's output fluctuations somewhat depend on those in the United States.

Second, as depicted in figure 2.1, the evidence for a common business cycle in the small East Asian economies is strong, as reflected by the β_5 coefficients for REA1$_j$ in equation 2.2. For all the EA$_1$ countries shown in table 2.4, the β_5 coefficients are significant. This coefficient is significant at the 1 percent level for six countries (Hong Kong, Indone-

Table 2.4
(continued)

j	U.S. (β_2)	Japan (β_3)	China (β_4)	REA1$_j$ (β_5)	Adj. R^2 (R^2)
Singapore	0.26	0.58	−0.13		−0.05
	(0.55)	(1.20)	(−0.45)		(0.10)
	0.19		−0.20	0.92[c]	0.40
	(0.52)		(−0.90)	(4.00)	(0.49)
Taiwan	0.57[a]	0.68[b]	0.14		0.30
	(1.99)	(2.35)	(0.82)		(0.40)
	0.60[b]		0.09	0.42[b]	0.34
	(2.14)		(0.54)	(2.66)	(0.43)
Thailand	−0.40	1.74[c]	0.30		0.36
	(−0.88)	(3.78)	(1.09)		(0.46)
	−0.57		0.18	1.43[c]	0.63
	(−1.63)		(0.85)	(6.10)	(0.68)
China	0.58	−0.19			0.04
	(1.65)	(−0.51)			(0.14)
	0.57			0.02	0.03
	(1.63)			(0.08)	(0.12)
EA$_1$	0.02	0.61[b]	−0.01		0.11
	(0.06)	(2.26)	(−0.08)		(0.26)
EA$_2$	0.31	0.45[a]			0.18
	(1.49)	(2.07)			(0.26)

Sources: International Monetary Fund, *International Financial Statistics*; Central Bank of China.

Notes: The dependent variable is annual output growth of the respective EA$_2$ countries.; *t*-statistics in parentheses.

EA$_1$ = Hong Kong, Indonesia, Korea, Malaysia, Philippines, Singapore, Taiwan, Thailand.

EA$_2$ = EA$_1$ + China.

REA1$_j$ = EA$_1$ excluding country *j*.

a. Significant at the 10% level.

b. Significant at the 5% level.

c. Significant at the 1% level.

sia, Korea, Malaysia, Singapore, Thailand) and at the 5 percent level for Taiwan. The Philippines' coefficient is significant at the 10 percent level.

Third, Japan has an important effect on the business cycles of its smaller neighboring countries. Japan's output changes have a significant impact on five out of eight East Asian countries—Hong Kong, Indonesia, Korea, Taiwan, and Thailand. Malaysia is close to significance at the 10 percent level. Only the business cycles of the Philippines and Singapore seem not to be linked to Japan's. For EA$_1$ as a whole, the impact of Japan's business cycle is significant at the 5 percent level. For

EA$_2$ the impact of the Japan's business cycle is significant at the 10 percent level.

Fourth, our estimates show that the United States, Japan, and the EA$_1$ countries collectively do not significantly influence output fluctuations in China, whose business cycle seems to be relatively uncorrelated with those in other Asian countries. Why should China be comparatively immune from exogenous shocks originating abroad? First, China is a very large continental economy with a modest, albeit growing, degree of openness in trade in goods and services. Second, insulated by capital controls, China's domestic countercyclical policies have successfully stabilized its very high GDP growth rates (see chapter 5). Also from table 2.4, modest fluctuations in China's own output growth do not much impinge on the smaller East Asian economies. Consequently, despite China's rapid growth and increasing relative size, it has been an important stabilizing macroeconomic influence in the increasingly integrated East Asian economy.

Measuring Exchange Rate Effects

Despite the positive correlation of East Asian and Japanese outputs, their business cycles are far from being totally synchronized. Because of the asymmetric impact of changes in the yen/dollar exchange rate, Japanese and East Asian business cycles could diverge. The impact of a higher yen is to depress growth in Japan while stimulating it in the rest of East Asia. A weaker yen stimulates Japan's economy while depressing growth in the smaller East Asian countries.

In step 1 we measured interactive output effects while ignoring the exchange rate. Now we measure *only* the concurrent and lagged effects of the exchange rate on output in *each* of the East Asian countries. Concurrently, that is, within the year corresponding to our annual observations, changes in the yen/dollar rate affect the competitiveness of exports (table 2.5). But also with a lag, there might be some impact through exports and foreign direct investment.

After regressing different lag lengths of the yen/dollar exchange rate on annual output changes for every East Asian country, lags of two periods or longer become insignificant. Therefore regression equation 2.3 uses a maximum lag of just one year.

$$y_{j_t} = \gamma + \sum_{i=0}^{1} \beta_i e_{t-1}^{Y\$} + u_t \tag{2.3}$$

Again there is the problem of multicollinearity where successive time series data on the yen/dollar exchange rate tend to be correlated. For any one estimated coefficient, its standard error is "too large," leading to an underestimation of its true t-value. However, the coefficients associated with each lag are still unbiased and efficient, and the overall fit of the model is adequately reflected in the R^2 and F statistics. To measure the cumulative or long-run effect of a change in the yen/U.S. dollar rate, we can simply sum the two coefficients for the zero and one-year lag.

The results of so estimating equation 2.3 are reported in table 2.5. The negative impact of the yen/dollar exchange rate on the output in the EA_1 and EA_2 countries is strong, both significant at the 5 percent level. On the individual country level, changes of the yen/dollar exchange rate most strongly affect the newly industrialized economies (NIEs) and Thailand, which directly compete with Japanese enterprises in EA_2, in Japan, and in third markets. The coefficients of Hong Kong, Korea, and Taiwan are significant at the 5 or 10 percent level in the same period. The long-run coefficients—adding the impact of the concurrent and lagged period—of -0.29 for Hong Kong, -0.27 for Korea, -0.20 for Taiwan, and -0.33 for Thailand are all significant at the 1 percent level. Taken at face value, these are big numbers. For example, a 1 percent depreciation of the yen against the U.S. dollar would slow Thai growth by almost one-third of 1 percent.

In contrast, the coefficients for Indonesia, Malaysia, Philippines, and Singapore have the expected sign without being significant. However, the fact that a depreciation of the yen against the dollar affects them all (slightly) negatively means that the t-value for any one equation likely understates its true significance.

Although China's own long-run exchange multiplier is only significant at the 10 percent level, its net stabilizing influence on the other East Asian countries is better shown by comparing the highly significant regression coefficients for EA_1 and EA_2. Table 2.5 shows that the long-run multiplier for a change in the yen/dollar rate on the smaller East Asian economies collectively is -0.21 but drops to -0.17 when China is included. China is much less affected by changes in the yen/dollar rate than are the others.

The Crisis Years, 1997–1998
Could it be that our demonstration of the strength of fluctuations in the yen/dollar exchange rate is biased by an outlying observation? In

Table 2.5
Exchange Rate Determinants of East Asian Output, 1980–2001

	Yen/US\$$_t$ (β_2)	Yen/US\$$_{t-1}$ (β_3)	Adj. R^2 (R^2)	LRM
Hong Kong	−0.18[a]	−0.11	0.30	−0.29[b]
	(−2.53)	(−1.50)	(0.36)	(−3.19)
Indonesia	−0.05	−0.13	0.02	−0.18
	(−0.49)	(−1.29)	(0.11)	(−1.54)
Korea	−0.19[a]	−0.08	0.25	−0.27[b]
	(−2.46)	(−1.03)	(0.32)	(−2.83)
Malaysia	−0.01	−0.12	−0.01	−0.13
	(−0.12)	(−1.29)	(0.09)	(1.15)
Philippines	0.02	−0.08	−0.05	−0.06
	(0.27)	(−0.98)	(0.05)	(0.61)
Singapore	−0.05	−0.07	−0.03	−0.13
	(−0.57)	(−0.84)	(0.06)	(−1.14)
Taiwan	−0.15[c]	−0.04	0.32	−0.20[b]
	(−3.08)	(−0.69)	(0.38)	(−3.17)
Thailand	−0.11	−0.22[a]	0.27	−0.33[b]
	(−1.26)	(−2.50)	(0.34)	(−3.04)
China	−0.07	−0.08	0.04	−0.15[c]
	(−1.06)	(−1.09)	(0.14)	(−1.79)
Japan	0.01	−0.05	−0.02	−0.04
	(0.18)	(−1.22)	(−0.07)	(−0.81)
EA$_1$	−0.12[a]	−0.09[c]	0.32	−0.21[b]
	(−2.37)	(−1.83)	(0.38)	(−3.35)
EA$_2$	−0.09[a]	−0.08[a]	0.42	−0.17[b]
	(−2.75)	(−2.34)	(0.47)	(−4.10)

Sources: International Monetary Fund, *International Financial Statistics*; Central Bank of China.
Notes: The dependent variable is annual output growth; *t*-statistics in parentheses.
LRM = Long-term exchange rate multiplier.
EA$_1$ = Hong Kong, Indonesia, Korea, Malaysia, Philippines, Singapore, Taiwan, Thailand.
EA$_2$ = EA$_1$ + China.
a. Significant at the 5% level.
b. Significant at the 1% level.
c. Significant at the 10% level.

1997–1998 the steep downturn in output in EA_1 was coupled with a deep depreciation of the yen. After rising as high as 80 yen to the dollar in 1995, by June 1998 the yen had fallen to 147 to the dollar (figure 2.2). It then had to be propped up by the Bank of Japan and the U.S. Federal Reserve Bank jointly intervening to buy yen and sell dollars. This intervention was successful, and the yen began to rise well into the year 2000, a rise that corresponded with the economic recovery in EA_1. All of this is consistent with our model of the effect of the yen/ dollar rate on the collective output of the EA_1 countries.

But suppose the 1997–1998 downturn in EA_1 was mainly caused by an extraneous event: the excessive buildup of short-term dollar and yen liabilities in banks in Indonesia, Korea, Malaysia, Philippines, and Thailand, used for onlending at higher interest rates in their domestic currencies (see chapter 6). The resulting highly contagious currency attacks forced massive depreciations in the currencies of these countries against the dollar (and even against the fallen yen), which resulted in a wave of bankruptcies throughout their economies. The fall in output in these economies then spread to Singapore and Taiwan, creating the sharp regional downturn. (Because of strong countercyclical measures, China managed to avoid this fate while leaving its dollar exchange rate unchanged.) From this vantage point, the downturn was not primarily caused by the yen depreciation of 1996–1998. Therefore, to check for the robustness of the estimation results reported in table 2.4, the crisis years 1997–1998 are excluded from the estimation.

Table 2.6 reports the results of excluding observations from 1997 and 1998. The impact of the yen/dollar exchange rate on EA_1 and EA_2 remains strong and invariant (as in table 2.5). The long-run multipliers are significant for the region as a whole at the 5 percent level for EA_1 and 1 percent level for EA_2 even when the crisis years are left out.

At the individual country level in table 2.6, the output growth in the newly industrialized economies (NIEs) Hong Kong, Korea, and Taiwan is still affected strongly by fluctuations in the yen/dollar exchange rate. The coefficients of Hong Kong, Korea, and Taiwan are all significant. The long-run multipliers for these three countries are large.

The ASEAN core countries Indonesia, Malaysia, and Philippines are not as strongly affected, and the coefficients are insignificant. While the coefficient for Thailand remains high, it becomes insignificant in contrast to the overall sample reported in table 2.5. Table 2.6 also underlines the special positions of China and Singapore, which were not very strongly affected by the yen/dollar fluctuations. Overall, tables

Table 2.6
Exchange Rate Determinants of East Asian Output, 1980–2001 (Crisis Years 1997–1998 Excluded)

	Yen/US$$_t$ (β_2)	Yen/US$$_{t-1}$ (β_3)	Adj. R^2 (R^2)	LRM
Hong Kong	−0.18[a]	−0.11[b]	0.21	−0.29[a]
	(−2.30)	(−1.28)	(0.29)	(−2.63)
Indonesia	−0.01	−0.06	−0.08	−0.07
	(−0.11)	(−0.55)	(0.02)	(−0.50)
Korea	−0.17[b]	−0.05	0.11	−0.22[b]
	(−1.98)	(−0.51)	(0.18)	(−1.80)
Malaysia	0.00	−0.08	−0.07	−0.08
	(0.09)	(−0.79)	(0.03)	(0.59)
Philippines	0.01	−0.10	−0.03	−0.09
	(0.12)	(−1.13)	(−0.06)	(−0.79)
Singapore	−0.05	−0.07	−0.05	−0.12
	(−0.54)	(−0.74)	(0.05)	(−0.97)
Taiwan	−0.17[c]	−0.06	0.35	−0.23[c]
	(−3.36)	(−1.14)	(0.41)	(−3.21)
Thailand	−0.07	−0.15	0.02	−0.23
	(−0.68)	(−1.32)	(0.11)	(−1.65)
China	−0.07	−0.09	0.05	−0.16
	(−1.10)	(−1.26)	(0.14)	(−1.65)
Japan	0.12	−0.03	−0.07	0.09
	(0.37)	(−0.75)	(0.03)	(1.54)
EA$_1$	−0.11[b]	−0.08[b]	0.15	−0.19[a]
	(−1.90)	(−1.21)	(0.23)	(−2.32)
EA$_2$	−0.09[a]	−0.08[b]	0.26	−0.17[c]
	(−2.27)	(−1.80)	(0.32)	(−3.14)

Sources: International Monetary Fund, *International Financial Statistics*; Central Bank of China.
Notes: The dependent variable is annual output growth; *t*-statistics in parentheses.
LRM = Long-term exchange rate multiplier.
EA$_1$ = Hong Kong, Indonesia, Korea, Malaysia, Philippines, Singapore, Taiwan, Thailand.
EA$_2$ = EA$_1$ + China.
a. Significant at the 5% level.
b. Significant at the 10% level.
c. Significant at the 1% level.

2.5 and 2.6 strongly support our view that the common EA_1 business cycle is generated largely by fluctuations in the yen/dollar exchange rate.

However, this is not to deny that the frenzy of overborrowing in foreign currencies from 1994 to 1996 was an important factor contributing to the crash of 1997–1998. But this seems to be (one hopes) a one-time event. Nevertheless, the depreciation of the yen over 1996–1998 definitely made the downturn worse. More generally, fluctuations in the yen/dollar rate seem to be a continual (rather than a unique) source of disturbance, generating cyclical fluctuations in the East Asian economy.

Combining Output and Exchange Rate Effects
In steps 1 and 2, interactive output effects (table 2.4) and exchange rate effects (table 2.5) were estimated. We observed that the NIEs Hong Kong, Korea, and Taiwan are strongly affected by fluctuations of the yen/dollar exchange rate; for the ASEAN core countries this effect is much weaker. Nevertheless, the impact on the smaller East Asian countries as a group (EA_1) is strong. How can this strong impact be explained?

The answer lies in the pattern of East Asian division of labor. Within the East Asian production chain, the ASEAN core countries have assumed the role of subcontractors or suppliers for the industrially more developed NIEs—Hong Kong, Korea, and Taiwan (Urata 2001). This intra-Asian pattern of the division of labor contributes to the synchronized business cycle. If the yen/dollar rate changes, the NIEs are more directly affected than are the ASEAN core countries, but the ASEAN core countries are still affected indirectly by intra–East Asian income effects.

The Relative Shrinkage in Japan's Economy
As shown in table 2.2, EA_1 trade with Japan has substantially declined since the early 1980s. While in 1980 almost 20 percent of EA_1 exports went to Japan, by 2001 the value had fallen to 10 percent. The relative fall in imports from Japan is less pronounced but similar. This relative decline of EA_1 trade with Japan would suggest that the impact of the yen/dollar exchange rate on EA_1 trade has weakened and will further weaken if this development continues. But two other considerations offset this effect of declining Japanese trade with East Asia.

First, fluctuations in the yen/dollar exchange rate not only affect trade with Japan but also affect the competitiveness of EA_2 exports in third markets. As the yen depreciates, the exports of Hong Kong, Korea, Taiwan, and perhaps eventually China lose competitiveness against Japanese competitors in the United States and Europe. However, as shown in table 2.2, the United States and the rest of the world still (in 2002) make up 48 percent of EA_1 exports and 41 percent of EA_1 imports. This suggests that these third-market effects account for a crucial part of the impact of the yen/dollar rate on East Asia. Against this effect, however, is the relative shrinkage of Japan as a supplier into third markets if Japan's economic malaise were to continue. (Again we note an apparent recovery in Japan's economy in 2004.)

Second, although the Japanese economy may continue its relative decline, the *leverage effect* of fluctuations in the yen/dollar rate on the rest of East Asia could still increase. Table 2.1 shows the remarkably increasing economic integration of the smaller East Asian countries with each other. Thus a common external disturbance, that is, a change in the yen/dollar rate, has an increasing impact on their common business cycle as they become more integrated. To some (unknown) degree, this leverage effect could well offset (into the indefinite future) continual relative shrinkage in the size of Japan's economy. As long as the yen/dollar rate fluctuates, we don't expect the synchronized East Asian business cycle to disappear any time soon.

Japan's Interaction with the Smaller East Asian Economies: A Summary

To summarize the main sources of instability in the East Asian economy, table 2.7 is a taxonomy of the macroeconomic impact of events in Japan's economy—changes in the yen/dollar rate and Japan's business cycle—on the income of EA_1. There are four possible combinations

Table 2.7
Economic Interaction between Japan and EA_1

	Upswing in Japan	Downswing in Japan
Yen appreciation	① +/+	③ −/+
Yen depreciation	② −/+	④ −/−

Notes: + indicates a positive impact on y_{EA1}, and − indicates a negative impact on y_{EA1}. EA_1 = Hong Kong, Indonesia, Korea, Malaysia, Philippines, Singapore, Taiwan, Thailand.

of changes in the yen/dollar rate and upswings or downswings in Japan's income. The plus signs indicate an expansionary effect on EA_1, and the minus signs indicate contraction.

Case 1 is the best outcome for EA_1 countries. The yen appreciates against the dollar while Japan's economy is expanding. The positive income effect and exchange rate effect reinforce each other to stimulate aggregate output. But discrete episodes are difficult to identify in the data.

Case 4 is the worst outcome for the EA_1 countries. Yen depreciation is aggravated by an economic downswing in Japan. This case was observed during the 1997–1998 crisis, when Japan's income turned down as the yen fell.

Case 2 applied in 1986–1987 and again in the early 1990s up to 1995. In each episode the strong yen was accompanied by a recession in Japan, widely characterized as high-yen induced recession (*endaka fukyô*). While the recessions had a negative effect on the EA_1 economies, the yen appreciations boosted growth, with this exchange rate effect predominating. The EA_1 economies experienced high growth in both cases.

Case 3 seems to apply from mid-1995 through 1996. Japan's output increased as the yen declined. The initial net effect on EA_1 was positive. But eventually the falling yen, which bottomed out at 147 to the U.S. dollar in June 1998, helped provoke the Asian crisis, putting us back into case 4.

Again we learn that the exchange rate effect usually dominates the income effect. This is an important empirical regularity to keep in mind when we discuss whether a deep devaluation of the yen would permit Japan to export its way out of its current slump.

2.4 Conclusion

Our message is clear: to boost the Japanese economy, the yen should not be depreciated below some rough measure of purchasing power parity (PPP) with the dollar. More generally, ongoing fluctuations in the yen/U.S. dollar rate around PPP increase the volatility of the business cycle in the smaller East Asian economies. They would be much better off if the yen were permanently tethered.

Other economists have recognized how fluctuations in the yen/ dollar rate destabilize economies in the ever more integrated East Asia region. But their common policy "solution" is to give the yen more weight in the exchange rate baskets of the nine EA_2 countries (William-son 2000; Kwan 2001). However, this proposed solution is misplaced. Why change the monetary and exchange rate policies of nine East Asian countries, including big ones like China and Korea, whose revealed preferences are to peg to the U.S. dollar (see chapter 1), when changing just Japan's would be sufficient?

Putting the matter more positively for Japan itself, chapters 3 and 4 show that the fluctuating yen has been a prime cause of Japan's low-interest-rate liquidity trap and its failure to escape from the ongoing slump. Thus, stabilizing the yen/dollar rate indefinitely in nominal terms would benefit both Japan and its East Asian neighbors: a win-win situation. But making any such exchange rate agreement credible would require the cooperation of the United States. Tethering the yen by the joint action of the U.S. Federal Reserve and the Bank of Japan is discussed in chapter 3.

3

Japan's Deflation and the Syndrome of the Ever-Higher Yen, 1971–1995

with Kenichi Ohno

Japan's macroeconomic problem has yet to be properly diagnosed. Throughout the 1990s into the new millennium, policymakers could not decide on the proper macroeconomic measures to combat the country's severe economic slump and deflation. This chapter and chapter 4 propose a unified explanation, with deep historical roots, of why the economy failed to recover after Japan's stock and real estate bubbles burst in 1991.

In this chapter we focus on the appreciating yen up to the mid-1990s as the main source of Japan's deflation and low-interest-rate liquidity trap. Then, by positing a negative risk premium in Japanese interest rates, chapter 4 explains why Japan's foreign exchange trap continued after 1995 even after the yen stopped appreciating secularly.

The problem was not purely "made in Japan." It arose from Japan's unbalanced mercantile relationship with the United States. Starting in the early 1970s, numerous trade disputes between the two countries created tensions that were (temporarily) resolved by the yen's going ever higher against the U.S. dollar up to 1995. By the 1980s this persistent pressure for the yen to rise was further aggravated by Japan's large current account (saving) surpluses as the counterpart of the United States' large current account (saving) deficits. The legacy is the expectation that trade and financial tensions will recur so that the yen could be higher 10, 20, or 30 years from now, with Japan's (wholesale) price level forced correspondingly lower and nominal interest rates on yen assets remaining more than four percentage points less than those on dollar assets. The Bank of Japan, whose monetary policy has been quite expansionary, is powerless to stimulate the flagging economy.

Abridged from Ronald I. McKinnon and Kenichi Ohno, "The Foreign Exchange Origins of Japan's Economic Slump and Low Interest Liquidity Trap," *The World Economy* 24 (March 2001): 279–315.

Before considering the strong international influences on Japan's economy, let us sketch the evolution of Japan's slump in the 1990s from a purely domestic perspective.

3.1   Japan's Domestic Economy in the 1990s

When Japan's bubble economy burst in 1991–1992, the sharp fall in the stock market and land values made inevitable a significant economic downturn, or at least a period of sluggish growth (by Japanese standards). Bad loans in the banking system, associated with the collapsing value of real estate and equity collateral, proliferated and impaired bank capital. The sharp decline in household wealth caused consumer expenditures to fall. Excess capacity induced business firms to curtail investment. Such economic travail is hardly surprising when asset bubbles burst.

More surprising is that for more than a decade Japan's economy did not recover. Figure 3.1 shows how sluggish Japanese GDP growth had become in the 1990s. Except for 1996, when annualized growth touched 5 percent, GDP growth since 1991 has averaged less than 1

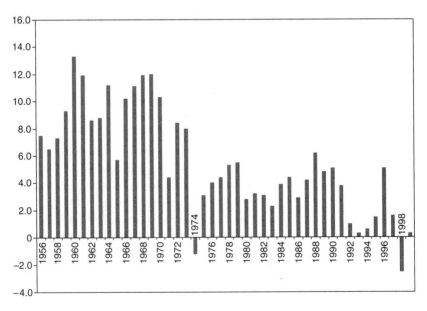

Figure 3.1
Japan's GDP Growth Rates, 1956–1999 (Yearly). (International Monetary Fund, *International Financial Statistics*)

percent per year. It was sharply negative in 1998, with negligible growth in 1999. Yet, among industrial countries, Japan had been the premier growth economy for the previous four decades. With the world's highest saving rates and seemingly endless capacity to adapt to, and dramatically augment, the latest industrial technologies, Japan's GDP grew at 6–12 percent in the 1950s and 1960s, and at a robust 3–5 percent in the 1970s and 1980s, when the rest of the industrial world was comparatively stagnant. Moreover, these basic virtues of private industry and thrift, and a highly skilled labor force with unmatched engineering capability in hi-tech manufacturing, remain intact. However, throughout the 1990s into 2000, domestic aggregate demand, both private investment and consumption, failed to recover.

The Fiscal Response

On the fiscal side, Japan's government responded with massive public expenditure programs designed to prime the pump of aggregate demand. Consequently, Japan's fiscal deficit in 1999 exceeded 10 percent of GNP. Table 3.1 shows that government gross debt rose from 58.2 percent of GDP in 1991, and the OECD projected it to increase to more than 114 percent of GDP in 2000[1] and 122 percent in 2001. This upward trend is completely out of step with other G-7 countries. Even Italy

Table 3.1
General Government Gross Financial Liabilities, 1991–2001 (percentage of nominal GDP)

| | 1991 | 1992 | 1993 | 1994 | 1995 | 1996 | 1997 | 1998 | Estimates and Projections | | |
									1999	2000	2001
U.S.	65.5	68.1	69.7	68.9	68.3	67.7	65.4	62.4	59.3	57.1	55.2
Japan[a]	58.2	59.8	63	69.4	76	80.6	84.7	97.3	105.4	114.1	122.1
Germany[b]	40.1	43.4	49	49.2	59.1	61.9	62.8	63.3	62.6	61.7	60.2
France	40.3	44.7	51.6	55.3	59.4	62.3	64.5	64.9	65.2	64.6	63.4
Italy	107.4	116.1	117.9	124	123.1	122.2	120.4	118.2	117.7	115.2	112.3
U.K.	40.1	46.9	56.2	53.7	58.9	58.5	58.9	56.4	54	51.2	48.6
Canada	80.9	88.2	96.8	98	99.2	98.9	94.1	91.7	86.9	82.5	78.5

Source: OECD Economic Outlook, December 1999, 226.
Notes:
a. Includes the debt of the Japan Railway Settlement Corporation and the National Forest Special Account from 1998 onward.
b. Includes the debt of the German Railways Fund from 1994 onward and the Inherited Debt Fund from 1995 onward.

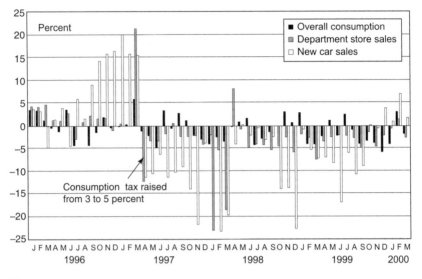

Figure 3.2
Japan's Consumption Expenditures, 1996–2000 (Change from Same Month of Previous
Year). (Management and Coordination Agency; Department Stores Association; Japan
Automobile Dealers Association)

has succeeded in putting its similarly large debt ratio on a downward
trajectory.

Offsetting this fiscal "expansion," the yen appreciated sharply in
1994–1995, peaking out at a highly overvalued 80 to the U.S. dollar in
April 1995, and depressed both exports and private domestic investment. However, in 1996 when the yen fell and became less overvalued,
output growth spurted to 5 percent. Recovery seemed at hand.

In April 1997, believing that this fiscal pump priming had worked
but concerned with the out-of-control debt buildup, the government
of then Prime Minister Ryutaro Hashimoto seized the opportunity to
increase the general sales tax from 3 to 5 percent and to close other
tax loopholes. This tax increase sent the still sluggish economy into a
severe tailspin from mid-1997 through 1999. Figure 3.2 shows the remarkable falls in overall Japanese consumption as well as in the sub-
categories of department store and new car sales during this period.
Figure 3.3 shows the sharp rise in Japanese unemployment in the late
1990s. Because of his party's electoral losses from the slumping economy, Hashimoto had to resign in July 1998. Since then, new public
spending programs, largely infrastructure investments, have been con-

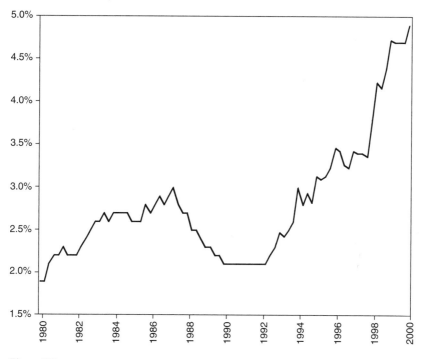

Figure 3.3
Japan's Unemployment Rates, 1980–2000 (Quarterly). February 2000 estimate of unemployment rate was used for 2000Q1. (International Monetary Fund, *International Financial Statistics*; OECD Quarterly Labour Force Statistics)

tinually introduced. Japan is still under pressure from the U.S. Treasury and from some commentators (e.g., Posen 1998) to engage in yet more Keynesian-style fiscal stimuli.

Because Japan is already in a serious debt trap, several more years of public-sector fiscal stimulus is simply not sustainable. Taking a more consolidated approach to public-sector gross debt by including the deteriorating position of local governments, and then presuming that fiscal deficits continue as in 1998–2000 out to 2005, David Asher and Robert Dugger (2000) produce the results shown in table 3.2. Assuming a 4 percent interest charge on existing public debt, they calculate that total public-sector debt/GDP will reach over 220 percent by 2005, a number not yet seen in peacetime in any industrial country.

Even table 3.2 does not tell the whole story. Japan has an aging population and an underfunded social security system, whose liabilities were not counted as part of the gross debt figures shown in tables

Table 3.2
Projected Public-Sector Borrowing for Japan (Fiscal Stimulus plus Debt Service), 1997–2005 (billions of U.S. dollars)

	1997	1998	1999	2000	2001	2002	2003	2004	2005
Needed fiscal stimulus	2.4	51.6	46.1	54.6	54.9	54.0	48.6	46.6	44.0
Debt service (4% rate)	18.4	19.2	22.1	24.5	27.2	31.4	36.3	42.0	50.8
Total borrowing need	20.8	70.8	68.2	79.1	82.0	85.4	84.8	88.7	94.8
Total public-sector debt		551.0	613.0	680.0	762.0	847.0	947.0	1049.0	1163.0
Total public-sector debt/GDP		112%	124%	136%	151%	166%	184%	202%	221%

Source: Asher and Dugger (2000).
Note: Projections assume that fiscal stimuli continue.

3.1 and 3.2. Nor were the huge contingent government liabilities from bad private bank loans counted, now estimated to be about $1 trillion.[2] Also not included in the count is the bad loan portfolio of the government itself, through its Fiscal Investment and Loan Program for housing, agriculture, economic development, and so on. Thus, even though virtually all public debt is internally held because of massive private-sector saving, further fiscal expansion, which would add massively to the existing public debt, is too risky.

With huge liquid savings balances, Japan's households are not currently liquidity-constrained. This is in contrast to what a static Keynesian public spending multiplier, which supposes that most agents are liquidity-constrained, would project. Nevertheless, ordinary Japanese still worry about the disarray in the public finances for their social security—pensions, medical care, and so on—in the longer run. Thus, in the face of huge public-sector deficits and unsustainable debts, current private spending has weakened further (personal saving has increased) as people decide to protect their own social security: a form of Ricardian equivalence. Thus has the string run out on further fiscal expansionism.

The Monetary Response
Monetary policy is also at an impasse as Japan enters the new millennium. However, a decade earlier, the tight money policy of the Bank of Japan had been effective in bursting the asset bubble. The sharp contraction in the monetary base in 1991–1992—a contraction that had more drastic and prolonged deflationary consequences than the Bank

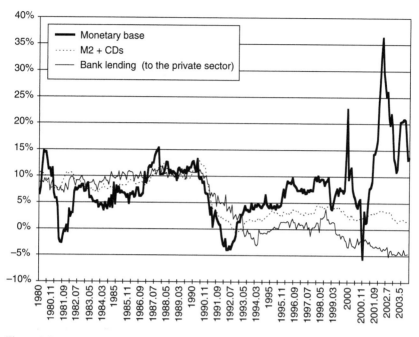

Figure 3.4
Growth of Bank Credit and Monetary Aggregates, 1980–2003. Twelve-month growth rates are computed. M2 is broad money including savings deposits, and CDs are certificates of deposit (Bank of Japan)

of Japan intended—is shown in figure 3.4. By 1994, however, monetary policy became expansive: base money subsequently has grown between 4 and 10 percent per year. Because this monetary growth has been much faster than the sluggish growth in nominal GDP, the velocity of base money has fallen sharply (see figure 3.5). So, this resurgence of monetary growth failed to restimulate income growth.

The admonition from the Great Depression of the 1930s against "pushing on string" should be recalled. Monetary policy can restrain overheating, but it is less effective in stimulating a weak economy with strong deflationary momentum into recovery. From 1994 the stimulative effect of the Bank of Japan's strong expansion in base money was ultimately frustrated by a breakdown in the monetary transmission mechanism. From a purely domestic perspective, Japan's broken money has three closely related aspects:

• *The low-interest-rate trap.* Starting with short-term interest rates of a little over 2 percent in 1994–1995, the Bank of Japan reduced the

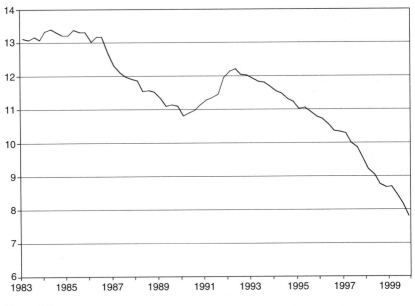

Figure 3.5
Velocity of Monetary Base, 1983–1999. Monthly numbers were averaged to obtain quarterly numbers. (Seasonally adjusted quarterly GDP figures, Economic Planning Agency; seasonally adjusted monetary base numbers, Bank of Japan)

overnight bank lending rate to just 0.5 percent in 1996. It then announced its now famous zero-interest-rate policy in April 1999; these facts are shown in figure 3.6. With the zero-interest floor, the Bank of Japan has no further leverage over the economy in this dimension.

• *The fall in bank lending.* Despite (or because of) the ultra-low interest rates, commercial bank lending was stagnant, growing less than 1 percent per year after 1994 and then falling from 1999 on. In the 1980s, by contrast, bank lending had grown faster than the monetary aggregates (figure 3.4).

• *Excess reserve holding by financial institutions.* As interest rates on interbank lending fall to near-zero levels and the demand by nonbanks for credit remains weak and unprofitable, the opportunity cost of commercial banks (and *tanshi* brokers, who are also authorized to hold deposits with the Bank of Japan) to hold excess reserves, also falls to zero, and their holdings rise (figure 3.7).

The upshot is the infamous liquidity trap for monetary policy. Not only can short-term interest rates not be cut further to stimulate the

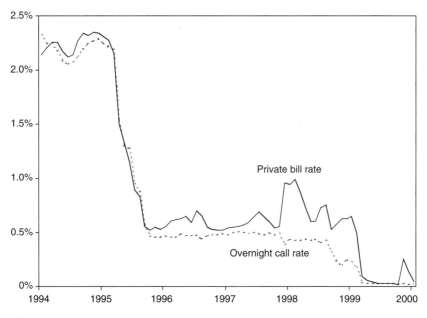

Figure 3.6
Japan's Short Rates, 1994–2000. (International Monetary Fund, *International Financial Statistics*)

private sector, but the demand for (velocity of) base money itself has become indeterminate. The traditional multiplier link from the creation of base money to bank credit creation has been broken. (Problems with the market for long-term bonds when interest rates are low are considered later.)

When monetary policy is caught in a liquidity trap, increased public expenditure is the textbook solution for overcoming a slump because government expenditure can increase without bidding up interest rates. But given the parlous state of Japan's public finances and the worries of the populace about their future social security, the fiscal route is not sustainable. From this purely domestic perspective, it's no wonder that Japan's leaders are discouraged.

Japan's economy is still fragile, but a leading official in the ruling coalition has admitted that its government has run out of policy options: "'It is very difficult to know what to do to achieve clear economic recovery,' said Chikara Sakaguchi, policy chief of the New Komeito party, a member of the ruling coalition" (*Financial Times*, May 5, 2000, 4).

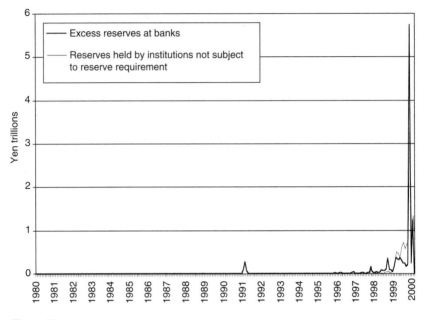

Figure 3.7
Japan's Excess Reserves, 1980–2000. (Bank of Japan)

3.2   The Syndrome of the Ever-Higher Yen

Before deciding on policies to sustain economic recovery in Japan, one
must first properly diagnose what has gone wrong. Here, an international perspective is called for. Among industrial countries, Japan is
unique in having relative deflation—and the expectations of continued
deflation—arising out of its peculiar political-economic relationship
with the United States over the past three decades.

In textbooks on international finance, national monetary policies are
usually presumed to be independently determined, and then exchange
rates adjust to these policies. For most industrial countries with floating exchange rates, this textbook view is surely right. In Euroland for
example, if the European Central Bank announced a massive easing of
monetary policy—a big expansion of commercial bank reserves with
the intention of driving short-term interest rates toward zero—then
the euro would fall precipitously in the foreign exchange markets. Similarly, if the Bank of England announced a major monetary expansion
beyond any measure consistent with its internal inflation target, the
pound sterling would fall like a rock.

But Japan is different. In April 1999 the Bank of Japan announced its now famous zero-interest-rate policy with a monetary expansion that has left commercial banks swimming in excess reserves. Yet, even as the economy has remained depressed, the yen has remained very strong in the foreign exchanges. From April 1999 through April 2000, the yen rose from about 120 to 107 to the dollar despite massive intervention by the government to sell yen and buy dollars. Japan's official exchange reserves increased by more than $80 billion as the government desperately struggled to keep the yen from rising. Chapter 8 discusses further the extraordinary increase in exchange reserves into the new millennium in Japan as well as in several other East Asian countries.

The yen/dollar rate remains unpredictably volatile in the short and medium terms, and the yen has depreciated substantially from its peak in 1995. Nevertheless, the continual pressure in the foreign markets for the yen to rise is of very long standing. This expectation generates a fear of deflation that dampens current spending by Japanese households and businesses while driving nominal interest rates toward zero. How these perverse exchange rate expectations came about is deeply rooted in the history of mercantile interaction between Japan and the United States, what McKinnon and Ohno (1997) called the syndrome of the ever-higher yen.

As defined by *Merriam-Webster's New Collegiate Dictionary*, a syndrome is "a group of signs and symptoms that occur together and characterize a particular abnormality; and a set of concurrent things (as emotions or actions) that usually form an identifiable pattern." But people ensnared in a syndrome, say, policymakers in Japan and the United States, need not realize what has happened to them nor understand the economic consequences.

Under the old Bretton Woods parity system for exchange rates from 1949 to 1971, Japan's exchange rate was fixed at 360 yen/U.S. dollar. In that era of Japan's highest economic growth, unmatched before or since, the parity regime was highly credible with no evidence of expected yen appreciation despite Japan's substantial encroachment on U.S. markets. Indeed, starting with the Dodge Line Program in 1949 to stabilize the highly inflationary Japanese economy of 1946–1948, keeping the rate at 360 yen/dollar was widely seen as the necessary anchor for Japan's monetary policy for more than 20 years.

Mercantile Pressure from the United States

Then the exchange rate regime changed. Worried about the United States' declining international competitiveness, President Nixon abrogated the dollar's last links to gold in August 1971; he also imposed a surcharge on all imports of manufactured goods into the United States. He insisted that this surcharge would remain in place until trading partners in Europe and Japan appreciated the dollar value of their currencies. Similar to other industrial countries, Japan let the yen appreciate by 17 percent by the end of 1971, and the surcharge was removed.

After 1971 U.S. mercantile concerns became more narrowly focused on the rapidly growing Japanese economy with its large trade surpluses. While Japan displaced the United States as the dominant supplier in many manufacturing industries worldwide, its home markets remained relatively closed to foreign competition. U.S. grievances that Japan was an unfair international competitor were compounded by the emergence of Japan's trade surpluses in the mid-1970s. The result was innumerable trade disputes between the two countries.

Then the yen appreciated enormously, if episodically, from 360 until it briefly touched 80 to the dollar in April 1995. Figure 3.8 shows

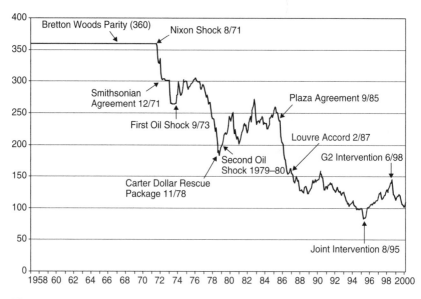

Figure 3.8
Nominal Yen/U.S. Dollar Exchange Rate, 1957–2000. (International Monetary Fund, *International Financial Statistics*)

the four main episodes (1971–1973, 1977–1978, 1985–1987, and 1993–1995) of upward ratchets in the yen associated with major trade disputes. We hypothesized that these interactions of the U.S. and Japanese governments in their conduct of commercial, exchange rate, and monetary policies resulted in the ongoing expectation that the yen would normally appreciate, if only erratically, in the longer run. What mechanism propagated this syndrome and continued the expectation of a rising yen into the mid-1990s?

No matter how much the dollar fell, at least some U.S. officials typically looked at Japan's trade surplus and saw further room for yen appreciation. Since the Nixon shock in 1971, various secretaries of the Treasury—notably Blumenthal in 1977, Baker in 1985–1987, and Bentsen in 1993—have suggested that the dollar was too high against the yen. Often these attempts to talk the dollar down were accompanied by intense negotiations aimed at forcing Japan to open or share this or that market or to impose "voluntary" restraints on Japanese exports. Trade disputes were particularly intense during the four episodes when the yen ratcheted upward. For example, in the first four months of 1995, when the U.S. trade representative tried to negotiate numerical targets for Japan to buy U.S.-made automobiles and components by threatening to impose high tariffs on U.S. imports of Japanese autos, the dollar fell particularly sharply, from 95 to 80 yen (figure 3.8).

In addition to talk by secretaries of the Treasury, why should trade disputes themselves cause the yen to appreciate? In the middle of a dispute, foreign exchange traders saw a higher yen ameliorating, or perhaps forestalling, protectionist threats from the United States. And in the short run, a rising yen does indeed improve U.S. competitiveness vis-à-vis Japan, although it washes out in the long run when purchasing power parity is restored as the Japanese wholesale price level falls relative to that of the United States. Figure 3.9 shows Japan's wholesale price level rising more slowly than the U.S. price level after the mid-1970s and then falling absolutely after 1985.[3] Consequently, purchasing power parity for the yen/dollar rate drifted steadily downward from the mid-1970s through the late 1990s, as shown in figure 3.10.

These mercantile concerns of the U.S. government and industrial lobbies have been shared by economists, perhaps the majority of them, who espouse an exchange rate doctrine based on the elasticities model of the balance of trade. Into the 1990s they tried to convince U.S. policymakers that devaluing the dollar would in itself reduce the U.S.

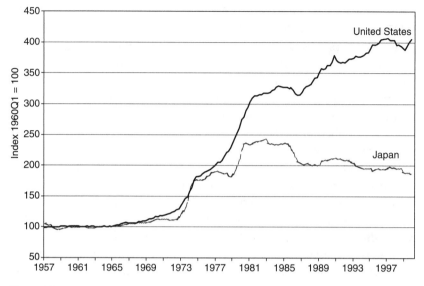

Figure 3.9
Wholesale Price Level of Tradable Goods, 1957–2000. (International Monetary Fund, *International Financial Statistics*)

trade or current account deficit, and that exchange rate changes can be treated as a rather "clean" and acceptable instrument of economic policy.[4] Japan has had the biggest current account surpluses, about the same size as the U.S. current account deficits, in the late 1980s.

True, U.S. mercantile pressure on Japan has been in remission since April 1995, when the yen peaked out at 80 to the dollar, a level so overvalued by the PPP criterion (figure 3.10) that U.S. officials worried about a collapse in the Japanese economy. The "normal" U.S. mercantile pressure ceased, and the U.S. government signaled, by joint interventions with the Japanese government to drive the yen down in the summer of 1995, that it would accept a much lower value of the yen (McKinnon and Ohno 1997, ch. 11). Indeed, the then Treasury Secretary Robert Rubin, unlike his predecessors, subsequently reaffirmed several times that he was in favor of a strong dollar. So did his successor, Lawrence Summers.

However, U.S. mercantile pressure for yen appreciation could return. Figure 3.11 scales each country's current account against its own GDP. It shows the remarkable persistence of Japan's current account surpluses since the early 1980s and U.S. current account deficits since the mid-1970s. Because of huge U.S. government deficits in the 1980s,

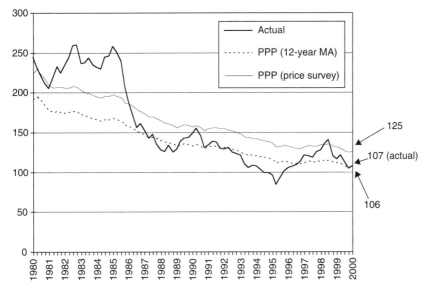

Figure 3.10
Actual and Purchasing Power Parity Yen/U.S. Dollar Rates, 1980–2000. The PPP yen/
U.S. dollar rate is calculated in two ways: the first assumes an equal tendency for overvaluation and undervaluation during the last twelve years; the second takes the price
survey result of manufactured goods in 1992Q2 as the base (150 yen/U.S. dollar). (International Monetary Fund, *International Financial Statistics*; *Japan Economic Journal*)

the U.S. current account deficit peaked at about 3 percent of GNP in
1986–1987 (Japan's surplus at that time was about 4 percent of its
GDP), and U.S. mercantile pressure, sometimes called Japan bashing,
was very intense. In the late 1990s, U.S. private saving declined (perhaps because of the boom in stock market asset values) so that the U.S.
current account deficit surged to an unprecedented 4 percent of GDP
by 2000.

In the new millennium Japan is not proportionally as big a creditor
to the U.S. as it was in the mid-1980s, although it is still the largest.
And from the mid-1990s to 2000, the U.S. "Goldilocks" economy of
high growth coupled with (over)full employment undoubtedly muted
much protectionist concern about job losses from surging imports.
Nevertheless, not much disruption in the U.S. economic machine need
occur before industrial lobbies come out in full force to complain about
unfair foreign competition and undervalued foreign currencies. However, after the high-tech bubble burst in 2001, China more than Japan
became the focus of U.S. mercantile concerns (see chapter 5).

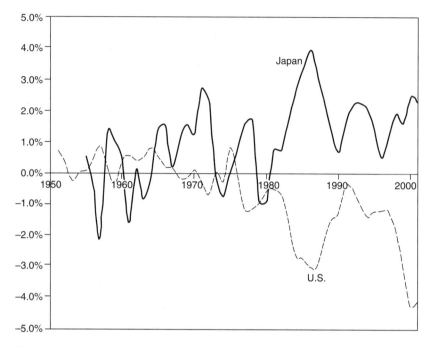

Figure 3.11
Current Account to GDP Ratio, 1950–2000. (Estimates for 2000 and 2001, *The Economist*, April 29, 2000; U.S. estimate for 1999, International Trade Administration)

3.3   Cumulative Currency Risk in Japanese Financial Institutions

Even though U.S. mercantile pressure to get the yen up has not been officially active since 1995, currency risk still contributes to today's upward pressure on the yen. For more than 30 years, Japan has run current account (trade) surpluses (figure 3.11). Correspondingly, Japanese financial institutions have accumulated financial claims on the rest of the world. But the world is still on a dollar standard in the sense that most international capital flows outside Europe are denominated in dollars, so most of these claims on foreigners are interest-bearing dollar assets.

However, as Japan's current account surpluses continue, the proportion of dollar assets in the portfolios of Japanese banks and insurance companies increases. Figure 3.12 shows some very preliminary estimates for banks and insurance companies, of the order of 12–16 percent. As time passes, Japanese financial institutions see heightened currency risk in acquiring yet more dollar assets, which could sud-

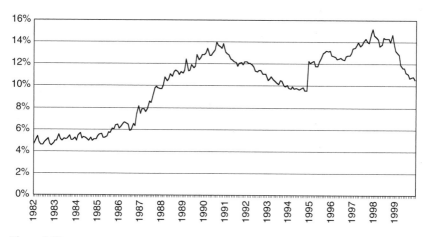

Figure 3.12
Foreign Assets as a Percentage of Total Assets in Japanese Deposit Money Banks and Insurance Companies, 1982–2000. Deposit money banks: domestically licensed banks and foreign banks in Japan, Shinkin banks, Norinchukin Bank, Shokochukin Bank, and Zenshinren Bank; insurance companies: life and nonlife. (Bank of Japan)

denly lose value if the yen appreciates. This reluctance to continue acquiring dollar assets then uncovers Japan's current account surplus as its matching private capital outflow diminishes: see chapter 8. Thus the yen tends to jump because of the problem of conflicted virtue, discussed in the introduction.

When upward pressure on the yen is strong, Japan's government absorbs some of the currency risk by acquiring dollar reserves (largely U.S. Treasuries) with the proceeds from selling yen-denominated "finance bills." The government, more narrowly the Ministry of Finance, thus becomes a substitute international financial intermediary for financing Japan's current account surplus, sometimes on a large scale. For example, from April 1999 to April 2000, the official accumulation of $80 billion of exchange reserves was almost three-quarters of the current account surplus.

With this official intervention, the private sector is relieved of the risk of adding to its own dollar assets. But insofar as private financial institutions begin to doubt that the government will continue such a rapid buildup of dollar reserves to keep a lid on the yen's dollar value, they become even more reluctant to acquire dollar assets and could even try to unload what they have already accumulated. This reluctance puts more upward pressure on the yen, resulting in a vicious circle strengthening the expectation of an ever-higher yen and keeping Japan's nominal interest rates low.

Sustaining Yen Appreciation 1971–1995: A Summary

To sustain an ever-higher yen against the dollar, national monetary policies in the two countries must be consistent with the relative deflation in Japan. For 1971–1995 consider the propagation mechanism in five highly stylized stages:

1. At the center of the world dollar standard, the U.S. Federal Reserve System independently determines U.S. monetary policy—the U.S. price level and interest rates—while paying little or no heed to exchange rates, economic conditions abroad, or foreign official interventions against the dollar (McKinnon 1996).

2. A mercantile dispute erupts between Japan and the United States. But trade sanctions against Japan are averted by the yen's appreciating in the foreign exchanges, making Japan's exporters less competitive in the short run. The Bank of Japan hesitates to flood the market with liquidity to bring the yen back down.[5]

3. Once the yen has risen, the Bank of Japan tolerates relative deflation in the medium term in order to sustain the higher dollar value of the yen. But eventually the relative fall in Japan's price level restores its mercantile competitiveness.

4. Trade disputes recur, leading to further yen appreciations that continually force Japan into relative and eventually absolute deflation, thus reinforcing expectations of an ever-higher yen.

5. In financing Japan's current account surplus, the increasing currency risk from the buildup of dollar claims within Japan eventually dampens capital outflows, putting more upward pressure on the yen even when U.S. mercantile pressure is in remission.

The Constraint on Yen Depreciation

We have argued that the spot yen need not naturally depreciate in the face of excess domestic liquidity as long as the future yen is expected to be (erratically) higher. Indeed, upward pressure on the yen in the foreign exchanges has been so great that it is difficult and almost impossible for the Japanese government to contain it. Nevertheless, to stimulate the slumping but very large Japanese economy, unrestrained monetary expansionists (e.g., Hoshi 1998; Krugman 1998; Meltzer

1998; and Svensson 2000, 2001) advocated sharply depreciating the yen below its current PPP rate.

Counterfactually, suppose the devaluationists could get their way. Even more massive interventions by the Bank of Japan somehow force the yen to depreciate sharply. Would this stimulate Japan's income and output while springing the zero-interest liquidity trap? This would fail on several counts:

• *The domino effect on incomes and exchange rates.* Other Asian currencies would be forced to depreciate (further). In particular, the finely balanced position of China, where the yuan/dollar rate has been stable for more than six years, would be undermined (see chapter 2).

• *Protectionist responses from other industrial countries.* With Japan's trade surplus again burgeoning in the new millennium, a deep devaluation of the yen from its current PPP of about 106 yen/dollar would impose too much mercantile pressure on industrial competitors.

• *The expectations effect.* The fear of future yen appreciation could still remain and even be strengthened if expectations about the long-term value of the yen were little changed in the face of current discrete depreciation of the yen.

3.4   Springing the Liquidity Trap

The basic problem, which has been misdiagnosed by devaluationists, is not so much the level of the yen (as long as it does not differ appreciably from its current PPP). Instead it is the uncertainty associated with possible fluctuations in its dollar value. This uncertainty can be partitioned into the fear of secular appreciation (the syndrome of the ever-higher yen), and the negative risk premium in interest rates on yen assets associated with purely random fluctuations in the yen/dollar exchange rate (see chapter 4). In the remainder of this chapter, we focus on the first question: how to quash the fear of an ever-higher yen.

In proper long-term perspective, it is the yen's *forward* value (as measured by the interest differential between Japan and the U.S. at every term to maturity), and not the spot value, that is too high. Once the problem is properly diagnosed, the solution for ridding Japan's economy of its deflationary psychology is straightforward: credibly stabilize the yen's dollar value into the indefinite future.

Unilateralism Is Not Enough

Why can't the Japanese government then solve the problem unilaterally by simply announcing a target value for the yen, say, its current PPP, into the indefinite future? The problem is a lack of credibility. In the liquidity trap, where the domestic demand for base money is indefinitely large, the Bank of Japan's monetary policy is helpless to stimulate the economy or to prevent the yen from rising (Okina 1999). And when the yen has been strong in the foreign exchanges, direct intervention by the Japanese government alone (not joint with the U.S. government) to sell yen and acquire dollars has met with only indifferent success in dampening yen appreciation. That is, the government sometimes succeeds in preventing the yen from rising in the short term but fails to quash the expectation that the yen is likely to rise over the longer term.

Figure 3.13 strips out interest rate earnings on existing dollar reserves and then plots quarterly changes in Japan's official foreign exchange reserves against the course of the yen/dollar exchange rate. One can see the very large interventions in 1986–1988, 1993–1995, and 1999–2000, three periods when the yen was tending to appreciate quite strongly. In the most recent episode, Japanese foreign exchange

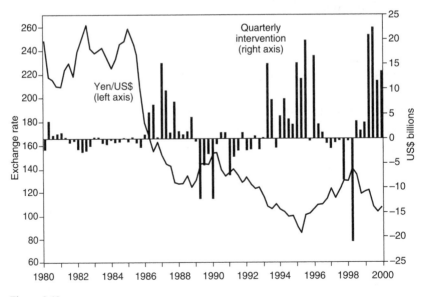

Figure 3.13
Yen/U.S. Dollar Exchange Rate and changes in Japanese Official Reserves, 1980–2000. (Jen 2000)

reserves increased from $222.5 billion in April 1999 to $305.5 billion in April 2000, about 37 percent. (When the yen had been fixed credibly at 360 per U.S. dollar from 1949 to 1969, total exchange reserve accumulation was only about $2 billion.) After Japan's asset bubble burst in 1991, its official foreign reserves were just $61.9 billion, so almost 80 percent of exchange reserves at the end of the decade had been accumulated during the depressed 1990s, during which there has still been some net yen appreciation. But even when the yen was not allowed to appreciate, the pressure on the government to prevent it was intense. Into the new millennium the private sector has no assurance that the government will be able to keep the lid on.

In effect, unilateral intervention by the Japanese government lacks long-term credibility. This lack of credibility stems from the fear that forces outside the control of the Japanese government, for instance, mercantile pressure from the United States and increasing currency risk within Japanese private financial institutions, will at some point force the government to give up its attempts to keep the yen from rising.

A Bilateral Approach

McKinnon and Ohno (1997) discusses policies that would unravel the syndrome of the ever-higher yen by rationalizing the mercantile-monetary interaction between Japan and the United States. At the risk of oversimplifying many institutional aspects covered in the book, our proposed economic pact between the two countries boils down to two complementary sets of policies:

• A *commercial agreement* limiting bilateral sanctions in trade disputes and ending (future) pressure from the United States to get the yen up.

• A *monetary accord* to stabilize the yen/dollar rate over the long term: the principle of virtual exchange rate stability.

Under the commercial agreement, the United States would forswear the use of Super 301 and similar bilateral trade sanctions against Japan, with all trade disputes to be adjudicated by the World Trade Organization. Japan would agree to finish liberalizing all aspects of its economy, including services and agriculture. Both countries would acknowledge that neither the current account surplus of Japan nor the current account deficit of the United States can be corrected by manipulating the yen/dollar exchange rate. A commercial agreement is necessary to be able to implement a monetary accord.

Under a monetary accord, the two countries would agree on a benchmark value for the yen/dollar rate, say, its current PPP rate, which is now about 120 yen/dollar. According to the principle of virtual exchange rate stability (McKinnon and Ohno 1997, 222), the two governments would always nudge the rate toward the benchmark but only do so actively if there were some sharp market movement in the wrong direction. For example, in early June 1998, the yen began to depreciate sharply, reaching 147 to the U.S. dollar by June 16 (figure 3.8). On June 17, the Fed and the Bank of Japan signaled joint or concerted intervention to reverse its course (New York Federal Reserve Bank 1998):

On June 17, the U.S. monetary authorities intervened in the foreign exchange markets, selling a total of $833 million against the Japanese yen. The operation, which was divided evenly between the U.S. Treasury Department's Exchange Stabilization Fund and the Federal Reserve System, was conducted in cooperation with the Japanese monetary authorities.... The yen continued to appreciate throughout the remainder of the New York session, climbing over five yen to 136 yen to the dollar before closing at 136.51 yen to the dollar.... Later, Treasury Secretary Rubin stated, "We are prepared to continue to cooperate in the foreign exchange markets, as appropriate."

This is not the only example of successful concerted intervention to stop the yen/dollar rate from moving in the wrong direction (by the PPP criterion). After the yen had been run up sharply from 95 in January to reach 80 to the dollar in April 1995, a concerted official intervention by the Fed and the Bank of Japan and other central banks stopped the run, and follow-up official interventions during the summer succeeded in driving the yen back down (figure 3.13) from what had become a grossly overvalued level that was seriously depressing the Japanese economy. This permitted a partial recovery of the Japanese economy in 1996, until the now infamous Hashimoto tax increase of April 1997.

Dominguez and Frankel (1993) document several other successful concerted official interventions to stop "wrong-direction" runs for or against the dollar since the Plaza Hotel Agreement of 1985. For official interventions to be successful, the authors emphasize, they must be *concerted and well signaled* so that the markets feel that follow-up actions will be forthcoming if necessary. Then only minor amounts of official foreign exchange reserves need be expended, with no significant changes in short-term monetary policies. And the successful interventions of June 17, 1998, and of the summer of 1995 fit this Dominguez-Frankel mold almost exactly.

Virtual Exchange Rate Stability

We define virtual exchange rate stability to be that associated with countries' agreeing on a long-run target for their (nominal) exchange rate but not necessarily attempting a hard short-term fix. The countries will work together to contain pressures that drive the spot exchange rate substantially away from the long-term benchmark; their commitment to a long-term target is not in question. (For a further discussion of this concept of virtual exchange stability for promoting the recovery of the smaller East Asian economies, see McKinnon 2000.)

How would our proposal for securing virtual stability in the yen/dollar rate differ from the already existing Plaza, or Plaza-Louvre, accords? The big omission from the existing Plaza-Louvre regime is that there is no restraint on long-term drift in the market exchange rate, followed by a similar albeit smoother drift in the PPP rate (figure 3.10). While the Plaza-Louvre accords encourage occasional concerted official interventions to stop wild movements in the market rate away from PPP in the short run, they do nothing to prevent the syndrome of the ever-higher yen over the longer term.

While keeping and perhaps strengthening the existing Plaza-Louvre conventions for concerted official interventions in the short run, our proposal would add a benchmark target for the long-term yen/dollar exchange rate.[6] The actual number the two countries chose, anywhere from 100 to 120 yen to the dollar, would be less important than the existence of the agreement itself.

Virtual exchange rate stability does not imply a commitment to stabilize the exchange rate in the short run within hard narrow bands. Nor does it attempt to target changes in the real exchange rate somehow defined, as per Williamson (1994) or Wren-Lewis et al. (1998). "Real" exchange rate targeting could be quite inconsistent with our objective of securing long-term stability in the nominal yen/dollar rate and Japan's (nominal) wholesale price index.

Instead, a benchmark parity for the nominal exchange rate is a device for harmonizing monetary policies between two countries in the longer term. But in the short run the two central banks would stand by to intervene directly and in concert in the foreign exchanges to reverse any sharp movements in the yen/U.S. dollar rate away from, say, 120. They would always reserve the right to occasionally nudge the rate toward the mutually agreed-on benchmark. If the yen/dollar rate is successfully tethered, this would have the important incidental impact of smoothing the collective business cycle in the smaller East Asian economies; see chapter 2.

3.5   After the Trap Is Sprung: The Transition

National monetary policies must eventually support any such long-run exchange rate target. But once the expectation of an ever-higher yen is successfully quashed, almost all the monetary adjustment would be in Japan. Little or no change in the Federal Reserve's policy of stabilizing the U.S. price level, the independent anchor, would be necessary or desirable. Because the purpose of long-term stabilization of the exchange rate is to end deflationary pressure and spring the liquidity trap in Japan, that is where the main monetary adjustment would take place. What would the transition look like?

An international pact to stabilize the yen/dollar exchange rate over the long term is politically difficult but technically straightforward. In contrast, once expectations begin to shift away from ongoing yen appreciation and deflation, successfully managing domestic Japanese monetary policy in the transition will be technically intricate. For analytical purposes, suppose deflationary expectations ended suddenly when the yen/dollar rate was virtually fixed at 120. What would happen?

• Nominal Japanese interest rates rise, and real interest rates fall, to world levels as the wholesale price level stabilizes. Holders of long-term yen bonds take a beating.

• New bank lending becomes profitable (see chapter 4) even though bank balance sheets remain a mess. But now a cleanup makes more sense. The banks can be "denationalized."

• Private investment increases as fear of a sudden yen appreciation and overvaluation is eliminated.

• As the price level stabilizes, private demand for new housing surges as the fear of ongoing decline in land values ends.

• The Bank of Japan may actually have to contract the monetary base to allow nominal interest rates to rise while keeping the exchange rate steady.

The last point needs some explanation. Once the foreign exchange value of the yen and future Japanese price level are securely anchored, whether the Bank of Japan should tighten or ease domestic monetary policy is, paradoxically, not clear. The possibly sharp increase in nominal interest rates would tend to reduce the demand for base money. If this effect dominates, the Bank of Japan would need to reduce the monetary base quickly in order to prevent capital outflows and a sharp depreciation of the yen below its agreed-on benchmark.

On the other hand, if the economy recovers sufficiently fast and the banking system is quickly recommercialized, the demand for base money would increase on net balance. Reprivatization of bank lending should proceed naturally as commercial banks offer positive nominal interest rates and bid funds away from the postal saving system. So, in the transition, the Bank of Japan must stand ready either to withdraw or to inject base money into the system, always being guided by pressure in the foreign exchanges.

With this exchange rate anchor, and after a successful transition, the economy should achieve approximate price level stability as measured by Japan's wholesale price index (WPI) but not necessarily by the consumer price index (CPI). Figure 3.14 shows the fall in Japan's WPI relative to its CPI. For many decades, the price of services in Japan has been rising relative to goods prices—the so-called Balassa-Samuelson effect. Since 1985 the Bank of Japan has been deceived by the relative stability in its CPI, while the WPI has fallen substantially and better

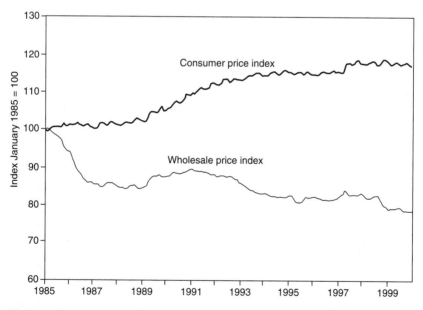

Figure 3.14
Japan's Consumer and Wholesale Price Indexes, 1985–2000. (International Monetary Fund, *International Financial Statistics*)

reflects deflationary pressure (along with falling land prices) in the economy overall.

Consequently, changes in the WPI are better (although not perfect) for deflating nominal into real interest rates (McKinnon 1979). The WPI is also more directly affected by the exchange rate. With exchange stability and economic recovery, the system would settle down to higher growth in Japan's CPI—say, 1 to 2 percent per year—while the WPI would remain approximately stable in the U.S. mode.[7]

The analysis in this chapter has focused on the institutional arrangements for eliminating expectations of an ever-higher yen. But the same arrangements of declaring and maintaining a long-term parity rate against the dollar would also curb short- and medium-term exchange rate fluctuations. In chapter 4 we show how this exchange rate stabilization would reduce or eliminate the negative risk premium in yen assets arising out of Japan's continual accumulation of dollar claims on foreigners, and thus improve profit margins in domestic bank lending.

4

Japan's Negative Risk Premium in Interest Rates: The Liquidity Trap and the Fall in Bank Lending

with Rishi Goyal

Japan's interest rates have been compressed toward zero because of pressure coming through the foreign exchanges. More than 20 years of current account surpluses have led to a huge buildup of claims, mainly in U.S. dollars, on foreigners. Because of ongoing fluctuations in the yen/dollar exchange rate, Japanese financial institutions will only willingly hold these dollar claims if the nominal yield on them is substantially higher than that on yen assets. From the mid-1990s to 2004, as U.S. interest rates have come down, portfolio equilibrium has been sustained only when nominal interest rates on yen assets have been forced toward zero. One consequence is the now infamous liquidity trap for Japanese monetary policy. A second consequence is the erosion of the normal profit margins of Japan's commercial banks, leading to a slump in new bank credit and an inability to grow out of the overhang of old bad loans.

After the asset price bubble burst in the early 1990s, Japan's economy was virtually stagnant, with a troubled banking sector for more than a decade. Chapter 3 described how the government resorted to expansionary monetary and fiscal policies. However, these standard stabilization tools failed to stimulate the economy. Most existing analyses have emphasized the need for broad-based structural reforms to clean up the banking sector and to liberalize various sectors of the economy. Others have emphasized the need for an even more expansionary monetary policy to halt deflation.

We believe that this emphasis on structural reform and further monetary (or fiscal) "expansion" is misplaced.[1] Here, we argue that long- and short-term nominal interest rates in Japan have been compressed

Adapted from Rishi Goyal and Ronald I. McKinnon, "Japan's Negative Risk Premium in Interest Rates: The Liquidity Trap and the Fall in Bank Lending," *The World Economy* 26 (March 2003): 339–363.

to historically low levels—the so-called liquidity trap—because of pressure coming through the foreign exchanges. This pressure has several facets. The first is the declining nominal interest rate on dollar assets from inflation stabilization in the United States in the mid-1990s and the extremely low U.S. interest rates from 2002 to 2004. The second is a *negative* risk premium in Japanese interest rates that has kept yields on yen assets well below those on dollar assets. The third facet is a residual fear, now possibly quite small, that the yen will resume appreciating secularly.[2] (The syndrome of the ever-higher yen from 1971 to 1995 was the focus of chapter 3.) This chapter focuses on the second facet: the domestic financial consequences of the negative risk premium arising from the cumulative effect of more than 20 years of Japanese current account surpluses.

As long-term interest rates have been pushed to very low values, short-term interest rates have been reduced to zero, and Japan has found itself in a liquidity trap: the Bank of Japan has been unable to halt deflation even though it has been increasing the monetary base at a high rate in the past few years; see figure 3.4 in chapter 3, and the more extensive depiction of Japan's very high growth in base money over the past decade in Shirakawa (2001).[3] In addition to the impotence of monetary policy at the zero lower bound of nominal interest rates, the compression of lending interest rates toward zero has squeezed bank profit margins. This compression has made new bank lending hardly profitable, and has made it practically impossible for Japanese banks, by themselves, to gradually write off old bad loans out of current earnings. In many countries beset by bad loan problems, the spread between deposit rates and lending rates has been raised so that banks have been able to gradually recover loan losses over time. In Japan, however, the compressed spreads have hindered banks saddled with sizable nonperforming loans from earning profits that could be used to restore their capital. It also explains the slump in new bank credit to Japan's private sector.

The rest of this chapter elaborates on and discusses these arguments. It presents the theory of the negative risk premium, along with supporting evidence and the theory's implications for the liquidity trap, and summarizes a more detailed analysis provided in Goyal (2001). It also discusses the consequences of compressed spreads for lack of profitability in the banking system and concludes with policy implications.

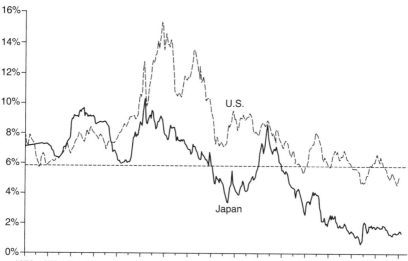

Figure 4.1
Long-Term Interest Rates on Ten-Year U.S. Treasuries and Japanese Government Bonds, 1970–2002. (International Monetary Fund, *International Financial Statistics*)

4.1 Theory of the Negative Risk Premium

Consider the plot in figure 4.1 of nominal interest rates on long-term U.S. government bonds and long-term Japanese government bonds. Note two properties. First, since the late 1970s Japanese rates have been well below U.S. rates. Second, since the early 1980s there has been a trend decline in the level of the interest rates in the United States and in Japan.

Uncovered interest parity suggests that the interest differential should correspond to expected yen appreciation; otherwise, there would be arbitrage opportunities. As figure 4.2 shows, the yen did appreciate from 1971 to 1995, as discussed in chapter 3. However, there has been no trend appreciation since the mid-1990s. The absence of such a trend may be rationalized either as the consequence of a strong U.S. economy and a strong dollar policy where U.S. mercantile pressure has been muted (unlike the main theme in chapter 3), or as the consequence of a stagnant real Japanese economy relative to a robust U.S. economy in a standard neoclassical growth model, as in Yoshikawa (1990). Even though there has been no trend appreciation since

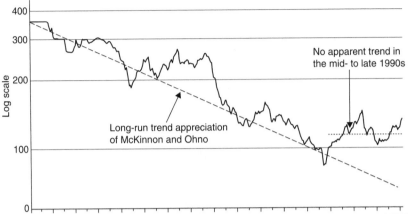

Figure 4.2
Nominal Yen/U.S. Dollar Exchange Rate, 1970–2002. (International Monetary Fund, *International Financial Statistics*)

the mid-1990s, Japan's long rates have remained much lower than their U.S. counterparts (figure 4.1).

To account for the sustained interest differential of about 4 percentage points between yen and dollar assets in the absence of trend yen appreciation, we postulate an augmented interest parity relationship:

$$i = i^* + \Delta s^e + \varphi \tag{4.1}$$

where i is the (endogenously determined) Japanese long-term nominal interest rate, i^* is the (exogenously given) U.S. long-term nominal interest rate, s is the yen price of \$1, Δs^e is expected depreciation of the yen, and φ is the risk premium on yen assets. The interest differential, $i - i^*$, from the 1970s to the early 1990s, was driven primarily by the negative Δs^e term, expected yen appreciation. Since the mid-1990s, $\Delta s^e \approx 0$ and the interest differential has been driven primarily φ, which is also negative.

φ is the excess yield that an investor demands for bearing foreign exchange risk. For a private Japanese financial institution holding net dollar assets, fluctuations in the yen/dollar exchange rate result in fluctuations in the yen value of the net dollar assets, and hence of the net worth of the financial institution. From the perspective of the institution whose liabilities are denominated in yen, dollar assets are riskier than yen assets. Thus, φ captures the excess yield, over and above expectations of ongoing yen appreciation, that a dollar asset must pay in order to induce the financial institution to hold it as the yen fluctuates.

It follows that φ is negative, for a creditor country such as Japan whose claims on foreigners are denominated mainly in dollars, on yen assets. Conversely, φ is positive for a debtor country whose debts are denominated in foreign currency. The size of φ depends on the share of net foreign currency assets or the net foreign currency debts and on the expected variance in the exchange rate. The larger the share of net foreign currency assets (debts), the more negative (positive) is φ. Hence, φ is inversely related to the net foreign currency asset position.[4]

These properties are in line with general cross-sectional evidence provided by Lane and Milesi-Ferretti (2001) showing an inverse relationship between real interest differentials and net foreign asset positions.[5] To see this, combine equation 4.1 with the familiar relative purchasing power parity equation, $\Delta s^e = p^e - p^{*e}$, where p^e is expected domestic inflation and p^{*e} is expected inflation in the rest of the world.[6] Fisher parity relates the real interest rate, r, to the nominal interest rate and expected inflation: $r = i - p^e$. Therefore, the real interest differential equals φ:

$$r - r^* = (i - \pi^e) - (i^* - \pi^{*e}) = (i - i^*) - \Delta s^e = \varphi \qquad (4.2)$$

Since φ is inversely related to net foreign assets (and, in particular, to net foreign currency assets in our theory), the real interest rate differential is inversely related to net foreign assets.

Not only does a larger net foreign currency asset share lead to a more negative risk premium of a creditor country, but declines in the value of domestic assets also result in a more negative risk premium. Shocks to domestic assets that lower the returns on and the market value of domestic assets result in a larger share of net foreign currency assets. This, in turn, results in a more negative risk premium because a larger share of the portfolio is subject to foreign exchange risk.

Being a creditor nation that does not lend much internationally in its own currency (conflicted virtue), Japan has a large negative risk premium. It has become more negative as running large current account surpluses continued throughout the 1990s into the new millennium (see chapter 8). Negative shocks to the Japanese economy in the late 1980s and early 1990s lowered the real return on capital in Japan relative to the rest of the world, so Japan invested more abroad (which

Table 4.1
Japan's Net Foreign Asset Position, 1980–2000 (billions of U.S. dollars)

	Total Net Foreign Assets	Private-Sector Net Position	Official Reserves
1980	12.52	−13.20	25.72
1985	130.38	103.15	27.23
1990	329.36	249.65	79.71
1995	817.60	632.42	184.82
1997	958.73	737.62	220.81
1998	1153.64	937.26	215.83
1999	829.12	540.10	287.66
2000	1157.93	796.82	360.99

Source: International Monetary Fund, *International Financial Statistics* (March 2002).

was reflected in large current account surpluses) and built up claims on the rest of the world. A substantial fraction of these claims was in foreign currencies (largely dollars), which resulted in a more negative risk premium in the 1990s through 2004.

In contrast, foreign currency claims on the rest of the world were small in the 1980s, and domestic growth rates were high. So, the risk premium term was small, and the interest differential between dollar and yen assets was explained primarily by expectations of yen appreciation. Since the mid-1990s, as Japanese growth has slowed and pressure for yen appreciation has eased, the interest differential is accounted for mainly by the negative risk premium.

Table 4.1 displays the rise in net foreign assets from 1980 to 2000. The breakdown between official reserves and private-sector net foreign asset holdings is also displayed. The table shows a large increase in Japan's net foreign asset position in the late 1980s and the 1990s. At the end of 2000, the total net foreign asset position stood at nearly $1.16 trillion, which is more than 20 percent of GDP, or about 8 percent of total assets.[7] A large portion of this position is held by the private sector, although accumulation of official reserves has played a large role from the late 1990s into the new millennium.

Table 4.1 displays the officially reported stock of net foreign assets. Unofficial estimates of the stock position, computed by cumulating current account surpluses, suggest numbers that are about 1.5 times as large as the official statistics.

Table 4.2 displays alternative estimates of Japan's cumulative current account surplus. The second column repeats the official net

Table 4.2
Alternative Estimates of Japan's Net Foreign Asset Position, 1980–2000 (billions of U.S. dollars)

	Official Estimate (IMF)	Lane and Milesi-Ferretti	Goyal	
			Cumulative Capital Accumulation Surplus	Capital Accumulation (6% interest rate)
1980	12.52	16.29	12.52	12.52
1985	130.38	101.49	138.43	135.54
1990	329.36	445.96	511.39	506.99
1995	817.60	1030.48	1099.86	1127.81
1997	958.73	1336.66	1277.93	1337.25
2000	1157.93		1653.18	1817.08

Sources: International Monetary Fund, *International Financial Statistics* (March 2002); Lane and Milesi-Ferretti (2001); Goyal (2001).
Note: Cumulative Capital Accumulation Surplus sums the balance on goods, services, and income. Capital Accumulation computes stocks from flow data (balance on goods and services only) as follows: Stock $(t) = (1 + i)$Stock $(t - 1) +$ Flow (t).

foreign asset position from table 4.1. The third column of table 4.2 displays the cumulative current account position from Lane and Milesi-Ferretti (2001). The fourth column updates their numbers to 2000. Both columns indicate numbers substantially higher than the official estimates. The final column cumulates the balance on goods and services only (the balance on income is excluded) using a 6 percent yield on assets. This yield comes from figure 4.1, where the return on long-term U.S. bonds was at least 6 percent until the late 1990s. These estimates suggest that the stock of net foreign assets, and hence the external exposure of Japanese financial institutions, is very large.

The share of net foreign assets that are in foreign currencies is difficult to ascertain. Some data are available through the Bank of Japan's Locational International Banking Statistics, which reports the balance sheet positions of banks and nonbanks vis-à-vis nonresidents in any currency. These are shown for selected years in table 4.3.

Note that, corresponding to the increase of Japan's net foreign asset position in tables 4.1 and 4.2, there is an increase in net assets vis-à-vis foreigners throughout the 1990s. A substantial portion of these net assets is in foreign currency. (Note also that the data in table 4.3 are less comprehensive and thus of lesser magnitude than those in tables 4.1 and 4.2.)

Table 4.3
Net Foreign Assets and Net Foreign Exchange Assets Positions of Japanese Banks and
Nonbanks vis-à-vis Nonresidents, 1990–2001 (billions of U.S. dollars)

	Total		Banks		Nonbanks	
	NFA	NFXA	NFA	NFXA	NFA	NFXA
1990	−17	−101	−184	−217	167	116
1994	305	−30	87	−180	218	150
1998	477	264	103	−41	374	305
1999	612	393	142	35	470	358
2000	656	401	127	21	530	380
2001	673	449	128	34	545	415

Source: Bank of Japan, Locational International Banking Statistics (2002).
Notes: The numbers reported for each year correspond to the end of September numbers.
NFA = Net foreign assets.
NFXA = Net foreign exchange assets.

The breakdown of foreign assets and foreign currency assets by banks and nonbanks (such as pension funds and insurance companies) is even more stark. Nonbanks hold the vast majority of the net foreign assets and net foreign currency assets. A very large fraction, 70 to 80 percent, of their net foreign asset positions is in foreign currency. Banks, on the other hand, borrowed heavily (in the short term) from abroad in the 1980s. This is reflected in their net liability position in 1990. However, after making large foreign exchange losses, they unwound much of their net short-term exposure while accumulating long-term foreign currency assets.[8] Their net foreign asset and net foreign exchange asset positions are not very large.

Absent detailed balance sheet data for banks and nonbanks, it is difficult to ascertain the share of net foreign exchange assets in total assets. Balance sheet data for banks are available; however, as shown in table 4.3, banks are not the primary holders of net foreign and net foreign exchange assets. For nonbanks such as life and nonlife insurance companies, basic balance sheet data suggest that about 12–14 percent of total assets are in foreign securities.[9]

The estimates of net foreign exchange assets and of exposure to foreign exchange risk are likely to be understated. First, as noted in table 4.2, unofficial net foreign asset positions for Japanese financial institutions, estimated from simple yet meaningful computations, are nearly 1.5 times as large as official estimates. Second, balance sheet data do not show the proportion of loans to foreigners or to multinational corporations for the purpose of foreign direct investment (FDI). Even if external FDI is denominated in yen, the investment is subject to foreign exchange risk if the proceeds from, or the success of, the investment is linked to the dollar. Third, the key variable for the foreign exchange risk premium is the share of net foreign exchange assets to performing (or healthy) domestic assets. If a large share of total domestic assets is at risk of becoming nonperforming, as is the case in Japan, then net foreign exchange assets become a larger share of performing assets and imply a more negative foreign exchange risk premium. As non-performing loans have ballooned in recent years, net foreign exchange assets of nearly 8 percent of total assets become a larger share of per-forming assets.

So, as Japan has run current account surpluses through the 1990s into the new millennium and has accumulated net foreign assets and, in particular, net foreign exchange assets, the risk premium has be-come more negative. This more negative risk premium has maintained the interest differential of 3 to 4 percentage points between yen assets and dollar assets even in the absence of trend yen appreciation. As U.S. nominal interest rates declined because of inflation stabilization in the United States, Japan's long rates have been compressed to very low values. Taking into account a term premium or liquidity premium, this compression of long rates has meant that short rates have been com-pressed to zero—a liquidity trap situation—and the Bank of Japan has been unable to halt deflation and reinflate the economy.

Portfolio Equilibrium in the Liquidity Trap

At the zero lower bound of nominal interest rates, $i = 0 = i^* + \Delta s^e + \varphi$. Recall that the left-hand variable, i, denotes the domestic currency re-turn on a domestic currency asset, and the right-hand expression, $i^* + \Delta s^e + \varphi$, denotes the risk-adjusted domestic currency return on a foreign currency asset.

On this uneasy edge of the liquidity trap, Japanese financial institu-tions are ambivalent about whether or not to hold dollar assets. On the one hand, at longer term, the yield can be as much as 4 percentage points higher (figure 4.1) than the near-zero interest rates on yen assets. Insurance companies, for example, are desperate for higher earnings in order to be able to fund their annuity obligations. On the other hand, dollar assets are seen to be much riskier than yen assets: the liabilities of the insurance companies, their annuity obligations, are in yen. Because the yen/dollar rate is free to fluctuate, any random

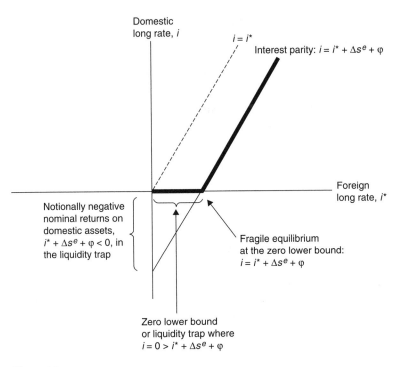

Figure 4.3
Negative Risk Premium and the Liquidity Trap

upward blip in the yen that reduces the yen value of their dollar
assets could wipe out their net worth. Thus, dollar and yen assets
are seen to be imperfect substitutes: the former are high yield and
high risk, the latter low yield and low risk. Nevertheless, in portfolio
equilibrium, some of both will be held as long as *risk-adjusted* interest
rates are the same, as per the preceding equality and as shown in figure 4.3.

Now suppose that this equilibrium is disturbed by an outside
shock—a fall in American interest rates or a new rumor in the foreign
exchange markets that the yen might appreciate. Given the existing
portfolio allocation between foreign assets and domestic assets, and
hence given a value for φ, a decline in $i^* + \Delta s^e$ due either to a decline
in foreign nominal interest rates, i^*, or to greater anticipated yen appreciation implies that risk-adjusted domestic currency returns on
foreign currency assets become negative. In other words, $i = 0 > i^* +
\Delta s^e + \varphi$.

Private Japanese financial institutions now become unwilling to hold so many foreign currency assets, so they sell them and buy yen assets. This portfolio reallocation implies a less negative risk premium because their exposure to foreign currency risk is reduced. However, it exacerbates pressure for yen appreciation.

At a time when the Japanese economy is already quite weak, an appreciation of the yen would further weaken it. To prevent this, the Japanese monetary authorities intervene in the foreign exchange markets to sell yen and buy dollar assets from Japanese private institutions, thus alleviating the pressure for the yen to appreciate. The risk premium is made less negative, so as to restore portfolio equilibrium at $i = 0 = i^* + \Delta s^e + \varphi$.

Figure 4.3 offers an illustration of this argument. The bold line shows interest parity above zero: $i = i^* + \Delta s^e + \varphi$. Since i is constrained below by zero, a fall in i^* (given $\Delta s^e + \varphi$) implies $i = 0 > i^* + \Delta s^e + \varphi$. But then intervention by the Bank of Japan to buy the now excess dollar assets (and reduce φ) restores risk-adjusted interest parity at the still zero domestic interest rate: $i = 0 = i^* + \Delta s^e + \varphi$. However, this is a fragile equilibrium because (1) any further decline in i^*, or (2) new accumulation of private dollar assets from the current account surplus, will lead to the same cycle of portfolio reallocation and foreign exchange interventions as we described. After official intervention to buy dollar assets in exchange for yen assets, the equilibrium currency risk premium will be less negative under (1), and it will be prevented from becoming more negative under (2).

An important, if incidental, consequence is that official dollar reserve accumulation becomes the main channel for financing Japan's current account surplus. For 1999 and 2000, when nominal interest rates were zero, official reserve accumulation was the primary channel for dollar finance of the current account surplus and for reducing what would otherwise have been an even more negative currency risk premium, φ (see table 4.1).[10] In the new millennium Japan's "nationalization" of capital outflows has gone even further (see chapter 8).

In summary, in the liquidity trap with a near-zero domestic interest rate, official foreign exchange interventions must continually adjust φ by reducing dollar holdings in the private sector in order to maintain private portfolio balance without the yen's appreciating. This scenario has serious implications for Japan's banking sector.

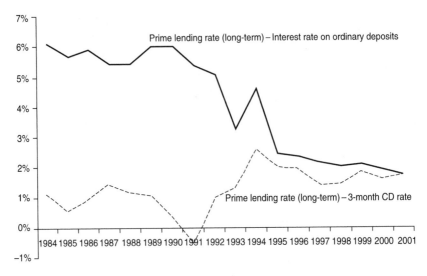

Figure 4.4
Japan's Ex Ante Profit Margins on Bank Lending, 1984–2001. (Bank of Japan, *Economic Statistics Annual*)

4.2   The Profitability of Banks

The compression of interest rates toward zero has an adverse impact on the profitability of new bank lending. Banks earn profits on the spread between their borrowing and lending rates. They accept various types of deposits such as demand deposits at zero interest rates and time deposits, and they borrow short-term from other banks. They typically lend long-term. As the (absolute) level of lending rates falls toward zero,[11] and as the spread between the short-term rates and long-term rates is compressed, banks will have very low profit margins on new loans.

Figure 4.4 shows the ex ante profit margin on new bank lending. Two measures are plotted. One is the difference between the rate on long-term loans for prime borrowers (the prime lending rate) and the ordinary deposit rate. This measure shows a decline through the 1990s. The other measure is the difference between the prime rate on long-term loans and the three-month certificate of deposit (CD) rate, which shows an increase in the 1990s relative to the 1980s and can be explained by deregulation of time deposit rates.[12] Though the latter measure has increased, it remains at low levels.

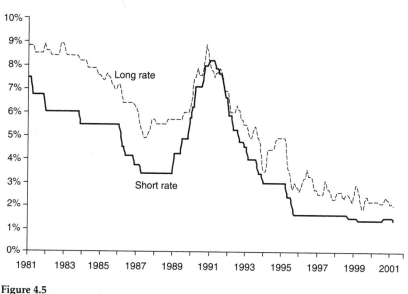

Figure 4.5
Japan's Prime Short-Term and Long-Term Lending Rates, 1981–2001. (Bank of Japan)

Alternatively, consider the ex ante profitability of bank lending to be the difference between the prime loan rate and the zero interest on demand deposits. Figure 4.5 plots the short-term and long-term rates for prime borrowers; it shows that both rates have declined in the 1990s. Significantly, the spread between the two prime loan rates has declined compared to the early and mid-1980s. In other words, the ordinary business of banking, of accepting demand deposits and making longer-term loans to high-quality borrowers, has become markedly less profitable.

Though ex ante measures of profitability show a decline, ex post measures of the actual profitability of bank lending are more difficult to calculate. Unless the cost of disposing of nonperforming loans is taken into account, one does not see a similar decline in actual bank profit margins. Figure 4.6a plots the interest margin on lending, the cost of maintaining assets or the expense ratio, and the realized credit cost. The interest margin on lending is defined as the difference between the yield on lending and the average rate on banks' interest-bearing liabilities. The expense ratio is defined as the ratio of general and administrative expenses to the average annual stock of interest-earning assets. Realized credit costs is the ratio of loan-loss provisioning and loan write-offs (or the disposal of nonperforming loans) to the

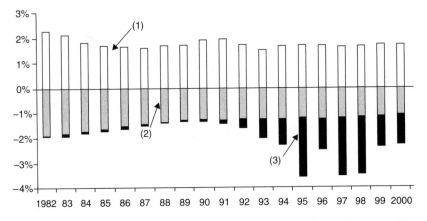

(1) Interest margin on lending = yield on lending – average rate on banks' interest-bearing liabilities
(2) Expense ratio = general and administrative expenses/balance on interest-earning assets
(3) Realized credit cost = disposal of nonperforming loans/average outstanding amount of loans

Figure 4.6a
Japan's Interest Margins on Lending, Expenses, and Credit Costs, 1982–2000. (Bank of Japan 2001)

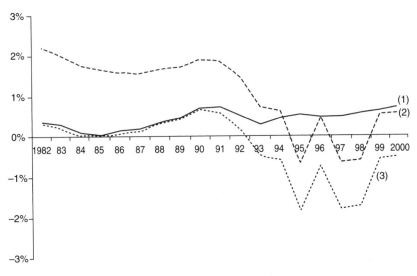

(1) Interest margin on lending net of general and administrative expenses
(2) Interest margin on lending net of realized credit costs
(3) Interest margin on lending net of general expenses and realized credit costs

Figure 4.6b
Japan's Ex Post Profit Margins on Bank Lending, 1982–2000. (Bank of Japan 2001)

average amount of loans outstanding, as shown by the darkest shading in figure 4.6a.

The interest margin on lending shows a slight decline in the 1990s. However, this decline was more than matched by a decline in general and administrative costs (or in the expense ratio). Hence, the ex post interest margin on lending net of general expenses displayed in figure 4.6b does not show a decline through the 1990s.

In contrast, realized credit costs or the costs associated with the disposal of nonperforming loans increased dramatically in the mid- to late 1990s. Consequently, ex post profitability suffered. This is displayed in figure 4.6b as an interest margin on lending net of realized credit costs, and as an interest margin on lending net of realized credit costs and general and administrative expenses. Both measures show negative returns in the mid- to late 1990s.

How does the compression of ex ante profit margins on lending square with the absence of compression in ex post profit margins not including bad loan write-offs? We think it quite likely that the accounting of interest income is flawed. While Japanese banks have disposed of a large number of nonperforming loans, new and larger amounts of them keep appearing on their books. This suggests that banks have not performed adequate risk assessments of their loan portfolios and they have not made sufficient allowances for future loan losses. It also suggests that banks may be "evergreening" these loans and capitalizing interest payments that they have not received. The effect is that their net interest income is possibly overstated and the reported ex post net margin does not decline. But profit margins remain at very low levels.

Very low profit margins or compressed profit margins imply that Japanese banks are not earning adequate profits to cover loan losses. Comparing Japanese profit margins on lending to the margins for U.S. banks is quite revealing (figure 4.7). U.S. banks have been able to run much larger profit margins and thereby have been able to cover losses on loans. Japanese banks have not been able to run as high profit margins and hence have been unable to cover loan losses by themselves. In the 1980s profit margins were low because of interest rate regulation. However, even after deregulation of the interest rate structure, Japanese banks have been unable to generate or maintain substantially larger profit margins.

Banks may want to raise lending rates. However, they have not been able to do so to any significant degree. One possibility is that if they raise them, the most creditworthy of their corporate clients will stop

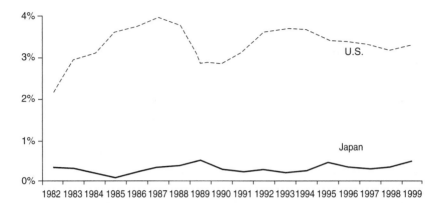

Figure 4.7
U.S. and Japan's Ex Post Interest Margins on Lending, 1982–1999. "Interest margin" is
yield on working assets minus cost of funds. (Bank of Japan, *Economic Statistics Annual*
and *Comparative Economic and Financial Statistics*)

borrowing from them and will instead raise credit by issuing low-yield
commercial paper. This will leave banks with less creditworthy clients.
In fact, yields on newly issued commercial paper have been very low
since the mid-1990s. They fell from around 2.5 percent before 1995 to
approximately 0.5 percent since 1996, suggesting that issuers of this
paper can access credit cheaply and need not pay higher interest rates
to banks.[13]

Another possibility is that small and medium enterprises, which are
the banks' primary clients, are already very heavily indebted and in a
precarious financial situation. Raising lending rates would raise their
risk of default. Bank lending shifted away from manufacturing firms
in the 1980s to primarily nonmanufacturing firms in real estate, finance, insurance, and services. In the 1990s lending to individuals
increased substantially as a share of total loans. By size of enterprise,
lending has been primarily to small nonmanufacturing firms.

With compressed lending rates and the zero lower bound on the
deposit rates, and hence with low profit margins on new commercial
lending, banks have an incentive to change their portfolio allocation
away from commercial lending and into government bonds, which
have a low transaction cost. This is indeed what has happened in
Japan. Loans outstanding have declined from the mid-1990s while
the amount in government bonds has increased quite substantially
(figure 4.8). Bank credit to the private sector has been shrinking in the
late 1990s into the new millennium, even though the monetary base

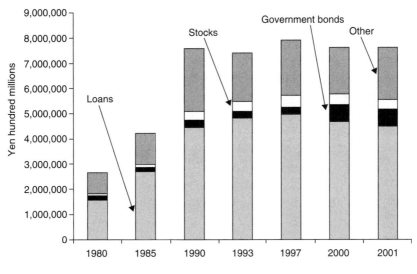

Figure 4.8
Assets of Japanese Domestically Licensed Banks, 1980–2001. (Bank of Japan, *Economic Statistics Annual*)

and broad money (M2 + CDs) have been increasing (see figure 3.4 in chapter 3).

4.3 Lending Spreads and Bad Loans: A Simulation

Compressed lending rates and low profit margins have made it practically impossible for Japanese banks, by themselves, to cover loan losses and gradually write off old bad loans out of current earnings. By contrast, U.S. banks have been able to gradually recover loan losses because their profit margins on lending have been much larger than has been possible for Japanese banks (see figure 4.7).

This section presents two simulation exercises to show the relationship between lending spreads and the share of nonperforming loans in a bank's portfolio, assuming that there are no *new* loan defaults. First, the lending spread required to recover a given share of nonperforming loans in T periods of time is computed. Second, given a particular lending spread, the evolution of the size of loanable funds is studied.

Consider an ultrasimple model of a bank. The bank has a given level of deposits and has made loans. Assume that a share of the loans has become nonperforming. Assume further that the nonperforming loans (NPL) are maintained on the balance sheet of the bank, that is, the nonperforming loans are not immediately written off. And suppose that no new funds come to the bank: there is neither a public injection of funds nor are there new deposits.

If the bank is to cover its loan losses, it needs to do so out of current profits. Given an initial share of NPL, in how much time can the bank cover its loan losses as a function of the lending spread?

The balance sheet of the bank may be described as follows:

Assets	Liabilities
Loans	*Deposits*
Nonperforming loans	
Performing loans	
Reserves	*Capital*

Let i_l be the lending rate, i_d the deposit rate, and τ the general and administrative cost per unit of assets. Let k be the capital adequacy ratio, and r the required reserve ratio. Let total liabilities be normalized to 1, and let the share of NPL at time t be NPA_t.

Assuming no new defaults, the bank's revenue per yen lent at time t is $i_l(1 - r - NPA_t)$. Assuming that no dividends are paid out on capital to the bank's owners, its cost at time t is $i_d(1 - k) + \tau$. Then its profit rate at time t, π_t, is given by

$$\pi_t = i_l(1 - r - NPA_t) - i_d(1 - k) - \tau \tag{4.3}$$

Assume that (positive) profits are used to write off loan losses. The evolution of the nonperforming loan share is given by

$$NPA_{t+1} = NPA_t - \pi_t \tag{4.4}$$

Given an initial share of nonperforming loans, NPA_0, and given i_d, τ, k, and r, we can compute the time to cover loan losses as a function of the lending rate, i_l. We do so by setting $NPA_T = 0$ and iterating backward using equations 4.3 and 4.4 (see the appendix at the end of this chapter).

Let $i_d = 0$, $\tau = 1.5$ percent, $k = 10$ percent, and $r = 2$ percent. These parameters roughly correspond to the situation in Japanese banks.

The results of this first simulation are shown in figure 4.9. It displays the time taken to reduce the share of nonperforming loans in the bank's balance sheet to zero as a function of the lending rate i_l (given a zero-interest deposit rate). As one would expect, the lower the lending

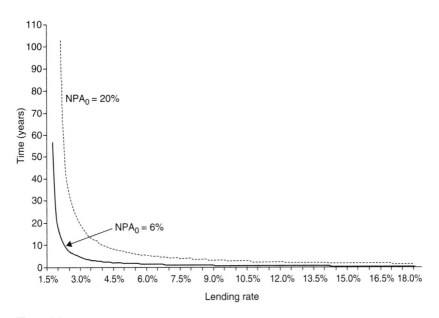

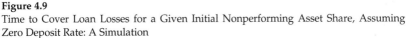

Figure 4.9
Time to Cover Loan Losses for a Given Initial Nonperforming Asset Share, Assuming
Zero Deposit Rate: A Simulation

spread, the longer it takes to cover loan losses. The larger the initial
share of nonperforming assets, the longer it takes to cover loan losses.
The time taken to cover loan losses increases exponentially as the lending spread declines.

By official estimates, the share of nonperforming loans is 6 percent
(Bank of Japan 2001). From figure 4.4, the ex ante profit margins are
approximately 1.7 percent. Given this spread, it will take more than 56
years to cover the loan losses. This computation assumes no new
defaults and no infusion of funds. If there is a continuing risk of default, as there most likely will be, then this is an underestimate and it
will take longer to cover the losses. Furthermore, in the past ten years,
there has been little change in the total deposit base of domestically
licensed banks. There have been public infusions of funds, but these
have been few and in times of (near) crisis.

Unofficial estimates of the share of nonperforming loans are as high
as 20 percent. For such high loan losses, it would take more than 100
years to recover losses at a spread of 2 percent. For spreads lower than
1.9 percent, the banks are running at a loss and are unable to cover
their loan losses. Indeed, the spreads required for Japanese banks to

make profits and cover losses are much larger than they have been able to generate. Figure 4.5 is also suggestive of their troubles, since the spread between short- and long-term rates has been about 0.5 percent, which is far smaller than the spreads that they need to restore financial health.

The exercise strongly suggests that low lending spreads are a key component of the problems faced by Japanese banks. Lowering τ and lowering r would reduce the lending spreads needed to cover loan losses, and in fact Japanese banks have been trying to lower τ by reducing personnel expenses. Reducing τ and r in the computations reduces the time needed to cover loan losses; however, the time needed remains high. For a 20 percent initial share of nonperforming loans and for τ and r both reduced to 1 percent, 40 years are needed to cover loan losses for a lending spread of 1.7 percent. For a 6 percent share, the time is 10 years. This computation assumes no defaults on new loans.

A spread of more than 3 percent, which U.S. banks have been able to generate, implies that a 6 percent initial nonperforming loan share can be covered in less than five years with the initial choice of parameters. After the crisis of the late 1980s and early 1990s, when many U.S. savings and loan banks were forced to liquidate, the ratio of nonperforming loans also rose significantly in the portfolio of U.S. commercial banks. However, with spreads over 3 percent, these banks have easily recovered their losses. On the other hand, with larger nonperforming loans and smaller lending spreads, Japanese banks face a much more difficult time in covering their losses.

With low lending spreads and large nonperforming loans, these computations suggest that many Japanese banks are losing money on their operations. In our second simulation, we calculate the impact on bank lending when the banks are unable to break even. How fast does the ratio of nonperforming to performing loans increase through time?

In our simple model, if the bank makes losses, $\pi_t < 0$, then its capital (or net worth) declines. To maintain a required level of capital, the bank must call in, or not renew, some of its performing (or good) loans to reduce its liabilities. As performing loans are called in, nonperforming assets rise as a share of performing assets. That is, the loan dependency ratio of nonperforming loans to performing loans worsens over time even if there are no new defaults.

We have computed and plotted this loan dependency ratio over time for the case of an initial nonperforming asset share of 20 percent. Let

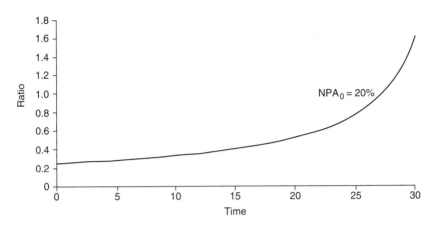

Figure 4.10
Ratio of Nonperforming Loans to Performing Loans When Lending Spreads Are Low and Profits Are Negative: A Simulation

total liabilities be normalized initially, that is, at time 0, to 1. Hence, nonperforming assets at time 0 are 0.20. As in the previous exercise, let the required reserve ratio be 2 percent and let the capital adequacy ratio be 10 percent of total liabilities. Let the lending rate i_l be 1.7 percent, the deposit rate i_d be 0 percent, and the general and administrative expense ratio τ be 1.5 percent.

Figure 4.10 plots the exponential increase in the ratio of nonperforming assets to performing assets over time. The ratio increases gradually at first, rising from 26 percent at time 0 (corresponding to nonperforming assets as a 20 percent share of total liabilities at time 0) to 29 percent in 5 years and 34 percent after 10 years. After that, the increases are much quicker, so the bad loan problem can fester for some years before it explodes.

4.4 Competition from the Government

An alternative interpretation, put forth by Fukao (2002), is that profit margins are low not because of pressure coming from the foreign exchange market, as we have argued, but in large part because government financial institutions have been lending at low interest rates, thus keeping commercial loan rates low. Most of this public intermediation is financed one way or another from the deposit base of the huge government-run postal savings system. In the 1990s doubts about the soundness of many commercial banks led many Japanese savers to

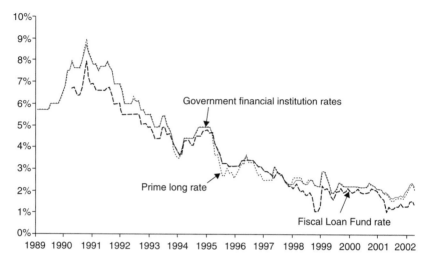

Figure 4.11
Japan's Lending Rates, 1989–2002. (Bank of Japan, *Financial and Economic Statistics Monthly*)

switch into postal savings deposits. But the question is one of causality or endogeneity. Is public intermediation driving the nonprofitability of commercial bank lending, or is public intermediation an endogenous response to a curtailment in (unprofitable) commercial bank lending? Fukao suggests the former, but we suspect that it may be the latter.

Figure 4.11 plots the prime long-term lending rate, the key lending rates of government financial institutions, including the Fiscal Loan Fund. The key lending rates of the government financial institutions move very closely with the prime long-term lending rate. The two are virtually identical for many periods. They also move very closely with the Fiscal Loan Fund rate, and have declined significantly over the 1990s. While the co-movement and the fall are apparent throughout the 1990s, the causality from one to the other is not.

Figure 4.12 plots the prime long-term lending rate with the middle rates on housing loans by city banks and the lending rates on private dwellings by the Housing Loan Corporation. The loan rates of city banks have moved nearly identically with the prime long-term rates and, since 1995, have been below the rates offered by the Housing Loan Corporation. Housing loan rates of the latter have declined in the 1990s, but it does not appear that the corporation is undercutting the profit margins of commercial bank lending.

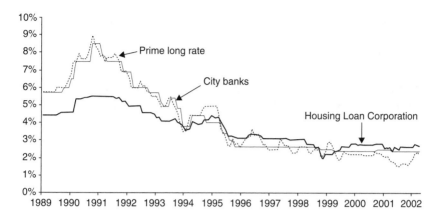

Figure 4.12
Japan's Housing Loan Rates, 1989–2002. (Bank of Japan, *Financial and Economic Statistics Monthly*)

On the loan side, commercial bank credit to private nonfinancial corporations has fallen in absolute terms since 1996–1997. As we have argued, commercial banks have instead increased their holdings of government securities. Loans from government financial institutions to private nonfinancial corporations rose in the early 1990s but have also fallen in absolute terms since 1998. In relative terms, a slightly larger share of loans outstanding to private nonfinancial corporations has come from government financial intermediaries. Their share of loans outstanding has risen from 11 percent in 1990 to 13 percent in 1997 and 14 percent in 2000 (Bank of Japan 2001).

On the deposit side, household saving has increased throughout the 1990s. In 1989–1990, 41 percent of these savings were held in domestically licensed banks, while 31 percent were in the postal savings system. The rest were mostly in financial institutions for agriculture, forestry, fisheries, and small businesses. By the late 1990s the share of savings held in domestically licensed banks had fallen marginally to 40 percent but had increased to 36 percent in the postal savings system. The increase in postal savings deposits came at the expense of the financial institutions for agriculture, forestry, and fisheries, and of financial institutions for small businesses.

To summarize, on the deposit side, there has not been much change. On the lending side, there has been an increase in the share of loans by government financial institutions, as Fukao (2002) has noted. But this change is not large, and there does not appear to be much evidence of undercutting of private lending rates by government financial institutions. Nevertheless, the evidence of government financial institutions' offering low rates and increasing lending to the private sector does not contradict our argument of pressures in the foreign exchange market compressing all interest rates toward zero and reducing bank profitability whether or not government financial institutions acting endogenously offset some of the decline in lending by commercial banks. Thus, the evidence presented by Fukao is consistent with our explanation.

4.5 Conclusion

One of the supposed truisms about Japan's economic malaise has been the failure of the government to take resolute action to clean up the balance sheets of the banks after the collapse of the bubble economy in 1991. After the string of bank failures in the United States in the 1980s, the U.S. government created the Resolution Trust Corporation in 1989. The RTC assumed dubious loans and wound up really bad banks. It also helped with the recapitalization of the wounded survivors, often by subsidizing a merger with, or acquisition by, a good bank. Although there have been several desultory attempts to inject more capital into distressed (and not so distressed) Japanese banks, nothing seems to work to stem the fall in new bank credit. Thus, with invidious comparisons to the earlier American example, the Japanese government is heavily criticized for not being thorough enough in restructuring commercial and other domestic banks.

However, our analysis of the negative risk premium and Japan's low-interest-rate trap suggests that such criticism of government regulatory inaction is seriously misplaced. Instead, macroeconomic phenomena have compressed bank lending (as well as deposit) rates toward zero so as to take away the "normal" margin of profitability on new lending. This compressed margin helps explain both the reluctance of Japanese banks to make new loans and their inability to gradually recapitalize themselves. In contrast, after the banking crises of the 1980s, most U.S. banks could gradually recapitalize because the spread between deposit and loan rates for several years was even higher than it is now, and much higher than in Japan currently.

A comprehensive restructuring of balance sheets, no matter how thorough, cannot end Japan's banking crisis. Under the currently compressed structure of interest rates on yen assets, commercial banks will remain reluctant to lend to high-quality borrowers that could alternatively issue very low-yield commercial bills in the open market. Decompression and a return to a more normal structure of nominal interest rates through macroeconomic reforms should precede serious balance sheet restructuring, which of course will ultimately be necessary.

Thus, ending the low-interest-rate liquidity trap is a necessary condition for recovery in Japan's banking system. If one accepts our hypothesis of the importance of the negative risk premium in contributing to Japan's low-interest-rate trap, then what should be done is obvious. The negative risk premium arises from (1) decades of accumulation of dollar assets in Japanese financial institutions, and (2) fluctuations in the yen/dollar exchange rate, which increase the risks to yen-based financial firms holding these dollar assets. Because running trade deficits cannot suddenly reverse the cumulative financial effect of 20 years of trade surpluses, the only immediate policy instrument for reducing the foreign exchange risk in Japanese financial intermediaries is to stabilize the yen/dollar exchange rate in a completely convincing fashion, as discussed in chapter 3.

For further details on how to credibly stabilize the yen/dollar rate into the indefinite future, and the macroeconomic consequences of doing so, see McKinnon and Ohno (1997) and Goyal (2001). Here it suffices to note that the solution, as well as the problem, is not one that the Japanese authorities are likely to be able to deal with on their own. Rather, to be credible, a long-term benchmark parity for the yen/dollar rate will require the cooperation of the United States. It would also be made easier if other East Asian countries, particularly China (see chapter 5), can stabilize their dollar exchange rates. This becomes more likely when the yen/dollar rate is stable—a virtuous circle.

4.6 Appendix

Case of Positive Operational Profits: $\tau_t > 0$
Combining equations 4.3 and 4.4 yields

$$NPA_T = (1 + i_l)NPA_{T-1} - i_l(1 - r) + i_d(1 - k) + \tau$$

Iterating backward to time 0 gives

$$NPA_T = (1 + i_l)^T NPA_0 - [i_l(1 - r) + i_d(1 - k) + \tau]$$
$$\times [1 + (1 + i_l) + (1 + i_l)^2 + \cdots + (1 + i_l)^{T-1}]$$

This equation can be used to compute the time T needed to cover loan losses of NPA_0 given $i_l, i_d, \tau, k,$ and r. This is done by setting $NPA_T = 0$. The equation then reduces to

$$i_l NPA_0 = [1 - (1 + i_l)^{-T}][i_l(1 - r) + i_d(1 - k) + \tau]$$

It can be solved for T. Alternatively, the equation can be used to determine the lending rate i_l needed to cover initial loan losses NPA_0 for a given time period of, say, 10 years.

Case of Negative Operational Profits: $\pi_t < 0$

Losses erode bank capital. Let k_t be bank capital at time t. Since losses erode capital,

$$k_{t+1} = k_t + \pi < k_t$$

Banks must maintain a certain capital adequacy ratio, denoted by k^*. So, its liabilities, which are deposits D_t, must shrink. Deposits must shrink such that $k_{t+1}/(k_{t+1} + D_{t+1}) = k^*$. Thus, the size of the bank $(k_{t+1} + D_{t+1})$ shrinks.

As liabilities shrink, so do required reserves and, more important, the performing assets. Performing loans are called in or are not renewed. Hence, nonperforming loans rise as a share of performing loans.

5

China: A Stabilizing or
Deflationary Influence in
East Asia? The Problem of
Conflicted Virtue

with Günther Schnabl

China's rapidly growing exports are mostly middle-tech, though increasingly high-tech, manufactured goods. The United States runs a huge and growing bilateral trade deficit with China, and the position of Japan has changed from being a net exporter to China in the 1980s and most of the 1990s to facing greater industrial competition from China today. China's smaller East Asian industrial competitors such as Taiwan, Korea, and Singapore also face difficult problems in restructuring their exports of producer goods to China while facing greater competition from Chinese consumer goods in third markets. However, China is a huge importer of primary products and industrial raw materials, and runs large import surpluses with the ASEAN group.

On the macroeconomic side, China has been a stabilizing influence. While maintaining steady high growth and exchange rate stability at 8.28 yuan/dollar since 1994, it has largely avoided, and thus dampened, the business cycles of its East Asian trading partners.

But potential clouds loom on this horizon. Since 1995, China has run moderate multilateral trade surpluses coupled with large inflows of foreign direct investment. The resulting balance-of-payments surpluses have led to a rapid buildup of liquid dollar claims on foreigners, both in official exchange reserves and, less obviously, in stocks held privately or in China's nonstate sectors. This increasing private dollar overhang leads to what we call the syndrome of conflicted virtue. If there is no threat that the renminbi will appreciate, private portfolio equilibrium for accumulating and holding both dollar and renminbi assets can be sustained.

However, many foreigners are upset with China's "excessive" mercantile competitiveness. They are urging China's government to appreciate the renminbi and to show greater future exchange rate flexibility, which could lead to repetitive appreciations. The result would be severe deflation throughout China's economy and a zero-interest liquidity trap, as in Japan, when it was forced into repeated appreciations of the yen in the 1980s into the mid-1990s.

5.1 China's Trade and Transformation since 1980

These days, even the most casual retail shopper must be impressed by the incredible proliferation of made-in-China labels on items from apparel to bicycles to toys, and to almost any middle-level electronic or mechanical gadget. From 2000 into 2004, China was the only truly booming part of the world economy. But in the older industrial economies this surge in exports provokes outcries that Chinese goods are too cheap. Is China the engine of growth or an economic threat in Asia?

In this chapter we sketch the broad dimensions of China's trade-led industrial expansion since 1980. We then consider China's monetary and exchange rate policies for accommodating this remarkable growth. Of course, when a large country like China grows unusually rapidly, industrial readjustment, sometimes quite painful, is inevitable in some neighboring countries.

But has China's growth made the East Asian macroeconomy less stable in a cyclical sense? We examine this issue empirically by looking at China's exchange rate policy and its own macroeconomic instability.

Since 1990, China's economic growth has been nurtured by large inflows of foreign direct investment (FDI), and since 1995 these have been coupled with trade surpluses, leading to substantial balance-of-payments surpluses overall. Is this financial regime sustainable?

We develop the idea of conflicted virtue, which applies to international creditor countries that cannot lend in their own currencies. We compare China's to Japan's earlier experience with conflicted virtue. Japan has a much longer track record of running balance-of-payments surpluses and building up liquid dollar claims on foreigners, both through its high-growth phase before 1990, and then in its subsequent deflationary slump and zero-interest liquidity trap of the late 1990s. Domestic monetary policy is then rendered ineffective for reflating the economy; for the foreign exchange origins of Japan's liquidity trap, see chapters 3 and 4, and McKinnon and Ohno (1997).

China's foreign exchange problem is uncomfortably similar to Japan's, yet it differs in some important respects, such as the huge

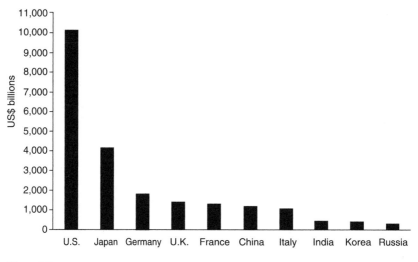

Figure 5.1
Nominal GDP, Ten Countries, 2001. (International Monetary Fund, *International Financial Statistics*)

inflow of foreign direct investment. We give alternative estimates of the buildup of liquid foreign assets, both government and private, in China and then discuss whether this increasing overhang, mainly in U.S. dollars, is sustainable.

China's economy is now huge. Although in terms of GDP per capita China still remains far behind the industrialized countries, because of its large population it has become the world's sixth largest economy. Today its nominal GDP (in U.S. dollars) is larger than Italy's and is just slightly smaller than the GDP of France (figure 5.1). If GDPs were compared at exchange rates reflecting purchasing power parities, that is, after adjusting for price differences in the respective economies, China would rank even higher.

Notwithstanding the already significant size of China's economy, a record of sustained high real growth rates portends an increasing impact on the world economy in general and that of East Asia in particular. With an average real GDP growth rate of almost 10 percent per year since 1980, the wakening giant is catching up fast (figure 5.2). In the 1990s, China outperformed the negligible growth rate of its ailing neighbor Japan and of its more robust trading partner the United States, which had only a 3 percent growth rate. Despite criticism about

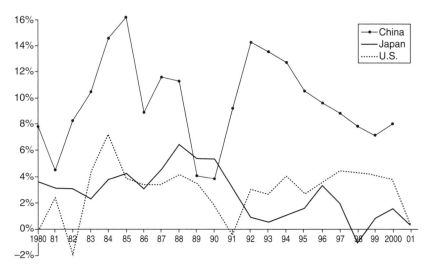

Figure 5.2
Real GDP Growth, China, Japan, and U.S., 1980–2001. (International Monetary Fund, *International Financial Statistics*)

the accuracy of official real GDP data, few doubt that China has become the world's most dynamic economy.

The country's trade performance reflects its growth dynamics. Exports plus imports are now equal to about 48 percent of China's GDP (compared to 15 percent in 1982). Although production for the large domestic market was the main driving force in the first decade of China's transition to a market economy, production for export and consumption of imports now add great momentum to the fast output expansion. As shown in figure 5.3, which plots Chinese, Japanese, and U.S. exports compared to the base year 1980, Chinese exports have expanded much faster than those of either Japan or the United States. This process has accelerated since the early 1990s, and today China has become the world's sixth largest exporting nation; within a few years, it is likely to surpass France, the U.K., and probably even Japan (figure 5.4).

Before 1994, China showed no sustained tendency to run trade surpluses: the net current account balance was sometimes positive and sometimes negative (figure 5.5). Since 1995 a more persistent tendency toward current account surplus, of about 1 to 2 percent of China's GDP, seems evident. But the net current account numbers are erratic,

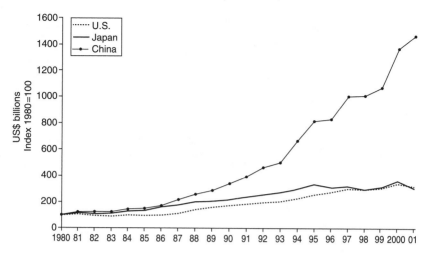

Figure 5.3
Nominal Exports, China, Japan, and U.S., 1980–2001. (International Monetary Fund, International Financial Statistics)

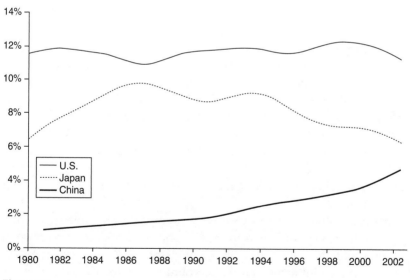

Figure 5.4
Exports/World Trade, China, Japan, and U.S., 1980–2002. Smoothed averages computed by Hodrick-Prescott filter. (International Monetary Fund, *International Financial Statistics*)

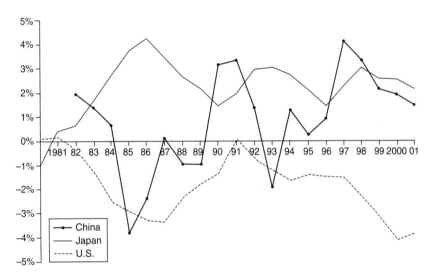

Figure 5.5
Current Accounts as Percentage of GDP, China, Japan, and U.S., 1980–2001. (International Monetary Fund, *International Financial Statistics*)

and there is no strong presumption that China will continue to run trade surpluses multilaterally.

Much more definite is the rapidly increasing *bilateral* trade surplus China is now running with the United States. It rose from virtually nothing in 1985 to more than $90 billion in 2002, exceeding even Japan's ongoing (but not increasing) surplus with the United States of about $70 billion, and rose to well over $100 billion in 2003. Figure 5.6 shows China's and Japan's bilateral trade surpluses since 1980 as a proportion of U.S. GDP. Just as striking is the sharp decline in Japan's large bilateral surplus with China in the 1980s to a sizable net deficit by 2001 (figure 5.7).

An alternative way of measuring these dramatic shifts in China's geographic trade patterns is to measure bilateral trade as a proportion of total trade, as shown in table 2.2 in chapter 2. As one might expect from its huge multilateral current account deficit, the United States has become China's most important export market. Although in 1980 only 5.4 percent of Chinese exports went to the United States, in 2001 the percentage had risen to 20.4 percent, with a strong tendency to rise further. At the same time, reflecting economic stagnation, the weight of Japan as an export market for China and as a source of imports into

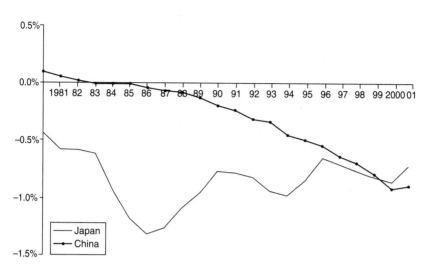

Figure 5.6
Bilateral U.S. Trade Balances with Japan and China as Percentage of U.S. GDP, 1980–2001. (International Monetary Fund, direction-of-trade statistics)

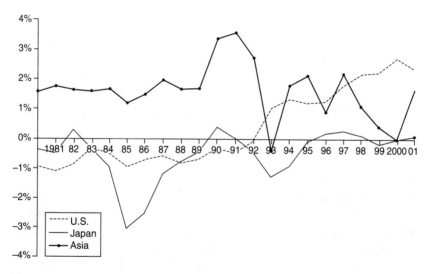

Figure 5.7
Bilateral Chinese Trade Balances with U.S., Japan, and Asia as Percentage of GDP, 1980–2001. "Asia" excludes Japan. (International Monetary Fund, direction-of-trade statistics)

Table 5.1
Chinese Trade with Japan, U.S., EA₁, and ROW as Percent of Overall Trade, 1980–2001

	Chinese Exports to				Chinese Imports from			
	U.S.	Japan	EA₁	ROW	U.S.	Japan	EA₁	ROW
1980	5.4	22.2	30.7	41.7	19.2	26.0	6.2	48.7
1985	8.6	22.3	36.4	32.8	12.2	35.7	13.9	38.3
1990	8.2	14.3	48.4	29.1	12.1	14.1	32.7	41.1
1995	16.6	19.1	36.8	27.5	12.2	22.0	32.6	33.3
2001	20.4	16.9	30.1	32.7	13.1	12.2	40.9	33.9

Source: International Monetary Fund, direction-of-trade statistics.
Notes:
EA₁ = Hong Kong, Indonesia, Korea, Malaysia, Philippines, Singapore, Taiwan, Thailand.
ROW = Rest of the world.

China has declined. Indeed, Chinese imports from Japan fell from 26 percent of total imports in 1980 to just 12.2 percent in 2001. Table 5.1 shows similar declines in the relative importance of the rest of the world (ROW), mainly Europe, although it is fairly balanced on both the import and export sides.

Given China's bilateral trade surpluses with the United States and Japan, from which country is it a net importer? While smaller East Asian countries by and large maintained their relative position as export markets, they have become China's most important provider of imports, bypassing the United States, Japan, and ROW. China's imports from its smaller East Asian neighbors (EA₁ in table 5.1) rose from 6.2 percent of overall imports in 1980 to a remarkable 40.9 percent by 2001. Collectively, the smaller East Asian countries now run trade surpluses with China, and these are more and more becoming their engine of economic growth. The fast integration of China into the East Asian production system displaces (in a relative sense) the dependence of the smaller economies on exporting directly to the more mature industrialized countries, United States, Japan, and ROW. More and more, China is dominating direct exports from East Asia to the United States and Europe.

In summary, a new geographical pattern in China's foreign trade has emerged. Exports are driven by strong import demand from the United States and, to a lesser extent, from Japan. China's smaller neighbors are an increasingly important input source for the fast-growing Chinese economy. Although Japan and Europe are still important

Table 5.2
Chinese Exports by Commodity, 1985–2000 (percent)

	AP	CM	CH	BM	MT	MM
1985	14.92	35.61	5.00	16.49	2.81	12.81
1990	11.40	14.13	6.04	20.61	17.45	28.23
1995	7.90	6.51	6.01	22.11	21.06	36.11
2000	4.92	4.93	4.78	17.38	33.08	34.34

Source: United Nations, *Yearbook of International Trade Statistics, Trade by Commodity.*
Notes: Numbers do not sum to 100% because the unclassified goods category is not reported.
AP = agricultural products, CM = crude materials including fuels, CH = chemicals, BM = basic manufactures (leather, wood, paper, textile yarn, iron and steel, nonferrous metals), MT = machines and transport equipment (power-generating equipment, machines for special industries, metal-working machinery, general industrial machinery, office machines, telecommunication and sound equipment, electric machinery, road vehicles), MM = miscellaneous manufactured goods (clothing and accessories, precision instruments, photo and optical equipment).

sources of foreign direct investment into China, their share of East Asian trade in general, and of China's in particular, is in decline. The remarkable transformation in the commodity composition of China's trade over the last two decades is consistent with these geographical changes in the overall trade balance statistics. In the early 1980s, Chinese commodity trade showed the characteristics of a developing country. Exports were largely agricultural products, raw materials, and basic manufactures (table 5.2). Imports were dominated by sophisticated manufacturing products such as machinery and transportation equipment (table 5.3).

Table 5.2 also shows that Chinese exports have shifted away from agricultural products and raw materials to manufacturing. In 1985, the year for which data first became available, agricultural products (14.92 percent) and raw materials (35.61 percent) accounted for about half of Chinese exports. Basic manufactures (leather, wood, paper, textile yarn, iron and steel, nonferrous metals) and chemicals were another 21 percent.

Today the composition of Chinese exports shows the characteristics of an industrialized country. In 2000 the relative weight of agricultural products (4.92 percent) and raw materials (4.93 percent) has fallen to less than 10 percent. The percentage of basic manufacturing products including chemicals has remained much the same, while the percentage of machines, transport equipment, and miscellaneous

Table 5.3
Chinese Imports by Commodity, 1985–2000 (percent)

	AP	CM	CH	BM	MT	MM
1985	4.41	7.99	10.45	27.95	38.95	4.52
1990	8.62	10.08	12.50	21.71	40.33	6.22
1995	6.90	11.39	12.76	22.06	39.70	5.98
2000	2.53	17.97	13.23	18.88	40.81	5.64

Source: United Nations, *Yearbook of International Trade Statistics, Trade by Commodity.*
Notes: Numbers do not sum to 100% because the unclassified goods category is not reported.
AP = agricultural products, CM = crude materials including fuels, CH = chemicals, BM = basic manufactures (leather, wood, paper, textile yarn, iron and steel, nonferrous metals), MT = machines and transport equipment (power-generating equipment, machines for special industries, metal-working machinery, general industrial machinery, office machines, telecommunication and sound equipment, electric machinery, road vehicles), MM = miscellaneous manufactured goods (clothing and accessories, precision instruments, photo and optical equipment).

manufacturing goods (clothing and accessories, precision instruments, photo and optical equipment) has risen to almost 70 percent.

The commodity composition of imports also shows marked changes, but more or less in the opposite direction. Table 5.3 shows the relative increase of raw materials imports from about 8 to 18 percent of total imports and some decline in imports of basic manufactures as China's own middle-tech industries have taken off. China looks more like an industrialized country and less like an agricultural developing one. Although average per capita income in China remains much lower than in the older industrial economies, the gap is narrowing. China's recent accession to the World Trade Organization will likely strengthen these trends.

5.2   China's Stabilizing Macroeconomic Role in East Asia

The impact of China's middle-tech industrial growth on other East Asian manufacturing countries has been strong and often difficult to adjust to. High-tech countries such as Japan, Korea, Singapore, and Taiwan can, in part, resolve the problem by moving further upscale. Others must sort themselves out in less obvious ways in finding their comparative advantages in exporting, where the Chinese market itself is becoming increasingly important. Mercantile complaints from the industrial world—including Europe, Japan, and the United States—

about "unfair" Chinese competition are commonplace. However, because of China's large size and rapid economic growth, substantial industrial restructuring in other manufacturing economies is inevitable no matter what the nature of the World Trade Organization's trading rules or the exchange rate regime might be.

Nevertheless, in some important respects, China has been an important stabilizing influence on the East Asian economy overall. Consider the cyclical stability of the smaller East Asian economies: Hong Kong, Indonesia, Korea, Malaysia, Philippines, Singapore, Taiwan, and Thailand. Let us denote these countries collectively by EA_1. Then, at the macroeconomic level, let us investigate China's impact on the stability of these countries.

The Exchange Rate Regime

A key aspect of the East Asian macroeconomy is the propensity of countries in the region (except for Japan) to informally peg their exchange rates to the U.S. dollar in noncrisis periods (McKinnon 2001a). For the developing countries of East Asia, this "fear of floating" is rational economically (see chapter 1). And from 1994 through 2003, China has kept its currency stable at 8.28 yuan/U.S. dollar.

Of course, during the crisis of 1997–1998, when the currencies of the debtor economies—Indonesia, Korea, Malaysia, Philippines, and Thailand—were attacked, they had to suspend their dollar pegs, and deep overshooting depreciations of their currencies of 50 percent or more followed. To try to preserve their international competitiveness, even the smaller net creditor countries of Singapore and Taiwan allowed their currencies to depreciate by 10 to 15 percent, although they did not have to. And the region's major creditor country, Japan, saw the yen depreciate by more than 30 percent from mid-1996 to mid-1998.

The cross-country spillover effects of such devaluations among closely connected trading partners, which are also mercantile competitors in third markets, was enormous. Although largely inadvertent, these beggar-thy-neighbor devaluations imposed severe deflationary pressure on the dollar prices of goods and services traded in the region (McKinnon 2001a). Fortunately, China did not devalue despite a loss of mercantile competitiveness against its neighbors and despite severe internal deflationary pressure. That China and Hong Kong withstood the foreign exchange storm and maintained their exchange rates lessened the exchange depreciations of the others. This quickened the pace at which the other currencies (except for the Indonesian rupiah) could recover much, although not all, of their pre-1997 dollar values. The steep regional downturn of 1997–1998 was thereby ameliorated.

Equally important, China's and Hong Kong's steadfastness sets a precedent for a possible return to a regime of more stable regional exchange rates. Malaysia pegged the ringgit at 3.8 to the dollar in September 1998, and since then the other crisis economies have intervened massively to smooth movements in their dollar exchange rates (see chapter 1).

However, the East Asian exchange rate system is hardly secure. The big problem is actual and potential fluctuations in the yen/dollar exchange rate—the "loose cannon" in the regional exchange rate system (see chapter 2). Japan's economy is still very large relative to China's, although China's is growing much faster (figure 5.8), and Japan is the most important source of foreign direct investment to other economies in the region. When the yen appreciates against the dollar as in 1986 or 1995, Japanese FDI surges and the others' exports become more competitive against Japan's. Similarly, when the yen depreciates against the dollar (as in 1997–1998), their output growth slumps because FDI

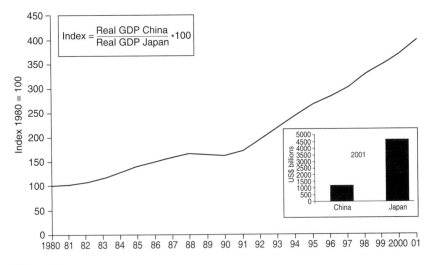

Figure 5.8
Relative Size of Japanese and Chinese GDP, 1980–2001. The base of 100 is arbitrary, and the line shows only China's real growth relative to Japan's, not the absolute size of the two economies. (International Monetary Fund, *International Financial Statistics*)

from Japan dries up and their exports become less competitive. Consequently, the wide fluctuations in the yen/dollar rate over the last 20 years or more have generated a synchronized, mutually reinforcing business cycle in the smaller East Asian economies (see chapter 2 and Kwan 2001). For more details on how to tether the yen/dollar exchange rate, see chapter 3 and McKinnon and Ohno (1997).

China's Role as a Regional Stabilizer

Despite these fluctuations in the yen/dollar exchange rate, China has assumed the role of a natural stabilizer in the increasingly integrated East Asian region. Not only has China's GDP growth been the highest in the region for the last two decades, but it has been also more stable than in any other East Asian country. Table 5.4 compares the coefficients of variation in the annual growth rates in GDP of the East Asian economies from 1980 to 2001. China's is the lowest, at 0.35, by a substantial margin.

Table 5.4
Annual Variation in Output Growth in East Asia, 1980–2001

	Mean	Standard Deviation	Variation Coefficient
China	9.55	3.35	0.35
Hong Kong	5.51	4.25	0.77
Indonesia	4.96	4.60	0.93
Korea	6.82	4.30	0.63
Malaysia	6.36	4.39	0.69
Philippines	2.52	3.73	1.48
Singapore	7.18	4.05	0.56
Taiwan	6.62	3.00	0.42
Thailand	5.99	4.97	0.83
Japan	2.67	1.89	0.71
EA_1	6.06	2.96	0.49
EA_2	7.46	2.13	0.29
EA_3	4.19	1.58	0.38

Sources: International Monetary Fund, *International Financial Statistics*; Central Bank of China.
Notes:
EA_1 = Hong Kong, Indonesia, Korea, Malaysia, Philippines, Singapore, Taiwan, Thailand.
EA_2 = EA_1 + China.
EA_3 = EA_2 + Japan.

The other East Asian countries show much greater variability in their rates of output growth; this is in large measure due to the strong impact of fluctuations in the yen/dollar exchange rate (see chapter 2). In table 5.4 the coefficient of variation for EA_1, that is, the aggregate growth in all the East Asian countries except China and Japan, shows the effect of this collective business cycle. For EA_1 alone, the coefficient is 0.49, but if China is added to EA_1 to form EA_2, the coefficient of variation drops to 0.29. China's growth rate is indeed more stable than that of the smaller East Asian economies.

If Japan is included in the collectivity of East Asian economies to form EA_3, the coefficient of variation in collective output growth rises to 0.38. By this measure, high variability in Japanese GDP growth is a source of instability to the region.

What are the reasons for China's greater macroeconomic stability? First, as is generally the case for a large economy, the openness of the Chinese economy is comparatively small. In the smaller East Asian countries in 2000, while international trade (exports plus imports) as a percentage of GDP ranges from 78 percent in Indonesia to 181 percent in Singapore. China's trade was only 48 percent of GDP. Because of the comparatively large size of China's domestic sector, external shocks play a less prominent role in its business cycle.

Table 5.5 demonstrates this point econometrically. Annual output growth rates in China and in EA_1 are regressed concurrently on Japanese output growth and on the yen/dollar exchange rate, and lagged

Table 5.5
Output and Exchange Rate Effects, China versus EA_1, 1980–2001

	Japan	EA_1	Yen/ Dollar$_t$	Yen/ Dollar$_{t-1}$	LRM	Adj. R^2 (R^2)
China	−0.14	−0.23	−0.10	−0.11	−0.21	−0.00
	(−0.28)	(−0.61)	(−1.17)	(−1.36)	(−1.07)	(0.19)
EA_1	0.80[a]		−0.12[b]	−0.05	−0.17[c]	0.50
	(3.01)		(−2.95)	(−1.92)	(−1.92)	(0.59)

Sources: International Monetary Fund, *International Financial Statistics*; Central Bank of China.
Notes: Yearly data; *t*-statistics in parentheses.
EA_1 = Hong Kong, Indonesia, Korea, Malaysia, Philippines, Singapore, Taiwan, Thailand.
LRM = Long-term exchange rate multiplier.
a. Significant at the 1% level.
b. Significant at the 5% level.
c. Significant at the 10% level.

one period. China has been relatively immune to output fluctuations in Japan as well as from fluctuations in the yen/dollar exchange rate: the regression coefficients of both are insignificant in China's case. However, both are significant for EA_1 (see chapter 2). Indeed, if the yen depreciates against the dollar by 1 percent, growth in EA_1 falls by 0.17 percent (table 5.5). That is, the long-run yen/dollar multiplier (LRM in table 5.5) is 17 percent for the smaller East Asian economies. Because China managed to smooth its own domestic output growth in the face of external exchange rate and other shocks, and because of its ongoing trade with its more vulnerable smaller neighbors, their cyclical volatility was thereby dampened.

The Post-1997 Keynesian Stimulus to China's Domestic Demand
However, China's stable growth cannot be attributed only to the momentum of its large domestic market. Particularly during the late 1990s, macroeconomic policy—a strong peg to the dollar coupled with an effective countercyclical fiscal policy operating on domestic aggregate demand—contributed significantly to economic stability in China itself and for the whole region.

Let us consider China's behavior during the crisis of 1997–1998 and its aftermath. China's exchange rate stabilization is not the whole story. Beginning in Thailand in June 1997 but extending to Korea in December 1997 and Japan in early 1998, depreciations in all these countries imposed strong deflationary pressure on China. Then, starting in March 1998, China took strong Keynesian measures to slow its internal deflation. Its New Deal encompassed a huge expansion of government expenditure on infrastructure and on mass residential housing. Since 1998 public works have increased by 20 percent per year. In 2001 and 2002, the (announced) stimulus package amounted to $18 billion (150 billion renminbi).

The Keynesian demand packages were financed by the sale of government bonds and by heavy borrowing from China's state-owned banking system in the form of so-called policy loans, which are not counted as a part of the official deficit. Excluding such loans, official yearly budget deficits rose from 0.7 percent of GDP in 1997 to 2.8 percent in 2000 and 2.5 percent in 2001, which greatly understates the true deficit if policy loans are considered to be government borrowing. This high level of fiscal spending seems to be sustainable into the near future. At the meeting of the International Monetary Fund and the World Bank in Ottawa in November 2001, China's finance minister, Xiang

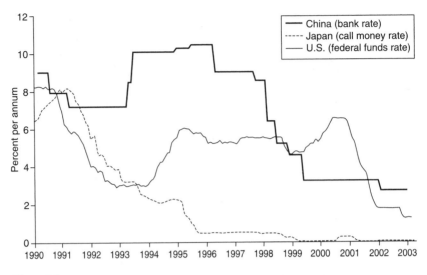

Figure 5.9
Money Market Interest Rates: China, Japan, and U.S., 1990–2003. "China bank rate" is
rate charged by the People's Bank of China on twenty-day loans to financial institutions.
(International Monetary Fund)

Huaicheng, stated that the country would continue its proactive domestic policy to spur the economy (Fidler 2001).

Further, the fiscal expansion was facilitated by a monetary expansion. Figure 5.9 shows the decline in China's interbank rate from 9 percent in 1996 to 2.7 percent by the end of 2002. Although this 2.7 rate is
slightly higher than in the United States (1.25 percent) and Japan (0
percent), it is in the context of a rapid growth in China's economy,
slow growth in the United States, and no growth in Japan. Indeed, in
China's case, fiscal and monetary policies can hardly be distinguished.
The People's Bank of China also eased the austerity policy, which had
been adopted in 1993, by pressuring the state banks to extend credit
for the construction industry, exporters, home purchases, and infrastructure projects as well as to the struggling state-owned enterprises.
The standard lending rate fell from 10 percent in 1997 to 5.3 percent in
early 2003. However, by 2004 China's economy showed signs of overheating, which would call for a Keynesian contraction to dampen aggregate demand.

China's Keynesian policy of economic expansion after 1997 can
be evaluated from several perspectives. First, many observers have
pointed out that China's murky banking sector is a considerable threat

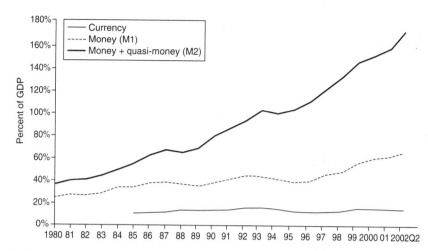

Figure 5.10
China's Monetary Aggregates, 1980–2003. "Currency" is currency outside the banking sector; "money" is currency outside the banking sector plus demand deposits other than those of the central government. "Quasi-money" is sum of time, savings, and foreign currency deposits of residents other than central government. (International Monetary Fund, *International Financial Statistics*)

to economic stability. The lending of the state-owned banks is not driven by mere profit considerations but by political constraints. The central government often uses the banking sector to support unprofitable state-owned enterprises. A large percentage of bank credits might eventually default. These nonperforming loans, which are estimated to be anywhere from 6 to 40 percent of GDP, could drive up the future cost of recapitalizing the banking system and thus should be considered government debt (McKinnon 1993a).

Is this explicit and implicit public debt manageable? If all components of public debt (official state debt and estimated nonperforming loans of the banks) are taken into account, China's public debt ratio is approximately 70 percent of GDP. Therefore, the recent anticyclical stabilization measures do not pose a substantial danger for the economy's stability. In contrast, Japanese public debt has risen to more than 140 percent of GDP, not including the cost of recapitalizing defaulting Japanese banks.

Second, the debt to GNP ratio is not the only measure of sustainability. The overall size of the financial system is equally important. In China monetary instruments still dominate the domestic financial system. Figure 5.10 shows the rapid buildup of M2, currency and bank deposits, from 1978 (just before China began liberalizing) through 2002. The current ratio of M2 to GNP approaches 180 percent, which is enormous by international standards and particularly so for a developing country. Thus China's financial system can cope with a rapid buildup of explicit and implicit government borrowing without resorting to printing money in the Latin American mode. Of course a rapid buildup of government debt is not sustainable indefinitely. But China has a lot of leeway for financing changes in government expenditures without provoking a general loss of confidence in the public finances and a flight from the currency.

Beyond budgetary leeway, however, *stationary expectations* about the price level, domestic interest rates, and the foreign exchange rate are also necessary for maximum effectiveness of countercyclical fiscal policy. This theoretical point was well established in the textbook Mundell-Fleming model (Mundell 1963) of how monetary and fiscal policy work themselves out in an open economy. If China had failed to stabilize its exchange rate while undertaking fiscal expansion, Mundell-Fleming predicts that the incremental capital inflows would have forced an appreciation of the renminbi, thus choking off the expansion. Since 1994, China's exchange rate has been stable, since 1996 its price level has been quite stable (figure 5.11), and since 1996 its

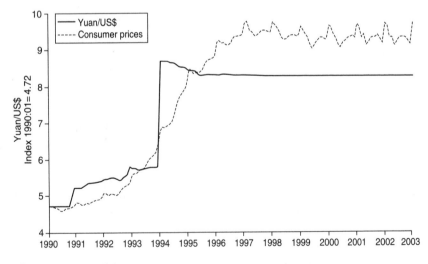

Figure 5.11
Yuan/U.S. Dollar Exchange Rate and Chinese Consumer Prices, 1990–2003. (International Monetary Fund, *International Financial Statistics*)

deposit rates of interest converged to low levels—below 2 percent in early 2003—as if expectations of future inflation and interest rates were also low.

Thus, in response to Premier Zhu Rongji's $1 trillion multiyear program of new public expenditure beginning in March 1998, confidence (stationary expectations) that there would be neither deflationary exchange rate appreciation nor flight from yuan-denominated assets necessitating a rise in domestic interest rates was central to the remarkable success in expanding domestic aggregate demand. The strong deflationary pressure from abroad arising out of the Asian crisis was successfully offset. Not only did this help maintain China's real economic growth, but it ameliorated the synchronized downturns in the other East Asian economies.

The policy of fixing the renminbi's exchange rate at some "traditional" level—8.28 yuan per dollar—is central to China's emerging role as the balance wheel in the East Asian system. During a major crisis, this policy limits competitive depreciations among the smaller East Asian economies and facilitates their return to exchange stability in its aftermath. On the other hand, stationary exchange rate expectations enable countercyclical fiscal policy within China itself to be more effective, thus helping to further dampen the regional business cycle. If China were to decide that a monetary-fiscal contraction had become necessary in 2004 or 2005 to prevent the economy from overheating, then raising taxes and slowing the growth in public spending for marginal infrastructure projects would work best in the context of a fixed exchange rate.

China's Impact on Other Countries: Deflation or Structural Adjustment?

China's rapid growth and increasingly large size are bound to cause problems of structural readjustment in other countries. But in a world economy with significant deflationary pressure, industrial competitors have, perhaps unsurprisingly, claimed that China is exporting deflation. Japan had been at the forefront of such complaints. Consider what the Japanese Minister of Finance Masajuro Shiokawa had to say early in 2003 (*People's Daily Online*):

Before the meeting of the financial ministers of the G7 to be held in Paris this year the Japanese financial minister announced by availing himself of all occasions that he would work out a so-called program combating the global disinflation. And he would ask the other countries to jointly adopt an agreement together with Japan in order to force China to inflate the exchange rate of the people's currency just as did the western countries in 1985 to force Japan to inflate the yen by adopting the "Plaza Agreement". When the meeting of the financial ministers of the "Seven Countries Group" was going on, Masajuro Shiokawa the Japanese Finance Minister once again condemned and protested China's people's currency.... "Too much importation of China's cheap goods has not only caused the currency constraint in Japan," he said, "but also the root-cause of the global economic depression."

Fortunately, as of early 2004, the Japanese government moderated its position, in part because of a resurgence of high-tech Japanese exports into the Chinese market and because of the belated recognition that any attempt to "talk" the renminbi up could cause a contagious upward spiral of the yen as well (see chapter 8). But influential groups in the United States and Europe continue to complain.

As long as China's economy provides a major and growing market for goods from all over the world, as well as for exporting to the rest of the world, the country's influence on the world economy on net balance is not deflationary *unless* its expansion forces a monetary contraction at home or abroad. Are either or both possible?

Consider first a situation where other countries could be forced into a monetary contraction. If the world were on a gold standard, as it was from the nineteenth century until 1913, there would be a problem. Under a gold standard China's rapid growth and demand for base money would necessarily be satisfied by a gold drain from other countries. With an inelastic supply of gold in the world economy, China's expansion certainly would impose deflation on other countries, much as the rapid growth of the United States and Germany in the late nineteenth century caused worldwide deflation from the 1870s to 1896.

However, for better or worse, most of the world is on a dollar standard, and the European countries are on a euro standard. In Asia, where exports, imports, and capital flows are overwhelmingly invoiced in dollars, the dollar standard predominates (see chapter 1). Governments strive (not always successfully) to keep their exchange rates stable against the U.S. dollar. And the meta central bank for the system is the U.S. Federal Reserve. Fortunately, Fed Chairman Alan Greenspan does not lack the means to keep feeding large amounts of base money into the world system through open market operations in the United States. Thus, the fact that China engages in a huge buildup of dollar exchange reserves, with Japan showing an even

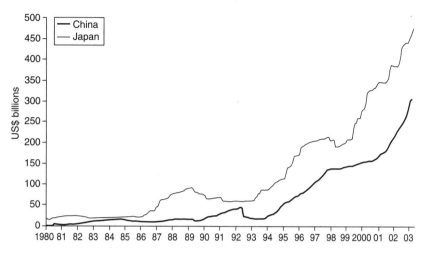

Figure 5.12
Official Foreign Reserves, China and Japan, 1980–2003. (International Monetary Fund, *International Financial Statistics*)

bigger buildup (see figure 5.12 and chapter 8), need not reduce the supply of base money anywhere else.

Worldwide deflationary pressure now mainly arises from the aftermath of the American bubble economy (1995–2000) and deflationary pressure in the United States, the central country. The nature of the world dollar standard makes it difficult for any country (except China) on the dollar's periphery to take independent action to reinflate. Mired in a deflationary slump, Japan is the extreme case with its zero-interest liquidity trap being tightened by the recent (2002–2003) fall in interest rates in the United States (see chapter 4). Let us hope that monetary expansion in the central country can pull peripheral countries out without the United States' falling into a liquidity trap itself. (And in mid-2004, both the United States and Japan are recovering fairly quickly.)

5.3   Conflicted Virtue: The Deflationary Threat

One of the peculiarities of the dollar's role as the key currency in East Asia is that creditor countries such as Japan and now China find it difficult to *lend* internationally in their own currencies. When they run balance-of-payments surpluses resulting in the buildup of liquid claims on foreigners, these claims are largely in dollars rather than in yen or renminbi. Why should this matter?

Currency risk, the risk that the dollar will fluctuate against the domestic currency, cumulates as these dollar claims get larger. The natural currency habitat of domestic nationals is their home currency, unless the country has an unusually flamboyant financial history of debasing the national money, as some Latin American and African countries do. But China has had a relatively stable financial history. Household consumption expenditures are in yuan, wages are paid in yuan, and claims on financial intermediaries such as banks (deposits) and insurance companies (annuities) are mainly in yuan. Unsurprisingly, households and business firms seek to accumulate most of their liquid wealth mainly in yuan because its real purchasing power over domestic goods and services has been quite stable.

Chinese firms and households will hold dollar assets only if there is a substantial business convenience in doing so, or if the interest rate on dollar assets is higher, or if they see a political need to hold dollar assets illegally offshore. The primary downside risk is for the renminbi to appreciate against the dollar and thus reduce the yuan value of their dollar assets. Depending on how sensitive domestic holders of dollar assets are to this risk, periodic runs from dollars into yuan could occur just on rumors of appreciation.

Notice that foreigners whose domestic currency habitat is dollars, or tied to the dollar, will not be so sensitive. Only foreign professional speculators would go out of their way to circumvent China's remaining capital controls in order to short the dollar in order to go long in the renminbi if they thought it might appreciate. In contrast, most Chinese holders of dollar assets, both legally inside the system of capital controls and extralegally outside them, are not speculators. But if they thought yuan appreciation was in the offing, they could be quite defensive about protecting their wealth positions. Thus, the potential speculative upward pressure on the yuan would come mainly from the domestic accumulation of foreign exchange.

However, for the world economy at large, the problem is more general. Any international creditor country that cannot lend in its own currency cumulates a currency mismatch that we call the syndrome of conflicted virtue, as discussed in the introduction.[1] Countries that are virtuous by having a relatively high saving rate tend to run surpluses in the current account of their international balance of payments, that is, lend to foreigners. But with the passage of time two things happen:

• As the *stock* of dollar claims cumulates, domestic holders of dollar assets worry more about a self-sustaining run into the domestic currency forcing an appreciation.

• Foreigners start complaining that the country's ongoing flow of trade surpluses is unfair and the result of having an undervalued currency.

Of course, these events interact. The greater the foreign mercantilist pressure for appreciation of the domestic currency, the greater the concern of the domestic holders of dollar assets. As runs out of dollars into the domestic currency begin, the government is conflicted because appreciation could set in train serious deflation ending with a zero-interest-rate liquidity trap, particularly if the domestic price level were already stable or falling slightly. But foreigners may threaten trade sanctions if the creditor country in question does not allow its currency to appreciate. That is the syndrome of conflicted virtue.[2]

Parallels with the Japanese Experience

The earlier Japanese experience with conflicted virtue is instructive (see chapters 3 and 4). Postwar Japanese industrial growth—although more oriented toward heavy industry such shipbuilding, steel, automobiles, machine tools, semiconductors, and so forth, than is China's current middle-tech expansion—was remarkably rapid. In the 1960s and 1970s industrialists and trade unionists in Europe and the United States became irate with the "unfair" competition from Japan. Compounding their adjustment problems, Japan in the 1980s began to run with large trade surpluses, which have continued to the present day. Beginning in the 1970s but intensifying by the mid-1980s, there developed intense mercantile pressure on Japan from its trading partners, particularly the United States, to get the yen up (McKinnon and Ohno 1997). And the yen rose all the way from 360 to the dollar in 1971 to 80 to the dollar in April 1995 (chapter 3).

These massive appreciations failed to eliminate Japanese trade surpluses, which simply reflected Japan's relatively high saving propensity compared to that of the United States. However, the appreciating yen did impose great deflationary pressure on Japan. In open economies, the ongoing current account surplus is all about net saving propensities, which are not predictably affected by exchange rate changes. But how the exchange rate moves eventually determines domestic inflation or deflation.

Nevertheless, most foreign and many Japanese economists genuinely believed, and still believe, that yen appreciation should have reduced Japan's trade surpluses. To some extent, the problem is doctrinal. Economists are largely in thrall to the old elasticities model of the balance of trade where an appreciation is presumed to reduce a country's exports relative to its imports. However McKinnon and Ohno (1997, chs. 6, 7) show that the simple elasticities approach to the trade balance is generally invalid in financially open economies—a point that was ignored by critics of Japan's exchange rate policy and is ignored now by the critics of China's policy of keeping its exchange rate stable. This false theory, combined with more immediate mercantile concerns, energized official U.S. policy to favor repeated yen appreciations.

Fortunately, in April 1995 the then U.S. Secretary of the Treasury, Robert Rubin, announced a strong-dollar policy and the end of U.S. arm twisting to get the yen up. Even so, the yen continued to fluctuate against the dollar: 20 percent annual swings in the yen/dollar rate are not unusual. Thus Japanese insurance companies, trust funds, and banks holding large stocks of dollar assets—which had cumulated to very high levels by the late 1990s—continued to see very high risk in holding such assets.

Within Japanese financial institutions, how does conflicted virtue lower interest rates on yen assets relative to those on dollar assets? The liabilities of Japanese financial institutions are mainly in yen, but they hold both yen and dollar assets. If the yen/dollar rate is free to fluctuate, these yen-based institutions see the dollar assets to be riskier. In order to maintain portfolio balance between riskier dollar assets and safer yen assets, they must see a higher yield on the former. But since the yield on dollar assets is given on world markets, the yield on yen assets is forced lower, reflecting a negative risk premium in Japanese interest rates (see chapter 4). Thus, when U.S. interest rates came down in the 1990s, Japanese interest rates fell toward zero.

The Bank of Japan responds endogenously to pressure coming through the foreign exchanges. By dramatically expanding the domestic monetary base from the mid-1990s to the present, it continually lowered interest rates on yen assets to limit the conversion of dollars into yen and thus limit upward pressure on the yen in the foreign exchanges. But dollar assets in private hands continued to accumulate because of Japan's ongoing trade surpluses. The result was that by the end of 1996 Japanese short-term interest rates had fallen close to zero (figure 5.9). Within this zero-interest-rate liquidity trap, the Bank of Japan can neither reflate the slumping economy nor prevent further conversions of private Japanese dollar assets into yen. To prevent the yen from appreciating, the Bank of Japan then enters the foreign exchange market to buy the "surplus" dollars. The result is the rapid increase in Japan's official exchange reserves shown in figure 5.12.

From 2001 into 2004 the foreign pressure on China to appreciate the renminbi is uncomfortably reminiscent of the earlier pressure on Japan. Ironically, until mid-2003, Japan's industrial and political leaders were the leading advocates of renminbi appreciation. The attempt of Japan's finance minister, Masajuro Shiokawa, to "demonize" the renminbi reflected a prominent segment of Japanese official and popular opinion. By 2004, however, a new Japanese export boom into the burgeoning China market and the realization that an appreciation of the renminbi would lead to further upward pressure on the yen have quieted Japanese calls for China to appreciate.

The view that China should appreciate its currency was also widespread in the Western financial press. Editorials in the *The Financial Times* (February 3, 2003) and *The Economist* (February 15, 2003) link China's burgeoning balance-of-payments surpluses to its fixed exchange rate. And this clamor continues into 2004. The editorials suggest that the renminbi should be appreciated discretely now; then, once China cleans up its banks, liberalizes its financial markets, and gets rid of its remaining exchange controls on capital movements, the renminbi should be floated, presumably with continual though erratic appreciation.

In resisting this external pressure China has one big advantage over Japan. The renminbi has been stable at 8.28 yuan/dollar from 1994 into 2004, including not devaluing in 1997–1998, thus limiting the great crisis. So, China cannot be fairly accused of manipulating its exchange rate; indeed it has grown into this external monetary standard in the sense that its price level has stabilized at that rate (figure 5.11). In contrast, the yen/dollar exchange rate has fluctuated so much that the Japanese government's credibility to pick any one rate to defend is more limited (but see chapter 3).

Direct Investment and the Dollar Overhang

In dealing with conflicted virtue, China has a disadvantage compared to Japan. Although its multilateral trade surpluses have been relatively small and really only began in 1995, since 1990 China has received

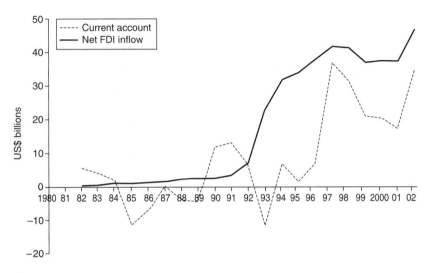

Figure 5.13
China's Current Accounts and Net Foreign Direct Investment Inflows, 1980–2002. "Net FDI inflows" are gross FDI inflows minus gross FDI outflows. (International Monetary Fund, *International Financial Statistics*)

large inflows of foreign direct investment. Figure 5.13 compares China's current account to FDI inflows. Since 1995, China's annual current account surplus has been about $20–$30 billion. In contrast, China's annual FDI inflows have been about $40 billion since 1997–1998, not offset by any significant outflows of FDI.

By comparison, Japan's annual current account surpluses are at about $100 billion for its much larger economy (figure 5.14). Gross FDI inflows into Japan have been small, but FDI outflows, particularly to the rest of East Asia, have been very large. Subtracting outflows from inflows, net flows of FDI into Japan have actually been negative, at about $25 billion per year. Insofar as Japan's net FDI abroad covers about one-quarter of its current account surplus, this part of the buildup of claims on foreigners is somewhat less liquid and thus is less of an overhang.

In contrast to Japan, China's buildup of liquid, mainly dollar, claims on foreigners has been much greater than its cumulative current account surpluses. The large inflows of FDI into China cumulate into a large stock of liabilities to foreign corporations, but these liabilities are very *illiquid* in the sense that they cannot be suddenly withdrawn. Be-

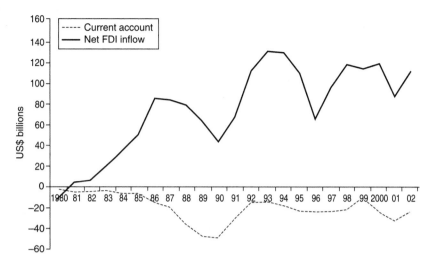

Figure 5.14
Japan's Current Accounts and Net Foreign Direct Investment Inflows, 1980–2002. "Net FDI inflows" are gross FDI inflows minus gross FDI outflows. (International Monetary Fund, *International Financial Statistics*)

cause China has not run current account deficits to match the inflow of FDI, its *liquid* dollar claims—some in official exchange reserves, and some private—are growing proportionately faster than in Japan.

These foreign exchange flows can be characterized by a simple balance-of-payments identity. Let CA be the current account surplus and let FDI be net foreign inflows of direct investment. The country's capital controls were not applied to FDI inflows in the form of joint ventures with local enterprises, which became very popular. We assume that other forms of foreign capital inflows into China, and FDI outflows from China, were restricted and their cumulated amounts are negligible. Let ΔOER be the change in official exchange reserves, largely U.S. Treasury bonds; and let ΔPFA be the change in private foreign assets, largely dollar claims against banks. Then, in any one year

$$\Delta\text{PFA} = \text{CA} + \text{FDI} - \Delta\text{OER} \tag{5.1}$$

Integrating backward to 1990 or earlier, and assuming no asset valuation adjustments, we then get China's international balance sheet position:

Liquid Assets	Liabilities and Net Worth
Official exchange reserves (OER)	Cumulated foreign direct investment (FDI)
Private foreign assets (PFA)	Cumulated current account surpluses (CA)

Table 5.6 approximates each side of this international balance sheet. We can then estimate China's private and official net holdings of liquid foreign assets both directly and indirectly from the left and right sides, respectively.

First, the right-hand side of the balance sheet provides *indirect* estimates of China's liquid foreign exchange assets. For 1990–2002 column 6 of table 5.6 cumulates China's current account surpluses and column 7 cumulates net inflows of foreign direct investment. Column 8 sums the two so that, at the end of 2002, China's net international liquid asset position is indirectly estimated to be $589.9 billion, whereas in 1990, when the economy was much smaller, it was just $24.4 billion. Figure 5.15 better shows the relative sizes of cumulative inflows of foreign direct investment, the cumulative current account, and cumulative multilateral trade surpluses in goods and services. Other than in the early 1990s, flows of foreign direct investment into China have been substantially larger than the current account balance. And the current account surpluses themselves have been somewhat smaller than the trade balance on goods and services, the main difference between the two being transfers to foreigners.

Table 5.6 contains mainly *direct* estimates of liquid foreign asset holdings (left-hand side of the balance sheet) from 1990 to 2002. Column 2, the least ambiguous, shows current stocks of official net foreign exchange reserves largely held with the People's Bank of China. Column 3 shows the officially reported net foreign asset position of Chinese commercial banks and other financial institutions. This foreign lending arises from the surprisingly large stock of internal dollar bank deposits held by Chinese nationals. Figure 5.16 shows that in the second quarter of 2002, these internal dollar deposits amounted to $150 billion, with household savings deposits being substantially greater than those of enterprises.

Finally, still on the left-hand side of the international balance sheet, column 4 of table 5.6 shows the most ambiguous item: cumulative errors and omissions that we have reclassified as cumulative unre-

Table 5.6
China's Cumulative Current Account Surpluses and Net Inward Foreign Direct Investment versus Estimated Holdings of Liquid Dollar Assets, 1990–2002 (billions of U.S. dollars)

	(1) Total Net Foreign Assets	(2) Official Reserves	(3) Net Foreign Assets of Banking Institutions	(4) Cumulative Unrecorded Capital Outflows[a]	(5) Total Liquid Foreign Assets (2)+(3)+(4)	(6) Cumulative Current Account Surplus	(7) Cumulative Net Inward FDI to China	(8) Alternative Estimate of Liquid Foreign Assets (6)+(7)
1990	21.7	28.6	5.1	3.2	36.9	21.7	2.7	24.4
1991	27.4	42.7	1.1	10.0	53.7	35.0	6.1	41.1
1992	30.6	19.4	6.4	18.2	44.1	41.4	13.3	54.7
1993	38.6	21.2	11.7	28.3	61.2	29.8	36.4	66.2
1994	58.8	51.6	7.1	37.4	96.1	36.7	68.2	104.9
1995	76.5	73.6	-3.4	55.2	125.4	38.3	102.0	140.3
1996	110.7	105.0	-4.3	70.7	171.4	45.5	140.1	185.6
1997	164.8	139.9	5.2	92.8	237.9	82.5	181.8	264.3
1998	181.7	145.0	17.9	111.7	274.6	114.0	222.9	336.9
1999	205.7	154.7	31.0	129.4	315.1	135.1	259.9	394.9
2000	243.0	165.6	59.6	141.1	366.3	155.6	297.3	453.0
2001	319.1	212.2	85.4	145.9	443.4	173.0	334.7	507.7
2002	383.4	286.4	107.8	138.3	532.6	208.4	381.5	589.9

Sources: International Monetary Fund, *International Financial Statistics;* col. (1)—banking survey.
Notes: a. Errors and omissions in international payment flows.
FDI = Foreign direct investment.

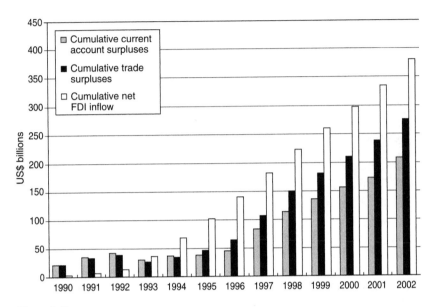

Figure 5.15
China's Cumulative Surpluses on Current Account, Trade, and Net Foreign Direct Investment, 1990–2002. (International Monetary Fund, *International Financial Statistics*)

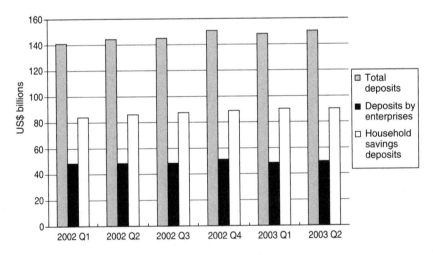

Figure 5.16
Foreign Exchange Deposits in Chinese Banking Institutions, 2002–2003. (People's Bank of China)

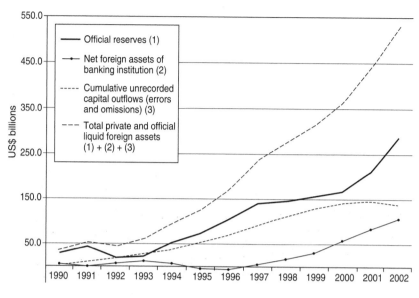

Figure 5.17
China's Liquid Foreign Assets, Capital Account Estimates, 1990–2002. (International Monetary Fund, *International Financial Statistics*)

corded capital outflows. Although this is seemingly arbitrary, students of international finance often classify errors and omissions this way, particularly if the country involved has controls on capital outflows. There could be unrepatriated export earnings, surreptitious transfers of money into foreign bank accounts in Hong Kong and elsewhere, and so on. At the end of 2002 these cumulative unrecorded capital outflows amounted to $138 billion, more than the officially recorded net foreign assets of banking institutions but still smaller than the government's exchange reserves. Figure 5.17 shows the evolution of these three forms of China's liquid claims on foreigners since 1990. At the end of 2002 the total of all three was $532.6 billion. Clearly, this direct estimate of China's holding of liquid foreign currency claims on foreigners can only be approximate because we treated errors and omissions as if they were unrecorded capital outflows.

Alternatively, by cumulating current account surpluses and inflows of FDI, total liquid dollar assets are indirectly estimated to be $589.9 billon at the end of 2002 (column 8 of table 5.6). Errors such as under invoiced exports, smuggled imports, or overstated FDI could clearly affect these indirect estimates as well. In spite of all of this, the direct and indirect estimates of China's international foreign liquid assets

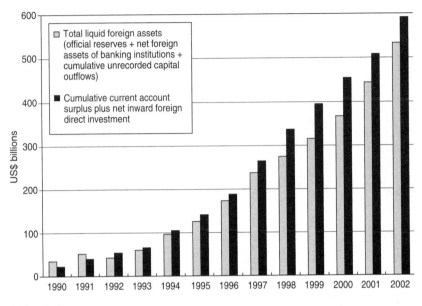

Figure 5.18
Alternative Estimates of China's International Liquid Asset Position, 1990–2002. (International Monetary Fund, *International Financial Statistics*)

seem to line up fairly closely, as they have since 1990 (figure 5.18). Thus we can have some confidence that China's total liquid foreign exchange assets at the end of 2002 were between $500 and $600 billion, with about half being privately held, or at least held outside of the government's direct control.

In what sense are China's huge private sector holdings of liquid dollar assets an overhang? Clearly, if private expectations are such that the exchange rate of 8.28 yuan/dollar will last indefinitely, then existing dollar claims—and further accumulation—can be held in rough portfolio equilibrium. GDP growth and growth in the size of renminbi bank deposits in China have been enormous (figure 5.10). Thus Chinese savers could easily accommodate further parallel growth in their dollar assets. But foreign pressure to appreciate the renminbi might upset what had been a rough portfolio equilibrium. A recent return flow of flight capital into China could well indicate that people are becoming less willing to hold onto their dollar claims (*Wall Street Journal* 2003):

Once viewed as a threat to the nation's economy, the movement of illicit capital in China is now tracking an unusual new pattern: flowing back into the country. For the first time [in 2002], the nation recorded a positive number, $7.79 billion under the balance of payments category called "errors and omissions" last year.... For as long as China has published such data, E&O has been negative, sometimes exceeding $10 billion annually.... The E&O figure also illustrates the pressure that Beijing is under to push up the value of its currency.... Bankers say Chinese companies and individuals may want to hold more yuan just in case Beijing allows the tightly controlled currency to rise in value.

This return flow of flight capital is consistent with the evidence shown in table 5.6 and figure 5.17: cumulative unrecorded capital outflows dropped from $145.9 billion in at the end of 2001 to $138.3 billion at the end of 2002. And the private sector seems to be increasingly reluctant to maintain its normal share of dollar holdings. Since 2000 the percentage increases in the official holding of exchange reserves have exceeded increases in private holdings (see chapter 8). Thus pressure to switch private dollar holdings into renminbi is occurring and could increase in the future.

In order to prevent the renminbi from appreciating, the People's Bank of China must intervene in the foreign exchange market to buy the excess dollars. Not sterilizing these interventions relieves the pressure: the domestic monetary base expands so as to drive down domestic interest rates relative to those on dollar assets. As long as interest rates on renminbi assets remain well above zero, such increases in the monetary base could be effective in expanding the domestic economy while slowing the growth of official exchange reserves. Nevertheless, China's buildup of foreign exchange reserves in 2003 has been so massive that the government has had to sterilize much of it in order to prevent runaway increases in domestic bank credit.

Unfortunately, the appreciation threat for China is a repetitive one, similar to the earlier Japanese experience with repetitive yen appreciations. As in Japan's case, China's surplus saving, its trade surplus, is unlikely to fall as its currency appreciates. Instead, economic growth would slow and China's price level would fall. Markets would anticipate that once the tradition of 8.28 yuan per dollar is undermined by an appreciation to, say, 7 yuan per dollar, further appreciations— particularly if the renminbi were floated—become very likely. By the principle of open interest parity coupled with a negative risk premium, such anticipations would bid down interest rates on yuan assets toward zero. China could then find itself in a deflationary liquidity trap like Japan's: monetary policy becomes helpless to reflate the economy or to slow the conversion of private dollar assets into renminbi.

(However, as figure 5.9 indicates, money market interest rates in China are still well above the near-zero interest rates prevalent in Japan.)

5.4   Conclusion

China has benefited enormously from the massive FDI inflows, largely in joint ventures with domestic enterprises, that have accelerated its access to modern technology and made possible a stunning export-led surge in the economy's overall productivity. However, from a financial and monetary point of view, we have emphasized the downside. By not running current account deficits of the same order of magnitude as the FDI inflows, China faces the syndrome of conflicted virtue arising from the rapid buildup of a liquid dollar overhang, much of which is in private or nonstate hands.

What should China do? Consider three medium-term options for rationalizing foreign trade and financial flows:

• It could take policy measures to reduce and even reverse its current account surplus: let imports expand more rapidly by reducing trade barriers faster than its World Trade Organization timetable requires and eliminate special incentives given to exporters.

• It could level the tax playing field so that FDI is no longer taxed at lower rates.

• It could reduce the financial magnitude of the FDI inflows by letting joint ventures finance more of their operations within China—by borrowing from Chinese banks or by issuing more stocks and bonds domestically.[3] The absorption of foreign technology would remain as a high as ever even if net financial inflows were substantially reduced.

What about macroeconomic management? By 2004 it appeared that China's economy had become overheated, with excess bank lending for real estate and some very marginal infrastructure investments. So, both monetary and fiscal policy need to become more contractionary in the near term: the *converse* of Zhu Rongji's great Keynesian expansion beginning in 1998.

On the monetary side, it makes sense to sterilize most of the buildup of official exchange reserves, much of which reflects a one-time portfolio shift from dollar assets into renminbi. The large new issues of central banks' bonds to commercial banks to soak up excess increases in the monetary base coming from large official interventions in the foreign exchanges is to be welcomed. In effect, such a policy recognizes the need for the government to reduce the liquid dollar overhang in increasingly nervous private hands as well as to slow undue expansion in domestic bank lending. Because China is still residually a socialist economy where the government leans on banks to lend one way or another, now is the time for further direct restraints on bank lending.

On the fiscal side, China has the long-term need to keep tax revenue well over 20 percent of GDP, if only to make the current buildup of internal debt sustainable. And tax revenue in 2004 has soared. In the long run, the impact of a general increase in taxes on aggregate demand is neutral. But in the near term, it is somewhat contractionary, and that is what is wanted in 2004 into 2005. Fortunately, at this macroeconomic juncture in China, good long-run policy is also good in the near term.

In the very short term, however, China must face the problem of conflicted virtue and work to defuse upward pressure on the renminbi in the foreign exchanges. Expectations are all-important in determining whether a given exchange rate regime is sustainable. China has gone through many anxious moments in keeping its exchange rate at 8.28 yuan/dollar. To the great benefit of the East Asian region, China withstood market pressure—and a lot of bad foreign advice—to depreciate the renminbi during the 1997–1998 crisis. Now, after ten years of exchange rate stability, the Chinese government should treat 8.28 yuan/ dollar as its long-term "parity" rate, which will not be altered by the ebb and flow of financial events into the indefinite future.

What about the possibility of making the exchange rate regime and the system of capital controls more flexible? Indeed, what should be the meaning of *flexibility* in this context? As financial constraints on international capital flows are loosened, it is natural to allow a soft band of variation around this central rate—say, from 8.2 to 8.4—in order to further devolve the clearing of international payments from the People's Bank of China to the commercial banks. As long as the Bank stands ready to intervene to drive any rate on the edge of the band back toward 8.28, and everybody assumes it will do so, actual intervention by the People's Bank of China should seldom be necessary. In noncrisis periods the commercial banks will act as stabilizing speculators (dealers) and take open positions in foreign exchange to nudge the market rate toward the central rate, as long as the central rate of 8.28 yuan/dollar itself is never in question.

6

The Overborrowing Syndrome and Economic Liberalization

with Huw Pill

Banks that enjoy government guarantees have an incentive to increase foreign borrowing and incur foreign exchange risks that are underwritten by the deposit insurance system. In the absence of capital controls, this moral hazard increases the magnitude of overborrowing and leaves the economy both more vulnerable to speculative attack and more exposed to the real economic consequences of such an attack.

While "bad" exchange rate pegs will tend to exacerbate the problem of overborrowing in emerging markets, it is not clear that flexible exchange rates always dominate fixed exchange rates. A "good" fix, one that is credible and close to purchasing power parity, may reduce the super-risk premium in domestic interest rates and thereby narrow the margin of temptation for banks to overborrow internationally. Contrary to the current consensus in favor of floating exhange rates as the lesson to be drawn from the 1997–1998 Asian crisis, a good fix may better stabilize the domestic economy while limiting moral hazard in the banking system.

The 1990s were marked by successive financial crises after countries had borrowed heavily in international markets. Following the financial turmoil in Mexico, East Asia, Russia, Argentina, Brazil, and Turkey, commentators began to question whether "globalization has gone too far" (Rodrik and Lawrence 1998) or whether the global capital market is a "benefactor or menace" (Obstfeld 1998). Should the scope of international financial liberalization be more restricted by capital controls? How does the nature of the exchange rate regime affect moral hazard

This chapter consolidates much of the earlier work contained mainly in two papers: R. I. McKinnon and H. Pill, "Credible Economic Liberalizations and Overborrowing," *American Economic Review* 87 (May 1997): 189–193, and R. I. McKinnon and H. Pill, "Exchange Rate Regimes for Emerging Markets: Moral Hazard and International Overborrowing," *Oxford Review of Economic Policy* 15 (Autumn 1999): 19–38.

in capital markets and the problem of international overborrowing or, depending on the perspective, overlending? These are the questions raised in this chapter.

The problem is not new. For economies undertaking economic liberalization, McKinnon (1973; 1993a) identified a phenomenon he labeled the *overborrowing syndrome*. Even if apparently well-designed macroeconomic trade and structural policies were being put in place in liberalizing economies, massive inflows of foreign capital often created severe macroeconomic imbalances that ultimately proved unsustainable. The entire reform process could be jeopardized if this capital were to be suddenly withdrawn, leading to declines in domestic asset values and a painful economic downturn. These massive inflows were often implicitly subsidized by governments. Because of government deposit insurance in the banks of both lenders and borrowers, coupled with government-guaranteed international credits by the export-import banks of the industrial economies, private lenders and borrowers were overly immunized from the social risks involved. Thus McKinnon advocated a carefully structured sequencing of reforms—the order of economic liberalization—where capital account liberalization came last, if at all.

The policy reforms favoring free trade, privatization, deregulation of domestic industry, and fiscal consolidation pursued by Chile in the mid-1970s led to massive capital inflows through 1981, followed by a financial crash and economic downturn in 1982–1983. In Mexico after 1988, similarly comprehensive real-side reforms attracted large capital inflows, which suddenly reversed during the December 1994 financial panic and steep 1995 downturn. In the new millennium Argentina faces the depressed aftermath of a reform program in the 1990s, during which it borrowed too much and subsequently had to retrench after a deep devaluation and default on its external debt in 2001.

This pattern is not confined to developing countries. After a dismal period of high inflation and public intervention in Britain in the 1970s, the Thatcher government undertook apparently successful industrial restructuring and fiscal consolidation in the early 1980s. Enthusiasm for Britain's changed economic prospects attracted capital inflows, increased consumption, and triggered a boom in residential and commercial real estate in the late 1980s that culminated in the bust of the early 1990s.

Although international overborrowing can be a problem in any economy, we are more concerned with the *transition* from economic repression to liberalization (McKinnon 1993a; Pill 1996; McKinnon and Pill 1996). When does an economy undertaking apparently well-conceived industrial and financial reforms suddenly become vulnerable to overborrowing?

6.1 A Fisherian Model without Exchange Rate Risk

Initially, we believed that the problem was a matter of getting the exchange rate right. However, we first abstract from monetary variables —the money supply, exchange rate, and price level—altogether, as did Conley and Maloney (1995). To focus the analysis one level deeper, we build a highly simplified Fisher two-period model of borrowing and investing based on real interest rates to show how the capital market could malfunction when, in moving from repression to reform, uncertainty about payoffs to new investments greatly increases.

In figure 6.1 the function $f(\cdot)$ portrays the prereform opportunity set, linking investments in period 1 (shown on the horizontal axis) to payoffs in period 2 (shown on the vertical axis), open to a representative firm-household with an endowment (m_1, m_2). In the standard Fisherian mode, $f(\cdot)$ displays diminishing returns overall; and because agents are identical, the capital market is redundant: point A represents the intertemporal consumption *and* production equilibrium, $c_1 = x_1$.

The expected economic gains from a real-side reform, such as a move to free trade, are portrayed by a new investment function $\hat{\alpha}g(\cdot)$, which shows a segment with much higher payoffs in period 2 from investments in period 1. Because $\hat{\alpha}g(\cdot)$ incorporates indivisibilities and increasing returns, the capital market is now critically important if the new export opportunities are to be exploited. Only after discrete setup costs (K in figure 6.1) are incurred, does further investment in $\hat{\alpha}g(\cdot)$ increase future output. Then, at a much higher level of average productivity compared to the traditional technology, diminishing returns from the economy's fixed factors of labor, land, and so on eventually set in at the margin.

Suppose, however, that the reforming economy remains financially repressed because of inflation and high-reserve requirements on financial intermediaries that are outside of our nonmonetary Fisherian model. Agents cannot borrow abroad. In this financially repressed economy (FRE), the potentially superior investment opportunities represented by $\hat{\alpha}g(\cdot)$ have setup costs that are too large to be self-financed

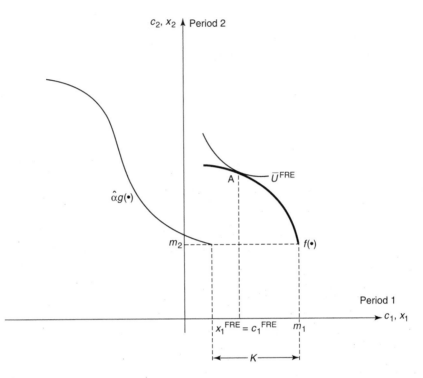

Figure 6.1
A Financially Repressed Economy

by individual firm-households. Thus, despite the trade reform, the economy remains mired close to A, which we call the FRE equilibrium.

Alternatively, when real-side reform occurs, suppose that the domestic (bank-based) capital market, but not international capital flows, is open—the so-called domestically liberalized economy (DLE) shown in figure 6.2. It assumes the payoffs in period 2 from inveseting in period 1 are known with certainty, so that moral hazard in the banks remains latent and the domestic capital market works efficiently. In this risk-free DLE economy, *some* agents borrow to invest in the superior $\hat{\alpha}g(\cdot)$ technology (point A), while others are confined to the old $f(\cdot)$ technology (point B). The latter become net depositors or lenders in the banking system.

At this double tangency equilibrium, represented by the points A and B in figure 6.2, the flow of funds from depositors to borrowers within the domestic economy must balance. In period 1 let N_M be the number of borrowers adopting the new technology, and N_T be the

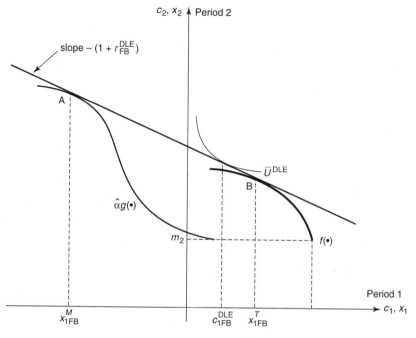

Figure 6.2
A Domestically Liberalized Economy, No Moral Hazard

number of depositors, agents staying with but partly disinvesting from the traditional technology. Figure 6.2 shows that each investor in the new technology borrows ($c_{1FB}^{DLE} - x_{1FB}^{M}$), a relatively large amount, and each of the more numerous lenders deposits ($x_{1FB}^{T} - c_{1FB}^{DLE}$), a relatively small amount. In period 1 the flow of funds is balanced between a small number of borrowers and a large number of depositors as follows:

$$N_M(c_{1FB}^{DLE} - x_{1FB}^{M}) = N_T(x_{1FB}^{T} - c_{1FB}^{DLE}) \quad \text{where } N_M < N_T \tag{6.1}$$

This double tangency, where both the new and old investment technologies coexist in the DLE, reflects the high setup costs (indivisibilities) of jumping to the new technology. The active bidding for investment resources to exploit the new, more productive investment technology drives up the rate of interest, as shown by the steep slope of the linear budget line, to induce some disinvestment in the old less efficient technology and to curb current consumption. Thus, in DLE without foreign capital flows, saving need not fall in period 1.

In this first-best (FB) equilibrium, where future payoffs to investment are known, everybody's welfare increases regardless of whether they are borrowers or depositors. Because firm-households are identical, their now higher utility—and, by implication, their consumption choices—must be the same, as shown by the tangency of $\overline{U}^{DLE}$ with the budget line in figure 6.2. Borrowers investing in the new technology gain from output in period 2, exceeding the cost of repaying their loans, whereas lenders, who all stay with the old technology, gain from the higher yields on their deposits made with the banks.

However, this state of bliss need not hold once uncertainty is introduced. By subsuming default risk on bank loans into an ex ante probability distribution of returns on investment, we sidestep the complex details of how macroeconomic management of the reforms affects future profitability. But a reforming economy may well be subject to more macroeconomic uncertainty than a repressed one. Let the random variable α modify the function $g(\cdot)$ so that $\alpha g(\cdot)$ is the actual investment payoff in period 2. Based on the best information available in period 1, the expected value of α is $\hat{\alpha}$, and $\hat{\alpha}g(\cdot)$ is the corresponding locus of expected (mean) invested outcomes, as shown in figure 6.3. (In the deterministic cases portrayed in figures 6.1 and 6.2, investment outcomes were known exactly.)

Because α now varies stochastically, figure 6.3 now represents possible investment equilibria in the old and new technologies in period 1 together with the corresponding *expected* payoffs in period 2 in the new, uncertain technology. (We assume this macroeconomic uncertainty does not affect investment payoffs in the traditional technology.) But how do nonbank firms decide what the returns to investment in the (radically) transformed economy likely will be? Here we posit a substantial informational asymmetry. Banks are special because they are at the center of the flow of funds in the economy, and collectively they can price credit and determine its availability to liquidity-constrained enterprises.

The upshot is that, in period 1, the aggressiveness of the banks' lending behavior offers an implicit signal to the nonbank sector of the likely success of the reforms, that is, of the mean realization of α. Domestic firm-households, perhaps naively, rely on these implicit signals from the "expert" banking system to generate their expectations of $\hat{\alpha}$. Besides enabling firms to finance their setup costs and so stimulate current economic activity, easy credit signals that new investments in the

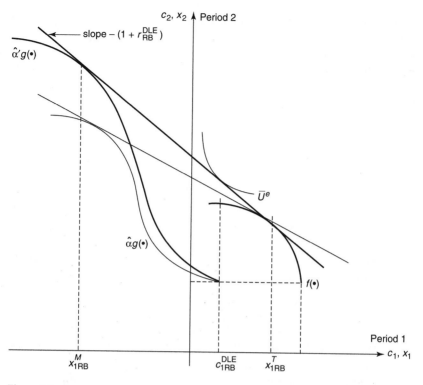

Figure 6.3
A Domestically Liberalized Economy with Moral Hazard and Rational Beliefs

reform technology will have high payoffs, which increases people's estimates of their future income.

If the banks' signaling is accurate, having them implicitly indicate how successful the reforms will be is efficient. In figure 6.3 portraying a DLE, $\hat{\alpha}g(\cdot)$, now gives the unbiased locus of expected investment outcomes in period 2, when banks are free from moral hazard. If firm-households are risk-neutral in this stochastic world, the double tangency of the borrowing-lending line with $f(\cdot)$ and $\hat{\alpha}g(\cdot)$ is the first-best solution, where expected two-period income is maximized.

The problem comes when banks exploit the potential for moral hazard implied by the implicit or explicit government guarantee of bank deposits. If prudential supervision is insufficient, risk-neutral banks will truncate the true probability distribution of future investment returns by unduly discounting the possibility of bad outcomes. They and their depositors know that if the overall reform program fails to deliver and leads to widespread bankruptcies and panic, the government will enter to bail out distressed institutions. Thus, ex ante, risk-neutral banks could run their loan programs overly optimistically as if the mean realization of α were $\hat{\alpha}'$, where $\hat{\alpha}' > \hat{\alpha}$. The result seen by non-banks is the unduly inflated investment payoff function $\hat{\alpha}'g(\cdot)$ shown in figure 6.3.

Unaware of the inadequacy of bank supervision, firm-households take this overly optimistic signal at face value and bid eagerly for funds to exploit the supposedly higher returns. The interest rate, as shown by the double tangency of the domestic interest rate with $\hat{\alpha}'g(\cdot)$ and $f(\cdot)$ in figure 6.3, is bid up higher than it would have been if the signal from the banks had been accurate. This corresponds to what Mordecai Kurz (1994) calls a *rational beliefs* (RB) equilibrium. Unlike a full rational expectations equilibrium, in our model nonbank agents with rational beliefs have insufficient information to reject a false signal from the banks. And under deposit insurance, loosely supervised banks prefer to gamble with the government's money.

Nevertheless, because the capital account of the balance of payments remains closed in the RB equilibrium shown for a DLE in figure 6.3, the false optimism about the higher returns to investment does not lead the economy into serious overinvestment or overconsumption. Although firm-households see their future income to be higher than it is likely to be, the sharp increase in the domestic interest rate above the first-best level (and probably far above international rates) restrains consumption and investment in period 1. Income and substitution effects offset each other, so current saving does not fall.

True, in period 2, when investment outcomes in the RB case turn out to yield less than anticipated, and high-cost bank loans must be repaid, bankruptcies could cause severe workout problems between debtors and creditors. But all of this is bottled up within the domestic economy. Moral hazard in the domestic banking system did not induce the nation as a whole to overborrow because, by definition, the capital account of the DLE remains closed—a crude fail-safe condition.

Opening the Model to International Capital Flows
Our analytical machinery also applies directly to an internationally liberalized economy (ILE), where the capital account is left open when credible real-side reforms are implemented. (We are still abstracting from currency risk and other monetary considerations as if domestic

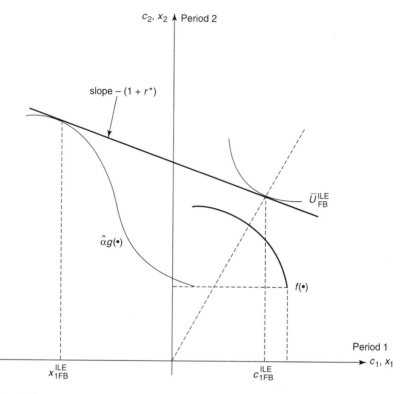

Figure 6.4
An Internationally Liberalized Economy, No Moral Hazard

and foreign real interest rates were directly comparable.) Now *all* identical firm-households become net borrowers in period 1 in order to surmount the discrete setup costs of investing to exploit the structural reforms. The pace of technical advance quickens.

Suppose first that the banking system has no moral hazard, that is, a strong regulatory system prevents banks from discounting bad macroeconomic outcomes. In an ILE, consumption rises (saving falls) in period 1 because income and substitution effects now pull in the same direction (figure 6.4). Not only does expected income rise into the indefinite future, but domestic interest rates fall to the world level r^*, as shown by the flatter slope of the linear budget line. The open international capital market allows people to borrow against their much higher incomes (accurately) expected in the future in order to increase consumption today.

Because all firm-households have access to foreign capital, all of them borrow in period 1 in order to invest in the new technology and enjoy higher income in period 2 (figure 6.4). The net inflow of foreign capital results in a deficit in the current account (CA) of the international balance of payments as all domestic agents spend more than their period 1 endowments. The CA deficit in period 1 is

$$CA = -N(c_{1FB}^{ILE} - x_{1FB}^{ILE}) \tag{6.2}$$

N is the total number of firm-households, and $c_{1FB}^{ILE} - x_{1FB}^{ILE}$ is the amount each borrower borrows in period 1.

As these loans are repaid in period 2, a corresponding current account surplus will be generated. The fall in saving in period 1, beyond that shown for DLE in figure 6.2, is simply part and parcel of the first-best solution: at the lower (world) interest rate, the reforming economy's resources for investment and consumption are optimally distributed intertemporally. In this international first-best solution (figure 6.4), welfare improves beyond what would prevail if the capital account had remained closed.

The potential for disaster arises when the capital market contains moral hazard *and* international financial flows are unrestricted. Now suppose that banks lend too exuberantly in period 1. They signal higher payoffs for investments than the reforms warrant, as per the investment schedule $\hat{\alpha}'g(\cdot)$ shown in figure 6.5. In the resulting rational beliefs (RB) equilibrium, as shown by the tangency of the world interest rate with the investment function $\hat{\alpha}'g(\cdot)$, saving declines further and the corresponding current account deficit mushrooms. Relative to the first-best equilibrium, first period (over)consumption increases by W, and (over)investment increases by V, in this RB equilibrium for ILE (figure 6.5).

Unless the economy experiences a lucky (upper tail) payoff to today's investments, the RB equilibrium in figure 6.5 is unsustainable. If the actual payoff is its true unbiased mean $\hat{\alpha}g(\cdot)$, firms will have trouble repaying investment loans, and households' debt burdens will escalate relative to their incomes. Widespread loan defaults could cause the domestic banking system to seize up and could also require a bailout from foreign indebtedness.

Although we have yet to introduce foreign exchange risk, because of moral hazard in banks associated with default risk coupled with inadequate regulation, the economy still can experience a crisis of overborrowing in international markets.

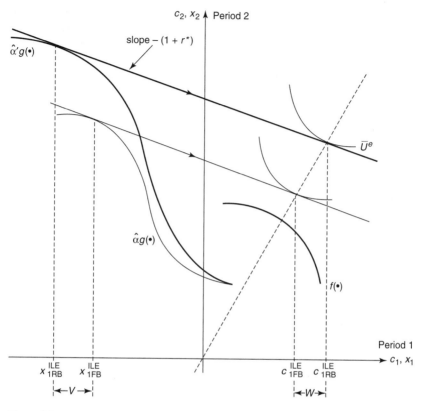

Figure 6.5
An Internationally Liberalized Economy with Domestic Credit Risk Only

6.2   Introducing Foreign Exchange Risk

Suppose that foreign and domestic monies differ so that there is exchange rate risk in addition to the domestic default risk analyzed heretofore. How does the choice of an exchange rate regime and the possible use of exchange controls over capital flows affect moral hazard in international financial markets? The current consensus in the academic literature, endorsed by the International Monetary Fund and other international organizations, is that one of the main lessons of recent emerging market financial crises is the need for more flexible exchange rate arrangements. Stanley Fischer (1999), who was the deputy managing director of the International Monetary Fund, stated the matter thus:

There is a tradeoff between the greater short-run volatility of the real exchange rate in a flexible rate regime versus the greater probability of a clearly defined external financial crisis when the exchange rate is pegged. The virulence of the recent crises is likely to shift the balance towards the choice of more flexible exchange rate systems, including crawling pegs with wide bands.

We explore this view and argue that, without introducing currency boards or otherwise completely ceding national monetary autonomy, well-designed programs of exchange rate stabilization can reduce the incidence of overborrowing manias, and thereby reduce the exposure of emerging markets to sudden reversals of investor sentiment leading to financial panics. Commonly held exchange rate objectives can even limit financial contagion, currency attacks spreading from one country to another, by helping to solve coordination problems among small open economies. However, no exchange rate regime, however well chosen, can obviate the need for prudential regulation of domestic banks against undue risk taking—regulation that may well cover international flows of short-term capital.

After credible real-side reforms, our Fisherian model focused on banks' overestimating domestic investment productivity irrespective of the exchange rate regime. However, from the recent emerging market crises, especially those in East Asia, banks also took excessive risks in the way they financed themselves in the foreign exchanges. While it is certainly the case that controlling overborrowing involves more than simply getting the exchange rate right, it is equally true that the exchange rate cannot be ignored.

Banks enjoying a government guarantee of their liabilities have an incentive to speculate on exchange rate developments because, as with the credit risks discussed in the previous section, they are protected from the full implications of adverse outcomes. Therefore, moral hazard could lead banks to take unhedged foreign exchange positions: they borrow in foreign currency and onlend to domestic residents at much higher interest rates in domestic currency, while implicitly transferring most of the currency risk incurred onto the government through the deposit insurance scheme.

We assumed earlier that real interest rates were equalized internationally in the absence of exchange risk. However, real interest parity for borrowing in *domestic* currency requires both uncovered interest parity and relative purchasing power parity to hold continuously (Frankel 1992). The empirical evidence in support of such propositions—even for small, open economies such as the emerging markets in question—is weak. Consequently, here we reintroduce the exchange rate into our simple Fisherian model of overborrowing by relaxing the assumption that RIP holds.

To do so, it is useful to recall a number of identities that decompose cross-country real interest rate differentials. As a benchmark, consider the world real interest rate r^*, which can be related to the world nominal interest rate i^* and the expected world inflation rate $E\pi^*$. To avoid complications associated with Balassa-Samuelson effects in consumer price indices (Pill 1995), define π and π^* to be rates of inflation in broad tradable goods price indices, i.e., as approximated by wholesale price indices.

$$r^* = i^* - E\pi^*$$
$$r = i - E\pi \tag{6.3}$$

We earlier assumed that the domestic real interest rate r was equal to the world real interest rate, $r = r^*$, because of RIP. However, after reintroducing the exchange rate into the model, interest rates may differ across currencies.

First, consider the covered interest parity (CIP) condition, relating nominal interest rate differential on bank deposits to the forward exchange rate premium of the same term to maturity. Let the spot exchange rate be S and the forward rate be F, both measured as domestic currency/foreign currency. The forward premium on foreign currency is f, where $f = F - S/S$. In the absence of controls over foreign capital flows or domestic interest rates, we have

$$i = i^* + f \tag{6.4}$$

When there are no barriers to international financial flows, covered interest parity, as defined by equation 6.4, must hold in portfolio equilibrium.[1] Otherwise, banks and other financial institutions, acting as covered interest arbitrageurs, could make unbounded profits while avoiding risk altogether.

Collectively, covered interest arbitrage by all banks is what makes the forward foreign exchange market in the course of determining f. For any one bank, CIP also implies that borrowing in foreign currency while hedging the position in the forward market is equivalent to borrowing in domestic currency.

For example, suppose that, as is normally the case in an emerging-market economy, the deposit rate in domestic currency in, say,

Thailand, is greater than if the same Thai bank accepted dollar deposits. That is, $f > 0$ and $i > i^*$. If a Thai bank were to accept cheaper dollar deposits, say, 30 days' duration, but hedged the transaction by buying dollars 30 days forward, the cost in baht of buying the dollars forward would be just f percent greater than buying them spot. The lower interest paid on the dollar deposits spot would just be offset by the higher cost of the forward cover. Consequently, when CIP holds, and banks are forced to hedge all their foreign exchange borrowing in the forward market, the incentive of banks with moral hazard for additional overborrowing related to the exchange rate is eliminated. The analysis collapses straightforwardly back to the previous simple model of figure 6.5, in which moral hazard is affected only by domestic credit risk.

However, in many, if not most, emerging-market countries, the regulatory and supervisory institutions are too weak to impose and enforce 100 percent hedging against domestic banks assuming foreign exchange risk. Consequently, banks with moral hazard have an incentive to borrow unhedged in foreign exchange at a lower interest rate, transferring the resulting foreign exchange risk to the government through the deposit insurance scheme. This will lead to (further) overborrowing for the country as a whole. To best characterize the margin of temptation for banks to borrow unhedged in foreign currencies, we develop the concept of the super-risk premium.

6.3   The Super-Risk Premium

What determines the nominal interest differential between baht and dollar deposits? This can be expressed using the uncovered interest parity relationship between the expected nominal depreciation $E\hat{e}$ and the interest differential,

$$i - i^* = E\hat{e} + \rho_{\text{currency}} \tag{6.5}$$

This is not a riskless arbitrage relationship like covered interest parity because nominal exchange rate developments are uncertain and introduce risk into the relationship. This is captured by the currency risk premium, ρ_{currency}. The currency risk premium represents the extra return required by investors to hold domestic rather than foreign currency assets. It reflects the correlations between returns on financial assets and other shocks to the income and consumption streams of wealth holders. In emerging markets interest rates and price levels are typically more volatile than those in industrialized countries. Insofar as the private sector of the emerging-market economy has built up significant short-term foreign currency (dollar) debts, as in many East Asian economies before 1997–1998, the risk from exchange rate fluctuations, especially depreciations, will seem greater. Consequently, wealth holders demand more compensation for holding emerging-market assets, and the interest rates on assets denominated the currencies of emerging-market debtor economies have to be higher to maintain international portfolio balance. The lower panels of figures 6.6–6.11 show that before the 1997–1998 crisis Korea, Thailand, Malaysia, Indonesia, Russia, and Brazil had interest rates as much as 10–12 percentage points higher than those on dollar assets.

The existence of a risk premium also reflects the inherent asymmetry between national monies at the center and on the periphery. In Latin America, Asia, and much of Africa, the U.S. dollar is the international standard of value for invoicing goods and services in foreign trade, and for denominating most of international capital flows (McKinnon 1979). The dollar is also the safe-haven currency into which nationals in emerging markets fly in the face of a domestic financial crisis. Thus, to measure $\rho_{currency}$ at different terms to maturity, interest rates on U.S. dollar assets are the natural standard of reference as the "risk-free" return in the international system. Moreover, for many emerging markets, the international price level in dollar terms is the main determinant of the domestic price level, given the exposure and openness of the formal sectors of the economy. (The European Union now provides a large, stable monetary safe harbor of its own, within which the dollar's asymmetrical role is less important.)

Equation 6.5 can be interpreted from this dollar standard perspective. The greater the volatility in Thailand's interest rates and price levels relative to those of the United States, the higher will be $\rho_{currency}$ in Thailand. This is close to saying that the greater the volatility of the baht's exchange rate against the dollar, the greater will be the currency risk premium in Thai interest rates. Conversely, the more that Thailand succeeds in integrating its monetary policy with that of the United States so that its dollar exchange rate is naturally stable and its price level is aligned with the U.S. price level, the lower will be $\rho_{currency}$ and the closer will be the Thai and U.S. nominal interest rates.

The other component of the interest differential—the expected depreciation of the domestic currency, E$\hat{e}$—can be decomposed into two parts. First, within a managed exchange rate regime with a crawling or

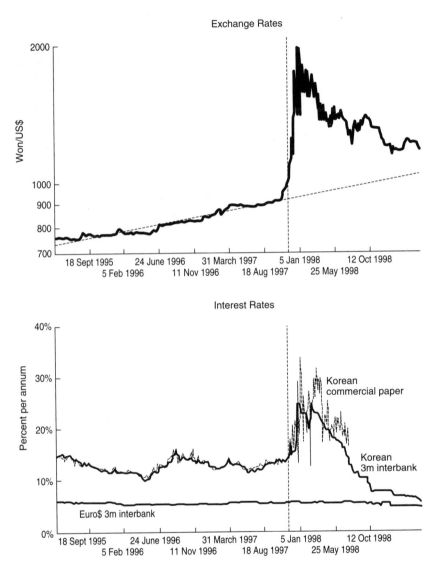

Figure 6.6
Korea's Exchange Rates and Interest Rates, 1995–1998. (International Monetary Fund, *International Financial Statistics*)

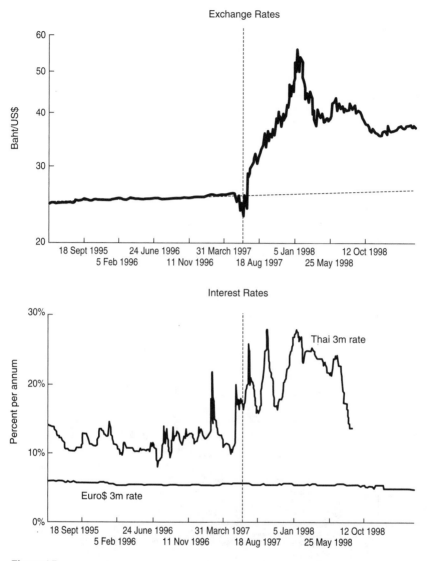

Figure 6.7
Thailand's Exchange Rates and Interest Rates, 1995–1998. (International Monetary Fund, *International Financial Statistics*)

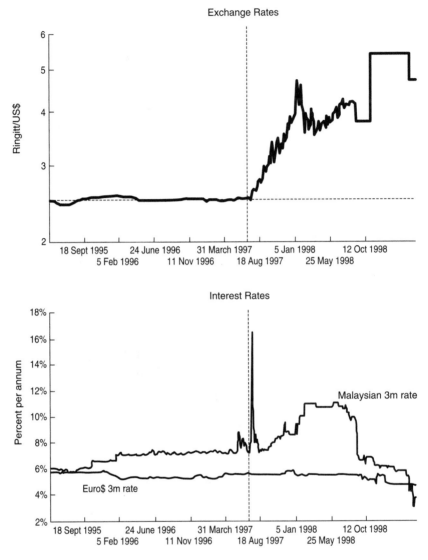

Figure 6.8
Malaysia's Exchange Rates and Interest Rates, 1995–1998. (International Monetary Fund,
International Financial Statistics)

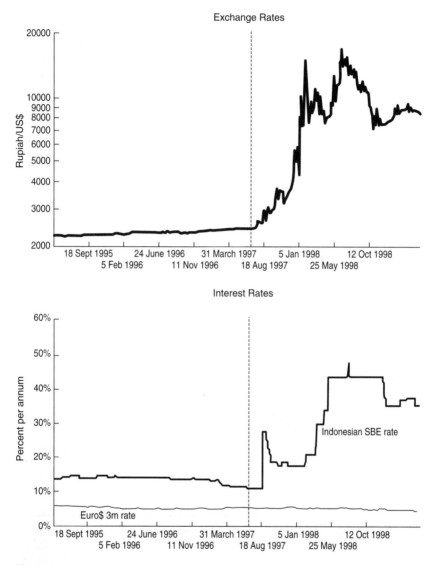

Figure 6.9
Indonesia's Exchange Rates and Interest Rates, 1995–1998. (International Monetary Fund, *International Financial Statistics*)

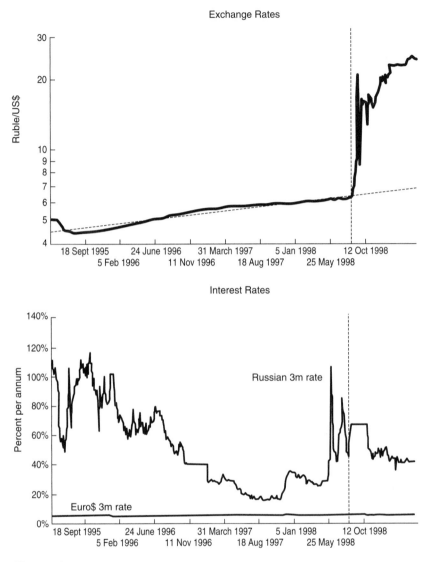

Figure 6.10
Russia's Exchange Rates and Interest Rates, 1995–1998. (International Monetary Fund, *International Financial Statistics*)

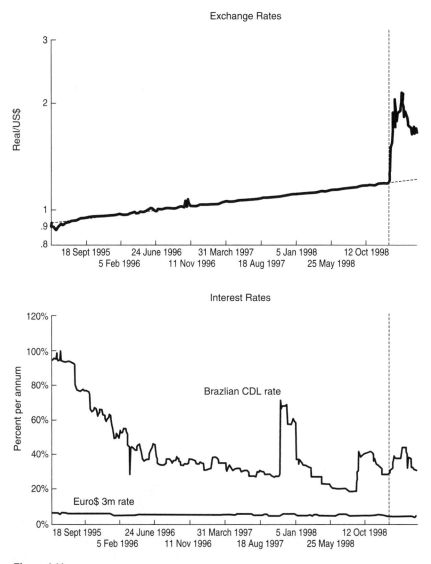

Figure 6.11
Brazil's Exchange Rates and Interest Rates, 1995–1998. (International Monetary Fund, *International Financial Statistics*)

constant peg (typical of East Asian countries, Mexico, Brazil, and most emerging-market economies), the exchange rate might change predictably and smoothly according to government's policy announcements and commitments, such as the downward crawl in the Indonesian rupiah before the 1997 crash. Second is the small probability of a regime change: a large, sudden devaluation whose timing is unpredictable:

$$E\hat{e} = E\hat{e}_{predictable} + E\hat{e}_{regimechange} \tag{6.6}$$

Although both types of expected change in the exchange rate in equation 6.6 widen the nominal interest differential in equation 6.5, it is plausible that $E\hat{e}_{regimechange}$ is part of the margin of temptation for banks with moral hazard to overborrow, while $E\hat{e}_{predictable}$ is not. If the exchange rate was expected to depreciate smoothly through time, even banks with very short time horizons will account for the higher domestic currency costs of repaying short-term foreign currency deposits. Therefore, we exclude $E\hat{e}_{predictable}$ from our measure of the super risk premium:

$$\rho_{super} = \rho_{currency} + E\hat{e}_{regimechange} = i - i^* - E\hat{e}_{predictable} \tag{6.7}$$

The super-risk premium, ρ_{super}, represents the margin of temptation for banks to overborrow in foreign exchange. It has two components: the currency risk premium, as defined, and the part of the interest differential arising from the small probability that the regime could change through a discrete devaluation.

The latter source of upward pressure on the interest rate on assets denominated in the domestic currency is sometimes called the peso problem. By borrowing unhedged in foreign currency, the domestic banks with deposit insurance and other government guarantees ignore downside bankruptcy risks implied by large devaluations whose timing is uncertain. In setting domestic nominal lending rates, the banks will only cover the "predictable" component of the expected depreciation within the currency regime.[2] In the special case where the nominal exchange rate is fixed, unhedged banks onlend at the international nominal interest rate plus a normal profit margin. For ease of macroeconomic exposition, this profit margin between deposits and loans is simply set at zero.[3] In equation 6.7, i represents the nominal interest rate that would be charged by a domestic bank that was borrowing in foreign currency but fully hedging its foreign exchange exposure. In contrast, a bank exploiting a government guarantee by borrowing unhedged in the international capital market will (in a competitive environment where bank profits are competed away) charge a lower rate i^* that does not incorporate the domestic super-risk premium and is simply the interest rate on foreign currency deposits.

This highlights our first regulatory dilemma. If the super-risk premium is high and the ability of the regulatory authorities to enforce hedging rules is imperfect, then there will be large differences in the perceived cost of capital to different financial agents and firms in the domestic market. Those that the authorities succeed in policing will face a much higher cost of capital than those that gamble and borrow unhedged. A declining market share could undermine the resolve of even conservative banks to hedge their foreign exchange positions.

6.4 "Good" versus "Bad" Fixes and the Real Interest Rate

To compare these results with our two-period model of real borrowing and lending in figure 6.5, we convert these nominal interest rates into real rates. The domestic real lending rate charged by a "well-behaved" fully hedged bank will be

$$r_{\text{hedged}} = r^* + (E\pi^* - E\pi + E\hat{e}_{\text{predictable}}) + \rho_{\text{super}} \tag{6.8}$$

In contrast, the domestic real lending rate charged by a bank exploiting its government guarantee and therefore not hedging its foreign exchange exposure will be

$$r_{\text{unhedged}} = r^* + (E\pi^* - E\pi + E\hat{e}_{\text{predictable}}) \tag{6.9}$$

A banking sector with moral hazard will charge a lower domestic real interest rate (equation 6.9) than one that is regulated to be fully hedged (equation 6.8).

Can domestic real interest rates differ from those prevailing on world markets? Suppose that relative purchasing power parity, defined with respect to the predictable component in the movement of the exchange rate, holds: the domestic (Indonesian) price level rises relative to the foreign (U.S.) only by the amount of the ongoing smooth depreciation of the rupiah so that $E\pi = E\pi^* + E\hat{e}_{\text{predictable}}$. Whether an unchanging peg or a downward crawl, let us call such PPP exchange rate regimes "good" fixes. Because the exchange rate regime seems secure enough, the small probability of a regime change and discrete devaluation is not incorporated into ongoing domestic inflation. Before the 1997 currency attacks, the Asian crisis economies—Indonesia, Korea, Malaysia, Philippines, and Thailand—and other noncrisis economies—Hong Kong, Singapore, and Taiwan—had fairly good fixes with sound macroeconomic fundamentals (see chapter 1). Among other things, a good fix implies

$$E\pi = E\pi^* + E\hat{e}_{\text{predictable}} \Rightarrow r_{\text{hedged}} = r^* + \rho_{\text{super}} \quad \text{and} \quad r_{\text{unhedged}} = r^*$$

$$(6.10)$$

The unhedged real borrowing rate is equal to the world's (center country's) real interest rate; and the hedged borrowing rate exceeds this by exactly the super-risk premium, ρ_{super}.

However with a bad fix, the domestic price level drifts up by more than the controlled rate of depreciation: $E\pi > E\pi^* + E\hat{e}_{\text{predictable}}$. Bad fixes have been common in Latin America, as in Chile 1978–1981, Mexico in 1992–1994, Argentina after 1991, and Brazil in 1996–1998, before their currencies were attacked. With unhedged borrowing and in the presence of a bad fix, the domestic real interest rate unambiguously falls below the world rate:

$$E\pi > E\pi^* + E\hat{e}_{\text{predictable}} \Rightarrow r_{\text{unhedged}} < r^* \tag{6.11}$$

With hedged borrowing, however, equation 6.8 shows that the domestic real interest rate could be higher or lower than the corresponding risk-free world rate. The ongoing domestic price inflation unambiguously reduces the real rate, but the super-risk premium could itself increase and more than offset this effect because the expectation of a regime change in the exchange rate is likely to rise as the current rate drifts further and further from the rate consistent with PPP. Thus, under a bad fix, the domestic real interest rate seen by hedged borrowers could be higher than the world rate and also higher than if there had been a good fix.

Indeed, a bad fix is precisely when the super-risk premium is a maximum. First, $E\hat{e}_{\text{regimechange}}$ is high because it is less likely that the fixed exchange rate can last. Second, ρ_{currency} is also high because of instability in the domestic price level and interest rates. Then, because of the huge difference in the cost of borrowing, hedged versus unhedged, regulatory discrimination through enforced hedging on some, but not all, borrowers may become unsustainable.

The super-risk premium, that is, the financing penalty imposed on hedged borrowers, is endogenously determined by monetary and fiscal considerations (not modeled here) as well as by regulatory ones. To the extent that the economy (currency area) as a whole accumulates unhedged foreign exchange liabilities, ρ_{super} increases and so does the penalty on hedged borrowers or ones that are just borrowing in the domestic currency. Strengthening the government's regulatory mechanism to enforce hedging against exchange risk can be likened to a public good. It limits adverse spillover effects from agents that have moral hazard to those that do not, as well as limiting overborrowing.

6.5   The Interaction between Credit and Currency Risk

To isolate the effect of domestic credit risk on overborrowing, the world real interest rate was previously given as if the same currency circulated at home and abroad, that is, as if currency risk were absent. Without moral hazard in domestic banks, borrowing at the foreign real interest rate r^* yielded the first-best solution, the socially optimal use of inflows of foreign capital (figure 6.4).

With a separate domestic currency, however, this first-best solution must be suitably risk-adjusted. Now the appropriate domestic cost of foreign capital is $r^* + \rho_{super}$, that seen by fully hedged borrowers under a good fix. (The issue of exchange rate flexibility is discussed later.) The first-best solution involves firm-households borrowing, either in domestic currency or fully hedged in foreign currency, at the interest rate $r^* + \rho_{super}$. This leads to a tangency solution with the undistorted investment function $\hat{\alpha}g(\cdot)$ (figure 6.12). With this risk adjustment and no domestic investment distortion, there is no overborrowing. The first-best solution for ILE (figure 6.5) is replicated, albeit with the domestic real interest rate adjusted for foreign exchange risk by the super-risk premium.

However, even if foreign borrowing is fully hedged under a good fix, domestic credit risk could still elicit moral hazard in domestic banks, leading them to behave too optimistically, as if the investment function were $\hat{\alpha}'g(\cdot)$. The tangency solution with $r^* + \rho_{super}$ leads to overborrowing in an international rational beliefs equilibrium, even with the domestic real interest rate properly adjusted for currency risks (figure 6.12). Again, overinvestment is denoted by V and overconsumption by W.

Suppose that this (distorted) expected domestic investment function $\hat{\alpha}'g(\cdot)$ remains unchanged, but foreign borrowing by domestic banks is unhedged. In these circumstances, the real interest rate seen by

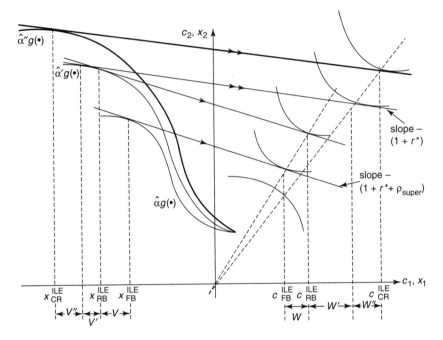

Figure 6.12
Moral Hazard with Currency Risk and Credit Risk

borrowers falls to r^*. Figure 6.12 shows how the lower level of domestic real interest rates leads to still more overinvestment, represented by V', and overconsumption, represented by W'.

Furthermore, the two risks now faced by the domestic banking sector—credit risk associated with the uncertainty about the productivity implications of real economic reform and currency risk resulting from the unhedged foreign currency denominated borrowing—may be interrelated. The interrelationships may dramatically raise the magnitude and riskiness of the overborrowing taking place.

Consider the situation where credit risk and currency risk are positively related. The most dramatic manifestation of this is when the cumulative bad loan positions of domestic banks induce a runoff in deposits. Because many of these deposits are in foreign currency, this forces a devaluation as the domestic banks bid for foreign exchange. In the event of an adverse productivity shock, the losses incurred by banks are now greater than they would have been in the pure real-side model discussed earlier. Not only does the bank suffer defaults by its borrowers that erode the bank's capital, but the associated devaluation of the currency imposes even larger capital losses because the bank's foreign exchange exposure is unhedged. Consequently, the probability of bankruptcy is increased and, by implication, the lower tail of the distribution for the productivity shock α that leads to bankruptcy is enlarged. Therefore a bank that enjoys government guarantees of its liabilities and is inadequately regulated against risk taking will truncate an even greater proportion of the ex ante distribution of investment returns. That is, ex ante it will disregard bad outcomes, which, with both currency and credit risk, are now a higher proportion of the total.

Figure 6.12 shows banks behaving (after this truncation) as if the investment payoff function were exaggerated to $\hat{\alpha}''g(\cdot)$, where $\hat{\alpha}'' > \hat{\alpha}' > \hat{\alpha}$. The tangency of this function with r^*, the non-risk-adjusted world interest rate, defines an international currency risk (CR) equilibrium where there is massive overborrowing—an additional V'' of overinvestment and W'' of overconsumption, beyond that observed in the scenario where banks did not exploit the correlations between productivity shocks and the exchange rate. Clearly, if domestic regulators allow banks and other financial institutions to assume both credit and foreign exchange risks simultaneously, the regime is unlikely to survive (a proposition supported by the evidence presented by Kaminsky and Reinhart 1999).

In many emerging markets (e.g., Korea and Thailand, where the crisis was triggered by a small number of high-profile bankruptcies), failures by bank borrowers appear to trigger the devastating currency devaluations that impose enormous capital losses on banks with unhedged foreign exchange exposures. Moreover, it is precisely the realization of adverse productivity shocks (and consequent bankruptcies) that is likely to trigger the collapse of foreign investors' confidence that is characteristic of the sudden, dramatic, and apparently irresistible currency crises of recent years. Therefore the confidence channel provides a further behavioral justification for assuming that adverse productivity shocks and precipitate exchange rate devaluations are likely to be positively related in debtor economies.

6.6 Interest Rate Differentials in Overborrowing Countries

Before such a crisis, how will the real interest rate differential evolve as overborrowing progresses? Contrary to the discussion in the previous section and the analysis in figure 6.12, conventional thought assumes a

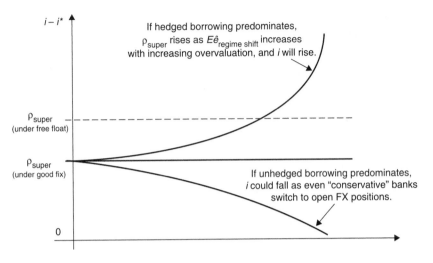

Figure 6.13
Evolution of the Super Risk Premium under a "Bad Fix"

"bad" fix with continuous real appreciation of the domestic currency. Because domestic price inflation is higher than any smooth depreciation of the exchange rate, there is growing overvaluation of the emerging market's currency. Ultimately the real overvaluation becomes unsustainable as the country's exports become uncompetitive on international goods markets. As real appreciation progresses, the super-risk premium rises because the expectation of a sudden devaluation of the exchange rate increases. According to equation 6.8, the domestic real interest rate associated with fully hedged borrowing in such a scenario would rise over time as the super-risk premium rises, causing a divergence of the domestic and international real rates. This is illustrated in figure 6.13.

However, in the event of such a bad fix, the nominal interest rate differential would behave quite differently depending on whether foreign borrowing is hedged or unhedged, as shown in the upper versus the lower graph in figure 6.13. According to equation 6.9, where there is moral hazard, domestic banks exclude the super risk premium when setting interest rates, since the risks implied are transferred to the government through the guarantee of insured deposits. Through time, this would imply that the domestic real interest rate converges to the world real interest rate, as previously "conservative" domestic banks (that have been hedging their foreign currency exposures) are forced by competitive pressures to pursue the riskier unhedged strategy.

The empirical validity of some of these assertions can be assessed, albeit in a simple manner, by investigating the interest differentials observed between the international capital market and domestic interest rates in the emerging market economies that suffered from currency and financial crises at the culmination of the overborrowing syndrome. If the investment function is exaggerated by exchange rate risk as per $\hat{\alpha}''g(\cdot)$ in figure 6.12 and most foreign (over)borrowing is unhedged, as the crisis approaches domestic nominal interest rates (on loans denominated in domestic currency) would tend to converge toward international nominal interest rates (on loans denominated in U.S. dollars), once the correction for a differential associated with any predictable preannounced crawl of the nominal exchange rate had been made. Where such a convergence took place, one would anticipate a large inflow of foreign capital (equivalently, a large current account deficit) and rapid growth of domestic investment and consumption before the crash occurs. (At this stage, no attempt is made to measure inflation expectations, so the results can be at best suggestive, because they focus on nominal rather than real rates.)

In contrast, and somewhat paradoxically, if exchange rate risk is not an important cause of overborrowing because most foreign borrowing is hedged, the spread between domestic and international rates should widen and the inflow of foreign capital should slow as the crisis approaches. As overvaluation grows under a bad fix, the super-risk premium increases because the probability of a sharp exchange depreciation rises.

To illustrate these points, we compare precrisis domestic interest rate data for Thailand, Malaysia, Indonesia, and Korea with the U.S. dollar interest rate (measured as London Interbank Offer Rate, LIBOR). These East Asian examples are then compared with Russia and Brazil in 1998, a year in which those two countries could more easily be identified within the bad fix group. To focus attention on the short-term hot money capital flows that are at the heart of analysis of the overborrowing syndrome, we choose to investigate three-month rates. Analysis of other maturities and of the relationship with other currencies (especially the Japanese yen in the East Asian context) would offer useful extensions, but this is left to future work.

Figures 6.6–6.11 show time series of exchange rates and interest rates. These cover the period from the beginning of September 1995 to the end of October 1998. The upper panel of each figure shows the development in the exchange rate against the U.S. dollar. As is clear, a predictable rate of crawl (generally very low) was typical of the East Asian countries' dollar exchange rates (shown by the dashed line). This modest expected depreciation of the exchange rate accounts for some of the spread between the three-month LIBOR on U.S. dollars and the corresponding domestic currency interest rates in Korea, Thailand, Malaysia, and Indonesia. Because the interest spread ranged between 2 and 10 percentage points, the super risk premium was still substantial, although there is some suggestion (e.g., in Indonesia) that the spread narrowed as the currency crisis approached.

Comparing the East Asian countries with Russia and Brazil reveals a dramatic difference. In both these countries, the nominal interest rate differential against the U.S. dollar narrowed very appreciably in the period preceding the currency and financial crises. This suggests that, in these bad fix countries, banks exploited the moral hazard offered by government guarantees and lack of regulation of foreign exchange positions to borrow unhedged and avoid paying the super risk premium. Their speculative currency positions drove domestic interest rates down and thereby exacerbated the magnitude and riskiness of borrowing from abroad to finance the ongoing current account deficit.

However, this purely descriptive empirical exercise does not discriminate fully between the two hypotheses: the role exchange rate risk plays in establishing the interest differential when foreign borrowing is hedged, and when it is unhedged.

6.7   Capital Controls and Bank Regulation

What light does our analysis shed on the question posed at the beginning of this chapter, namely, what is the appropriate exchange rate regime for an emerging market? Because domestic supervision and regulation are assumed to be insufficient to fully curtail moral hazard in banks, our policy proposals are inherently second-best. The best solution would be to implement regulatory reforms for directly limiting domestic credit risks and open positions in foreign exchange. Then, the choice of exchange rate regime, at least on the dimensions discussed here, would be of secondary importance.

However, even in our second-best world, a bad fix looks unambiguously bad in worsening the moral hazard problem. Domestic banks accepting unhedged foreign exchange deposits see the upward drift in the real exchange rate reducing their real interest rate below even the "risk-free" world interest rate. In addition, as $E\hat{e}_{regimechange}$ rises sharply, so does the super risk premium measuring the greater cost of capital (interest rates in domestic currency) seen by hedged borrowers compared to those with unhedged foreign exchange liabilities. Faced with having their economic positions completely undermined, normally conservative banks and firms would also begin to gamble by borrowing unhedged in world markets. Public morale for enforcing prudential regulations could crumble altogether, as in the Russian debacle in the summer of 1998.[4]

When potential moral hazard is extreme both in deposit-insured banks and in government-sponsored corporations, capital controls that prevent agents from taking positions in foreign exchange may well supplement domestic prudential regulations. In the order of economic liberalization, capital controls should be liberalized only after everything else, including macroeconomic stabilization and prudential bank regulation and control, is securely in place (McKinnon 1973; 1993a).

For example, China's commercial banks have had festering bad loan problems for many years, and many of its state-owned enterprises are loss makers. Wisely, the government has contained the moral hazard by ringing the country with capital controls so that bank and corporate short-term indebtedness in foreign currencies is negligible. Together with more stable macroeconomic policies leading to a good fix for the yuan/dollar exchange rate, this regulatory prudence has been rewarded with a negligible super-risk premium. From 1997 through 2003, interest rates on yuan-denominated assets in China were virtually the same as those on dollar-denominated assets in the United States.

In incompletely reformed economies, the case for capital controls as an extension of prudential regulations over the domestic financial system can hardly be faulted, even if difficult to implement in economies that are already highly dollarized, as is much of Latin America. But where successfully implemented, as in China or Malaysia at the present time, floating the exchange rate is simply not an option. By definition, banks and other important market-making institutions are restrained from taking open positions in foreign exchange. Thus the exchange rate cannot float freely. The government must make the foreign exchange market because private agents are now prohibited from doing so by the existence of controls. What sort of managed exchange rate regime should the government aim for?

First, the authorities must recognize that a forward market in foreign exchange cannot exist with capital controls in place. Banks, the natural market makers, are prohibited from covered interest arbitrage, which otherwise would make a forward market possible (equation 6.4). But domestic importers and exporters need some kind of official forward signal as to what their future foreign exchange earnings and costs in terms of the domestic currency are likely to be. (The need of banks and other financial institutions for forward cover is obviated if the controls themselves succeed in preventing them from having net foreign exchange exposure.) A good fix to the dollar, the effective international standard of value for most emerging market economies other than Eastern Europe, is an appropriate benchmark on which importers and exporters can base their hedging decisions (see chapter 1). Ideally, a stable dollar exchange rate could also provide an effective nominal anchor for the domestic price level, as was true in the high-growth East Asian emerging-market economies before the currency attacks of 1997 (McKinnon 2000).

With more erratic domestic inflation, however, a managed downward crawl—perhaps with a band around it—can help stabilize the real exchange rate seen by importers and exporters by making movements in the nominal exchange rate more predictable. With capital controls in place from the mid-1980s to the mid-1990s, both Chile and Israel successfully managed downward crawls without overborrowing. In inflationary economies, combining a crawling peg with capital controls dominates a bad fix without capital controls.

No doubt, capital controls are often very clumsy bureaucratically, and their effectiveness erodes as the economy liberalizes more generally; eventually they should be discarded. Nevertheless, in emerging-market debtor economies with original sin (see chapter 1), strong prudential regulation over banks should continue indefinitely. In particular, regulatory sanctions against banks' taking net open positions in foreign exchange should continue. With their potential moral hazard, banks are not appropriate vehicles to be international financial intermediaries.

Even so, banks remain very useful as money changers, making both the spot and forward exchange markets function more efficiently. Even if they were regulated so as to have no net foreign exchange exposure, they could still function freely as covered interest arbitrageurs, thus establishing an active forward market in foreign exchange (equation 6.4).

However, if banks cannot take net open positions in foreign exchange, they cannot be stabilizing speculators and take up the slack if the government were to withdraw from setting the foreign exchange rate. In other words, with draconian regulations in place to prevent banks from taking net open positions in foreign exchange, a free float is next to impossible. Without banks as stabilizing speculators, any exchange rate untethered by the government would behave too erratically.

6.8   Good Fixes versus Free Floats in Financially Open Economies

Now suppose our prototype emerging market economy is financially open, that is, it has no capital controls. Hedging against currency risk, at least in the short term, might now be possible if forward markets exist. Nevertheless, floating the exchange rate can be a dangerous option, because it would require relaxation of the prudential regulations over banks.

On the other hand, if the macro fundamentals are sound (in the sense that there is fiscal balance and no need to resort to the inflation tax), a good fix of the exchange rate is also an option. Chapter 1 shows that, before 1997, the East Asian economies, those that were subsequently attacked and those that were not, had good fixes for the exchange rates. From our fairly narrow perspective of minimizing moral hazard in international capital flows and mitigating the tendency toward overborrowing, how should the government choose between a good fix and a free float?

Referring to equation 6.7, this boils down to the question of which exchange rate regime minimizes the super-risk premium, the margin of temptation for domestic banks to accept unhedged deposits in foreign exchange. Would ρ_{super} be greater under a good fix or a free float? Under a good fix, PPP holds but, unlike a permanent fix such as under a currency board, the regime could change. In determining the size of the differential between deposit interest rates in domestic and foreign currency, the term $E\hat{e}_{regimechange}$ is a significant component. But so is $\rho_{currency}$, the penalty for having ongoing volatility in domestic prices and interest rates greater than the center country's.

Suppose an emerging-market economy had succeeded in integrating its monetary policy with that of the center country so that its nominal exchange rate as well as its internal price level and interest rates have been quite stable. Under such a good fix, both $E\hat{e}_{regimechange}$ and $\rho_{currency}$ would be quite moderate. For example, figure 6.8 shows that with its good fix, Malaysia's nominal interest rates were less than 2 percentage points higher than those of the United States before the 1997 attacks. If the authorities had decided to float the exchange rate, would this interest differential have narrowed further?

True, $E\hat{e}_{\text{regimechange}}$ could decline under floating as the danger of a discrete devaluation seemed more remote. But as the exchange rate begins to move randomly, which is one way of defining a free float, surely ρ_{currency} would rise. As the economy lost its nominal anchor, domestic price-level and interest-rate volatility would increase, and so would the currency risk premium.

To express this in another way, it has been argued (McKinnon 2000; and see chapter 1) that in financially open emerging-market economies, such as Thailand or Korea, that are fully integrated into the world trading system, the domestic price level needs to be aligned toward the international price level expressed in U.S. dollars. A good fix to the U.S. dollar achieves this objective. Allowing the domestic currency to float against the dollar from this starting point simply introduces noise into the domestic price level associated with portfolio shocks in the international capital market. Within the framework we have described, this noise is a pure cost. Not only does it make the domestic price level less stable directly, but it also reduces macroeconomic stability by introducing a risky margin on which banks enjoying government guarantees can speculate. This can lead to overborrowing and the type of crisis that has been common of late.

We conclude that floating need not succeed in reducing ρ_{super} and thus need not succeed in reducing the temptation to borrow unhedged in foreign exchange. With inadequate domestic prudential controls over foreign exchange exposure and domestic credit risk in a debtor economy, a floating rate could be suddenly attacked much like a fixed one.

From the broader perspective of monetary policy, however, giving up on a good fix loses the price-level anchor, which the smaller East Asian economies used quite effectively in their "miracle" growth phases. By all pegging to the same monetary standard before 1997, they also had mutual protection from competitive devaluations. One could go further and say that the super-risk premium in the interest rates of any one East Asian economy is lower when its neighbors—both trading partners and competitors—are on similar good-fix exchange rate regimes. (But collective exchange rate security goes beyond the purview of our single-economy model.) In assessing what went wrong in the Asian crisis economies, we would implicate the breakdown in domestic prudential bank regulations, including the premature elimination of capital controls, but we would not fault their good-fix exchange rate regimes.

Optimum Currency Areas
and Key Currencies:
Mundell I versus
Mundell II

The East Asian economies are increasingly integrated in trade and direct investment. More than 50 percent of their foreign trade is with each other (see chapter 2), and both the high growth and high level of trade integration are similar to what the Western European economies achieved in the 1960s. In the new millennium, the inevitable question arises, Is East Asia also an optimum currency area (OCA)? Despite the apparent success of the European Monetary Union, many writers familiar with the East Asian scene, such as Kwan (2001), think not. Taking the seminal papers of Robert Mundell as the starting point, this chapter first analyzes traditional theorizing on the pros and cons of international monetary integration and then suggests new approaches to the problem of international risk sharing in OCAs.

More than 40 years after Robert Mundell put forth the theory of optimum currency areas, the analytical consensus based on his celebrated 1961 paper has disintegrated. Part of the problem stems from a seeming contradiction in Mundell's own work. For offsetting asymmetrical macroeconomic shocks, his 1961 article leans toward making currency areas smaller and more homogeneous—rather than larger and more heterogeneous—while emphasizing the advantages of exchange rate flexibility. However, in a little-known article, "Uncommon Arguments for Common Currencies," Mundell (1973a) later argued that asset holding for international risk sharing is better served by a common currency spanning a wide area within which countries or regions could be, and perhaps would best be, quite different.

Paul De Grauwe (2003) characterizes the earlier Mundell as (implicitly) assuming an efficient market for determining how flexible

Revised and expanded from "Optimum Currency Areas and the European Experience," (2002) *The Economics of Transition* 10 (2): 343–364.

exchange rates vary through time. He suggests, in contrast, that the later Mundell (implicitly) assumed an efficient international market for allocating capital when exchange rates were fixed.

In this chapter, I first analyze the plausibility of the earlier Mundell's presumption that exchange rates adjust efficiently in response to asymmetric macroeconomic shocks across countries. I then focus on extending Mundell's later argument on capital market efficiency for international risk sharing against shocks to productivity, the international terms of trade, and so on. For specific classes of financial assets—money, bonds, and equities—I examine how the exchange rate regime and currency risk affect the incentives for international portfolio diversification.

Across nations or regions, the discussion of OCA theory will proceed on at least four levels:

• The long-standing debate on the optimum domain of fixed exchange rates in comparison to keeping them flexible when all currencies are treated symmetrically.

• The asymmetrical role of a key currency chosen from within an optimum currency area in securing exchange rate stability for the group.

• The subordinate debate on whether one needs complete monetary union (as in continental Europe) to secure an optimum currency area's internal domain.

• The important issue of whether a group of economies with close trade ties (as in East Asia) gain by collectively pegging to an outside currency such as the U.S. dollar.

The last issue is most relevant for East Asia. What are the advantages and disadvantages of pegging to the U.S. dollar in order in order to achieve exchange rate stability within the East Asian region? How is this linked to the net debtor or net creditor status of individual East Asian economies?

To encompass all four levels of analysis, a general algebraic model is devoutly to be wished. For a noble attempt to provide one, see Ching and Devereux (2000a; 2000b). Short of this, this chapter addresses issues on each level and provides a taxonomic analytical framework to show how they are interrelated. But first, let us reexamine the two Mundell models—Mundell (1961), or Mundell I, and Mundell (1973a), or Mundell II.

7.1 Mundell I and Stationary Expectations

Like most macroeconomists in the postwar period who had a Keynesian mind-set, Mundell in 1961 believed that national monetary and fiscal policies could successfully manipulate aggregate demand to offset private-sector shocks on the supply or demand sides—what Willem Buiter (1999, 49) called the "fine-tuning fallacy." Underpinning this belief was the assumption of stationary expectations. As a modeling strategy, Mundell assumed that people behaved as if the current domestic price level, interest rate, and exchange rate (even when it was floating) would hold indefinitely. Not only in his 1961 theory of optimum currency areas but in the standard textbook Mundell-Fleming model (Mundell 1963), stationary expectations underlie how monetary and fiscal policy work themselves out in an open economy. In several of his influential essays collected up to 1968, Mundell showed how the principle of effective market classification could optimally assign monetary, fiscal, or exchange rate instruments to maintain full employment while balancing international payments. He assumed that agents in the private sector did not try to anticipate future movements in the price level, interest rates, the exchange rate, or in government policy itself.

In addition to stationary expectations, Mundell I posited that labor mobility was restricted to fairly small national, or even regional, domains. And these smallish domains could well experience macroeconomic shocks differentially—asymmetrically, in the jargon of the current literature—from their neighbors. In these special circumstances, Mundell I illustrated the advantages of exchange rate flexibility in what has now become the standard textbook paradigm:

Consider a simple model of two entities (regions or countries), initially in full employment and balance of payments equilibrium, and see what happens when the equilibrium is disturbed by a shift in demand from the goods in entity B to the goods in entity A. Assume that money wages and prices cannot be reduced in the short run without causing unemployment, and that monetary authorities act to prevent inflation. . . .

The existence of more than one (optimum) currency area in the world implies variable exchange rates. . . . If demand shifts from the products of country B to the products of country A, a depreciation by country B or an appreciation by country A would correct the external imbalance and also relieve unemployment in country B and restrain inflation in country A. This is the most favorable case for flexible exchange rates based on national currencies. (510–511)

True, Mundell I carefully hedged his argument by giving examples of countries that were not optimum currency areas—as when the main shocks in the terms of trade occurred across regions within a single country—rather than between countries. He also worried about monetary "balkanization" into numerous small currency domains that might destroy the liquidity properties of the monies involved. Nevertheless, the economics profession enthusiastically embraced this delightfully simple paradigm, often without Mundell's own caveats. Textbooks took existing nation-states as natural currency areas, and argued that a one-size-fits-all monetary policy across nation states can't be optimal when labor markets are somewhat segmented internationally and when the composition of output varies from one country to the next, leading countries to experience macroeconomic shocks differentially.

Following Mundell I, McKinnon (1963) hypothesized that openness with potential currency area trading partners would militate toward having a fixed exchange rate between them. He argued that the more open the economy, the less tenable would be the Keynesian assumption of sticky domestic prices *and* wages in response to exchange rate fluctuations. For a small open economy, he also worried that the liquidity value of the domestic money would be impaired if its exchange rate, and thus its purchasing power over a broad basket of world goods, fluctuated. He *should* also have made the case that the more open economies are to each other, the less asynchronous would be their output fluctuations arising from demand shocks—a case made empirically and very neatly in a recent article by Frankel and Rose (1998).

Also operating within Mundell's 1961 framework, Peter Kenen (1969) looked at the conditions under which asynchronous macroeconomic shocks across countries would become less likely. If a country's output were more diversified, Kenen hypothesized, it would be a better candidate to have fixed exchange rates with its neighbors because shocks focused on this or that industry would offset each other in the aggregate—the law of large numbers. He concluded that "the principal developed countries should perhaps adhere to the Bretton Woods regime, rarely resorting to changes in exchange rates. The less developed countries, being less diversified and less-well equipped with policy instruments, should make more frequent changes or perhaps resort to full flexibility" (4).

Kenen's conclusion, that relatively undiversified, less developed countries—often with just one or two dominant export products—should retain exchange flexibility, is consistent with the earlier Keynesian Mundell I, who stressed asymmetric shocks in the face of internal price and wage rigidities. However, Kenen's conclusion is quite inconsistent with the later "forward-looking" Mundell II, who emphasized the need to promote asset diversification for international risk sharing.

In the 1960s, Mundell I, and almost all other economists, presumed that a flexible exchange rate would be a smoothly adjusting variable for stabilizing fluctuations in domestic output and employment, and would support domestic countercyclical policies, as prominent Keynesians such as James Meade (1955) argued. At the time, this presumption was also shared by monetarists such as Milton Friedman (1953) and Harry Johnson (1972), who were not macro fine-tuners but who wanted domestic monetary independence in order to better secure the domestic price level. Whatever policy a central bank chose, both groups believed a flexible exchange rate would depreciate smoothly if the bank pursued easy money, and appreciate smoothly if the bank pursued tight money. (Because economists had very little experience —except for Canada—with floating exchange rates in the 1950s and 1960s, the great volatility in generally floating exchange rates after 1971 was unanticipated.)

Thus, in the 1960s, Mundell I's "optimum currency areas" appealed both to monetarists and Keynesians, although for somewhat different reasons. As such, it became enormously influential as the analytical basis for open-economy macroeconomics, and for scholarly doubts as to whether Western Europe, with its diverse national economies and relatively immobile labor forces, was ready for a one-size-fits-all monetary policy.

In the 1990s the outstanding scholarly skeptic of the European Monetary Union (EMU) was Barry Eichengreen, whose many articles (with several co-authors) were consolidated in his book *European Monetary Unification* (1997). He acknowledged Mundell I's influence thus:

The theory of optimum currency areas, initiated by Robert Mundell (1961), is the organizing framework for the analysis. In Mundell's paradigm, policymakers balance the saving in transactions costs from the creation of a single money against the consequences of diminished policy autonomy. The diminution of autonomy follows from the loss of the exchange rate and of an independent monetary policy as instruments of adjustment. That loss will be more costly when macroeconomic shocks are more "asymmetric" (for present purposes, more region- or country-specific), when monetary policy is a more powerful instrument for offsetting them, and when other adjustment mechanisms like relative wages and labor mobility are less effective. (1–2)

Eichengreen and Bayoumi (1993) had used an elaborate econometric analysis to show this asymmetry: "A strong distinction emerges between the supply shocks affecting the countries at the center of the European Community—Germany, France, the Netherlands, and Denmark—and the very different supply shocks affecting other EC members—the United Kingdom, Italy, Spain, Portugal, Ireland and Greece" (Eichengreen 1997, 104).

Even today, the British press and many economists still argue that a one-size-fits-all monetary policy run from Frankfurt can't be optimal for both continental Europe and Britain. After all, aren't business cycle conditions in Britain sufficiently different to warrant a separate countercyclical response from an independent Bank of England? But whether sophisticated or not, writers in this vein, such as Martin Feldstein (2000) in "Europe Can't Handle the Euro," are definitely in thrall to the earlier Mundell.

On these conventional doctrinal grounds, some might object that the East Asian countries, with or without Japan, are too diverse to constitute an optimum currency area. In his book *Yen Bloc*, C. H. Kwan (2001) states Mundell I's 1961 argument this way:

The major cost associated with monetary integration arises from the abandonment of an independent monetary policy. By fixing its exchange rate to other members of the monetary union, a country joining a union automatically gives up control over its own monetary policy. When its economy is subject to an external shock, it has no choice but to follow the common monetary policy of the monetary union. Countries with similar economic structures can respond to a common shock with a common monetary policy, and the costs of giving up an independent monetary policy are relatively small. In contrast, countries with heterogeneous economic structures require different policy responses to common shocks, and the costs of sharing a common monetary policy are relatively large. For example, Japan and Korea, both oil importers, can respond to a surge in oil prices with same monetary policy. This, however, would not apply to Japan and Indonesia, where the latter is an oil exporter. . . .

In view of the diversity among these countries, it is unlikely that Japan, the Asian NIEs [newly industrialized economies, Hong Kong, Korea, Singapore, and Thailand], the ASEAN countries [Indonesia, Malaysia, Philippines, and Thailand], and China together and at once form an optimum currency area. Higher income countries such as those of the Asian NIEs have trade structures similar to that of Japan while lower income countries such as lower-income members of ASEAN and China have trade structures very different from that of Japan. (11–12)

Based on Mundell's 1961 analysis, Kwan concludes that East Asia collectively is not an optimal currency area, and that exchange rates within the East Asian area should remain flexible, albeit with the yen getting a higher weight in the currency baskets (see chapter 1). Kwan's careful analysis is in line with the plentiful literature showing that pre-euro continental Europe was not an optimum currency area either.

7.2   Mundell II and International Risk Sharing

In a not-much-later incarnation, Robert Mundell (1973a), now called Mundell II, jettisoned his earlier presumption of stationary expectations to focus on how future exchange rate uncertainty could disrupt the capital market by inhibiting international portfolio diversification and risk sharing. At a 1970 conference in Madrid on optimum currency areas, he presented two prescient papers on the advantages of common currencies. Perhaps in part because the conference proceedings were not published until 1973, these papers have been overshadowed by his 1960s masterpieces.

The first of these later papers, "Uncommon Arguments for Common Currencies" (1973a), is of great intrinsic interest because very early it emphasized the forward-looking nature of the foreign exchange market, which was then worked out in more analytical detail by his students: see, for example, Frenkel and Mussa (1980). As such, it counters the earlier Mundell idea that asymmetric shocks—those where an unexpected disturbance to national output affects one country differently from another—undermine the case for a common currency.

Instead, Mundell II showed how having a common currency across countries can mitigate such shocks by better reserve pooling and portfolio diversification. Under a common currency, a country suffering an adverse shock can better share the loss with a trading partner because both countries hold claims on each other's output. In contrast, under a flexible exchange rate inhibiting portfolio diversification, a country facing an adverse shock and devaluing finds that its domestic currency assets buy less on world markets. The cost of the shock is now more bottled up in the country where the shock originated. As Mundell II puts it,

A harvest failure, strikes, or war, in one of the countries causes a loss of real income, but the use of a common currency (or foreign exchange reserves) allows the country to run down its currency holdings and cushion the impact of the loss, drawing on the resources of the other country until the cost of the adjustment has been efficiently spread over the future. If, on the other hand, the two countries use separate monies with flexible exchange rates, the whole loss has to be borne alone; the common currency cannot serve as a shock absorber for the nation as a whole except insofar as the dumping of inconvertible currencies on foreign markets attracts a speculative capital inflow in favor of the depreciating currency. (115)

Mundell II's second Madrid paper, "A Plan for a European Currency" (1973b), makes clear his early enthusiasm for the great European experiment. With the formal advent of the euro on January 1, 1999, the forward-looking Mundell of the Madrid papers "triumphed" over his earlier Keynesian incarnation as the originator of the theory of optimum currency areas. But he is intellectual father to both sides of the debate.

7.3   Mundell I with and without Capital Controls

To better pin down the theorizing that differentiates Mundell I from Mundell II, Paul De Grauwe (2003) points out that Mundell I implicitly assumed an efficient foreign exchange market when exchange rates were flexible, whereas Mundell II implicitly assumed an efficient international capital (financial) market once exchange rates were convincingly fixed. Let us consider De Grauwe's distinction more closely by first considering Mundell I's implicit assumption of an efficient foreign exchange market.

In the 1950s into the 1960s, the major industrial countries (except for the United States) and most developing countries all had capital controls that limited the possibilities for international risk sharing. Thus it is not so surprising that Mundell I ignored international portfolio diversification as a way of dealing with asymmetric shocks. So let us reconsider what Mundell I must have meant by foreign exchange market efficiency, first in the presence of capital controls (Mundell IA), and then in the absence of capital controls (Mundell IB).

Mundell IA

Once a country imposes capital controls, a free float becomes impossible. Potentially important market makers such as commercial banks are constrained from taking open foreign exchange positions. Without private "stabilizing" speculators, the government, as normally represented by its central bank, must make the market and determine the exchange rate through official intervention. With capital controls in place, China is a recent case in point. The People's Bank of China has opted to keep its exchange rate constant at 8.28 yuan/U.S. dollar from 1994 into 2004, although in the 1980s and early 1990s it had opted to change its official rate with discrete controlled devaluations. But as long as capital controls remain, the Chinese government correctly recognizes that it must manage the exchange rate.

What do capital controls imply for Mundell I's presumption that exchange rate flexibility could be used to offset asymmetric shocks? According to his standard textbook paradigm, where aggregate demand shifts from the goods produced by country B to those produced by country A, the depreciation of B's currency (appreciation of A's) must be guided and implemented by a least one of the two governments. Through official interventions, B's government could nudge its exchange rate continually downward or devalue in one discrete jump if it could judge the "right" amount. Whatever its choice, efficiency in the foreign exchange market would depend on the government's intervening in the foreign exchanges to implement its fine-tuning strategy for maintaining domestic output and employment.

But even this is an oversimplification. A's government would have to agree to let its currency appreciate according to the decision of B's government to intervene. The symmetrical way Mundell set up his paradigm—the increase in the demand for the goods of country A being equal to the fall in demand for the goods of country B—could make this agreement easy to come by if both countries start off with balanced full employment before the shock occurs. Nevertheless, an intergovernmental coordination problem lurks behind the presumption of exchange market efficiency.

However, intergovernmental cooperation would be much more difficult to come by if there were, say, a fall in demand or negative supply shock in country B *without* any corresponding increase in demand in country A. Then, A's government would be reluctant to have its currency appreciate and so import deflationary pressure. The matter would be aggravated if both economies started with underemployment. Then a devaluation by country B to stimulate its exports into A's markets would have a beggar-thy-neighbor effect on country A and could lead to retaliation rather than cooperation. So much for exchange market efficiency.

The problem of intergovernmental cooperation and which governments should be responsible for setting exchange rates was not, and typically is not, addressed in the OCA literature. The national monies of a series of anonymous countries are assumed to be similar, with no one being dominant, and spillover effects are ignored. In practice, however, potential intergovernmental conflicts in setting exchange rates are largely resolved by choosing one national money to be the dominant key currency. Then other countries in the OCA peg to, or simply define their exchange rates in terms of, the key currency: they do not attempt to adjust their other bilateral exchange rates directly. In Europe from the 1970s into the 1990s, before the advent of the euro, the German mark was the key currency to which the other Europeans governments pegged, or at least tracked, with varying degrees of success.

But for the German mark (or any other currency) to fulfill this central role, three important conditions had to be satisfied. First, the German authorities, with the large and then very robust German economy behind them, passively allowed other countries, often inadvertently, to fix or adjust their exchange rates against the mark without Germany's retaliating. Within Europe, Germany had no separate foreign exchange objectives of its own. Second, with no exchange rate target, the German authorities could follow an independent domestic monetary policy for stabilizing the purchasing power of the mark in terms of real goods and services. Thus other European countries could treat the mark as a nominal anchor for their own price levels. Third, by the beginning of the 1970s, Germany no longer had capital controls, although most other European countries retained them into the late 1980s. Other European countries could comfortably hold some of their reserves in internationally liquid mark assets to facilitate stabilizing their exchange rates in terms of marks.

Mundell 1B

What about the efficiency of the foreign exchange market among countries closely connected in trade with flexible (or insecurely pegged) exchange rates if they all abandon capital controls, as was largely true in Europe after the Single European Act of 1987? Paradoxically, without capital controls, efficiency could well decline. There are two related problems (McKinnon 2004):

• *Excess volatility* from nonstationary expectations. Unlike the economic doctrines of the 1960s suggested, we now know that a floating exchange rate behaves like a forward-looking asset price (Frenkel and Mussa 1980). Agents in the foreign exchange markets continually look forward to what governments might do, or economic shocks that could happen, and often get it wrong. Because movements in market exchange rates can be much greater than in the underlying fundamentals, such volatility would be particularly disruptive among nations closely integrated in trade.

• *Aggravated currency asymmetry.* The need for a strong key currency for managing mutually consistent official interventions under capital controls, as discussed under Mundell 1A, is clear enough. However, this asymmetry among national monies would not disappear when capital controls are removed. The private foreign exchange markets would still select one central money to be the vehicle currency through which foreign exchange trading takes place, and to be the dominant invoice currency in trade in goods and services as well as for international capital flows. This key currency would then become definitive money for measuring foreign exchange risk seen by the weaker currencies on its periphery.

Under floating (necessarily without capital controls), these problems interact: excess volatility aggravates currency asymmetry. On the periphery of the key currency, however, debtor countries are affected differently than are creditors.

International debtors find that they cannot borrow in their own currencies—the problem dubbed "original sin" by Eichengreen and Hausmann (1999) (see chapter 1 of this book). As their debts cumulate in terms of the central money, they fear a possible speculative attack taking the form of capital flight and forced devaluation that could bankrupt domestic financial institutions. In order to forestall capital flight, they must then run with positive risk premiums in their interest rates. In Europe from the late 1980s into the mid-1990s, many economies around Germany—particularly Greece, Italy, Portugal, and Spain—had higher and more volatile interest rates than did Germany itself.

In mirror-image contrast, international creditor countries find that they cannot *lend* in their own currencies: the problem I called "conflicted virtue" in the introduction and in chapter 5. Outside of Europe, the rest of the world is on a dollar standard: the U.S. dollar is the dominant key currency. And the United States has exploited its central position by running current account deficits for more than 20 years. Thus an increasing number of countries, particularly in East Asia and most notably Japan and China, have become dollar creditors. But instead of building up claims on foreigners in their own currencies, they build up liquid dollar assets, which become an overhang in the face of any possible appreciation of the domestic currency. In order to forestall such massive conversions from the privately held domestic dollar assets into the national currency that would impose unwanted appreciation and deflation, they must run with *negative risk premiums* in their domestic currency interest rates. Not only do their central banks intervene heavily to buy dollar assets, but they are forced to continually cut domestic interest rates below international levels. The result could be a zero-interest-rate liquidity trap that renders the domestic central bank helpless to stem the deflation (for the case of Japan, see chapter 4).

A further consequence of this currency asymmetry is that the international capital market among countries that would otherwise constitute an OCA is impaired. As in East Asia before the currency crashes of 1997–1998, large interest differentials between debtor and creditor economies worsened moral hazard in banks and other financial institutions (see chapter 6). Japan as the region's main creditor had deposit interest rates close to zero. In contrast, heavy borrowing by Indonesia, Korea, Malaysia, Philippines, and Thailand in the early 1990s resulted in unsustainable buildups of short-term foreign currency indebtedness and high risk premiums in their interest rates. This interest differential aggravated the latent moral hazard in poorly regulated banks and other financial institutions, and induced them to overborrow in foreign exchange. (see chapter 6). (China wisely used capital controls to prevent international overborrowing.)

The upshot is that smooth adjustment under flexible exchange rates, as implicit in the efficient foreign exchange market imagined under Mundell I to support independent and differing national countercyclical policies among countries closely integrated in foreign trade, is an illusion. This is not to deny that exchange rate adjustment occurs when governments follow different macroeconomic policies. But movements in exchange rates, sometimes guided by official interventions and capital controls, are likely to be erratic at best, and may have serious negative spillover effects for unwary trading partners as disturbances are transmitted from one country to another.

7.4 Updating Mundell II's Risk-Sharing Argument: An Axiomatic Approach

Let us now analyze Mundell II's arguments that, in the absence of capital controls, credibly fixed exchange rates would encourage international portfolio diversification to share the risks from asymmetric economic shocks. When exchange rates are fixed, is Mundell II's implicit assumption of efficiency in the international capital market tenable?

In developing his formal model of risk sharing, Mundell II made no distinction among money, bonds, or equities. Indeed, his analysis proceeded as if the only financial asset in each of his two countries were some form of domestic money. And he considered risks arising only on the supply side, where supply shocks affected national outputs differentially. In this context, his risk-sharing argument is deceptively simple. However, if money is the only financial asset (no bonds or stocks), then risk sharing between two countries will still be incomplete, even when they are joined together by a fixed exchange rate. So we need to bring other forms of financial assets into the analysis.

First, however, let us ask whether a fully efficient international capital market with full international risk across regions or countries is ever possible. Purely theoretically, one could imagine an Arrow-Debreu economy with a complete set of cross-country contingent claims, that is, insurance contracts all specified in real terms. If country A experienced a shortfall in output from some specified natural disaster, then it would be compensated by country B, and vice versa. Similarly, if output increased fortuitously in country A, a contract would exist requiring its surplus to be shared with country B.

However, an Arrow-Debreu economy can't actually exist. Besides being inhibited by overwhelming complexity in writing such contingent contracts, any contracts actually negotiated would be fraught with moral hazard. In Arrow-Debreu insurance contracts, the precise meaning of every state of nature requiring a particular payoff would have to be prespecified. Otherwise, one country's citizens could slacken their work effort, reduce output, and try to exercise some (false) insurance claim on a neighbor.

Be that as it may, suppose these problems of complexity and moral hazard in writing such forward contracts could be overcome, that is, suppose a full set of such state-contingent claims on real resources were actually negotiable both within the domestic economy and for trade with neighboring countries. Then money itself would become redundant. There would be no point in carrying cash reserves forward, whether in domestic or foreign currency. Nominal exchange rate arrangements, whether fixed or floating, wouldn't matter. In this complete Arrow-Debreu model, all current and future "real" resources would have been fully bartered in the first negotiating period. Thus, full capital market efficiency in the Arrow-Debreu sense is a chimera.

In practice, the set of relevant financial assets available for sharing risk among nations is much more restricted. So let us proceed more inductively by restricting the analysis of international capital market efficiency to those kinds of noncontingent financial assets—bonds or stocks—that we observe in an integrated national financial market and that could potentially be traded internationally. To be realistic, the theoretical modeling must satisfy the following four restrictive axioms:

• *No claims contingent on states of nature.* Although private insurance markets exist at the microeconomic level, individual risks can largely be diversified away. Not so at the macroeconomic level when large supply shocks affect nations differentially.

• *All financial assets are nominal.* The intrinsic value of financial assets is only monetary. There are no "real" bonds indexed against inflation or tied to particular commodities.

• *Many goods.* Consumer and producer decisions span a wide variety of goods and services.

• *Stable fiat money.* Each national monetary authority strives, perhaps imperfectly, to stabilize the purchasing power of the national money in terms of a broad basket of consumable goods and services.

These axioms are symbiotically related. As per Arrow-Debreu, stable money isn't necessary if there are "real" bonds or a complete set of contingent claims on real output. We know, however, that in practice virtually no state-contingent bonds are actually issued and that there are no private issues of indexed "real" bonds; thus the first two axioms hold.

In contrast, broad markets for *noncontingent* nominal bonds, those whose payoffs are fixed in monetary terms without regard to states of nature, exist on a large scale, but only because buyers and sellers believe that the national monetary authority is committed to stable money. A holder of a fixed-interest nominal bond needs to be reassured ex ante that the bond's purchasing power at face value is known, at least approximately. Otherwise, broad and deep long-term bond markets can't exist.

Finally, theoretical models of open economies with just one, two, or even three goods naturally violate the third axiom. In such models, often with just one domestic good, the whole domestic price level jumps substantially in response to some supply shock or exchange rate change. But that is inconsistent with having a determinate demand for each domestic money. People will only hold the national money if there exists a broad diversity of goods produced at home or abroad whose average price defines its purchasing power, which the national government strives to stabilize (see the fourth axiom). In a literal one-good economy, people would have no incentive to hold money. More generally, in undiversified economies with just one or two specialty outputs, the authorities would target the price level in terms of a broad basket of importables.

Of course, the stable money axiom doesn't rule out the possibility of major changes in the *relative* prices of particular goods or (limited) exchange rate flexibility. But large discrete changes, or jumps, in the domestic purchasing powers of national monies are ruled out.

With these restrictive axioms limiting the potential array of financial assets available (in comparison to the unlimited array in an Arrow-Debreu economy), what can be said about the possibilities for international risk sharing against supply-side shocks under alternative exchange rate arrangements? To simplify the discussion, consider capital markets as if they contained just one financial asset at a time. Let us consider money, bonds, and equities in turn.

Money and Official Exchange Reserves

In the face of imperfectly correlated supply shocks, Mundell II's original (1973b) theoretical argument, where money is the only financial asset, still holds. If two countries share a common currency, Mundell II reasoned, the full stock of privately held money in country A could be exercised as a claim on country B's resources should A be hit with a sudden decrease in output, and vice versa. Under flexible exchange rates, however, privately held money in one country would not be an automatic claim on the resources of the other, at least not at par value.

In the absence of a common currency, however, governments could only ensure that the stock of privately held national domestic money would be fully convertible into foreign money at a fixed exchange rate by holding official exchange reserves, possibly on a large scale. Then, issues of national money would be fully backed by foreign currency assets, as when one of them adopts a currency board.

But even if the domestic stock of narrow money, say, M1, is fully backed by foreign exchange, it is simply not large enough for substantial international risk sharing. Ching and Devereux (2000a) derive this result more formally in the context of a model where money is the only asset in countries forming a monetary union. But it is intuitively obvious. The amount of narrow money individual firms and households wish to hold as domestic means of payment is small relative to their total stocks of bonds and equities and small even relative to the economy's total stock of short-term liquidity. In the United States the stock of M1, currency and checking accounts, is less than one-fifth of the total stock of private-sector liquid assets (M3), which also includes money market mutual funds, commercial paper, and short-term Treasury securities. And, narrower still, the U.S. monetary base—currency and commercial bank reserves held with the Federal Reserve—is less than half of M1, or only 5.4 percent of U.S. GNP.

Clearly, for financially sophisticated economies, a broader range of financial assets as vehicles for international portfolio diversification needs to be considered.

International Diversification in Bond Holdings and the Principal Agent Problem

Let us define fixed-interest bonds very broadly to include virtually all financial assets that are neither narrow money (M1) nor equities. (Because their payoffs are variable, common stocks might be considered natural financial instruments for international risk sharing; I consider them separately later.) Hence, the definition of a bond includes time deposits in banks and commercial bills as well as mortgages and corporate or government bonds.

A key aspect of the bond market is that most of the bonds held by households are not primary claims on ultimate borrowers. Instead, most of these claims are indirect claims intermediated through financial institutions—banks, money market funds, pension funds, insurance companies, and so on. And the size of these holdings is extremely large relative to narrow money. Under this broad definition, direct and indirect bond holdings are about 200 percent of GNP in the United States. Thus, if different regions (nations) suffer from asymmetrical supply shocks to regional outputs, default risk in the bond market is potentially substantial.

In principle, however, much of this default risk can be shared through portfolio diversification across diverse regions. Indeed, in regions with just one or two products, uninhibited portfolio diversification by financial intermediaries representing domestic households would result in *most* of their bond-type domestic assets being claims on foreigners. But this need not result in a net outflow of capital. Foreigners would happily own most of the domestic bonds issued by any (small) single-product economy as long as the rest of their portfolios were well diversified outside of the economy in question, thus leading to compensating capital inflows. Indeed, the less diversified the local economy is in its output structure, the more it has to gain in risk reduction by being plugged into a broader bond market encompassing economies very different from itself.

However, there is trouble in this potential paradise. Unless these diverse economic units are securely connected by a common money, exchange rate uncertainty (currency risk) will inhibit the international sharing of default risks.

At first glance, it is not obvious why the presence of currency risk should inhibit international bond portfolio diversification by households and nonfinancial firms. On the contrary, isn't currency risk just another risk that domestic bond holders could diversify away? Indeed, if the future purchasing powers of various national monies were (symmetrically) uncertain, wouldn't risk-averse households in any one country be given additional incentive (beyond their concern for limiting default risks) to hold bonds denominated in foreign currencies?

But for international or even domestic risk diversification, households could hardly manage their own bond portfolios directly. They would lose all the well-known economies of scale, including expert information collection, associated with risk pooling by financial intermediaries. Thus a household would prefer to hold general claims with a fixed monetary payout that are, say, an indirect claim on a bank's loan portfolio. Similarly, households seeking insurance would prefer an annuity fixed in nominal terms rather than directly holding some pro rata share of the insurance company's assets.

Reflecting this strong empirical regularity, let us assume that all the holdings of bonds by households are indirect, that is, general claims on a financial intermediary. Then the resulting *principal-agent problem* becomes the key to understanding why we observe so little international diversification in bond holdings across countries not joined by a common money. The household (the principal) cannot possibly monitor or control the individual investment decisions made by the financial intermediary (the agent). So it buys claims on the financial intermediary, such as a certificate of deposit, whose face value is fixed in monetary terms. And in noninflationary economies where foreign monies do not circulate in parallel with the domestic one, the simplest way of establishing the face value of the payout, that is, the intermediary's liability, is to choose the domestic money as the sole numéraire. Thus *the face value of bonds held by domestic nationals the world over is largely denominated in the local (national) currency.*

But households' demands to have their noncontingent assets fixed in the national currency poses problems for the financial intermediaries, who must eventually make good on these claims. Within the limited domain defined by the domestic currency, risk-averse intermediaries can freely strive to diversify their own asset portfolios to limit default risk. However, if they cross currency boundaries in making loans, they find themselves in the uncomfortable position of having liabilities with fixed face values denominated in the domestic currency when some of their assets are denominated in foreign currencies. Thus, in the foreign exchange markets, if the domestic currency were suddenly to appreciate against all others, such a financial intermediary could easily go bankrupt. So, various regulatory rules of thumb, especially for banks, force them to hedge in order to limit the extent of their net foreign exchange exposure. Although short-term foreign exchange risk can be hedged at some cost, long-term holdings of foreign bonds are less amenable to being hedged. A British retirement pension fund with long-term annuity liabilities fixed in sterling would lean strongly to holding fixed-yield sterling assets at a similar long term to maturity.

The bottom line is that the presence of currency risk inhibits international portfolio diversification in bond markets designed to share default risks arising out of asymmetric supply shocks. Insofar as smallish regions are more specialized in what they produce and thus subject to idiosyncratic output shocks, they would suffer more from allowing their exchange rates to float. Under flexible exchange rates, the inability of a small region to diversify away its default risks could lead to a risk premium in the whole structure of its domestic interest rates.

But much of the literature on optimum currency areas has argued just the opposite. Besides Kenen (1969), other authors have questioned whether regions or nations that are highly specialized in production should give up control over their own monetary policy and exchange rates. As Jeffrey Frankel (1999) has pointed out, Barry Eichengreen (1992) and Paul Krugman (1993) have gone one step further and worried that even a successful monetary and economic union might become less of an optimum currency area through time as its regions naturally become more specialized in what they produce. Eichengreen and Krugman point out that industrial production is now much more specialized across U.S. states than across European nation-states and that the latter will become more specialized as a result of the very success of European Economic Union. As reported by Frankel, Eichengreen and Krugman are essentially claiming that an economic entity might fail the criteria to be an OCA ex post, even if it had passed ex ante. Indeed, Krugman (1993) suggests that "theory and the experience of the United States suggest that EC regions will become increasingly specialized, and that as they become more specialized, they will become more vulnerable to region-specific shocks. Regions will, of course, be unable to respond with countercyclical monetary or exchange rate policy" (60).

Clearly, Eichengreen and Krugman were still in thrall to Mundell I's fine-tuning fallacy. But once risk sharing through portfolio diversification in bond holding is properly weighed, the case for a monetary union becomes even stronger as the constituent parts of the underlying economic union become more specialized in what they produce. Presumably, the productivity gain from greater regional specialization is one of the major benefits of having an economic cum monetary union in the first place.

Fortunately, we now have the example of the European Monetary Union (EMU) to show what happens when a country moves from floating or uncertainly fixed exchange rates to full monetary union. The great success of EMU was to move beyond an asymmetrical German mark zone to a common currency. Except for some differences in national banking regulations, EMU now comes close to the ideal of allowing unhindered portfolio diversification for international risk sharing. But systematically testing this proposition empirically is a major task far beyond the scope of this chapter. However, the great natural experiment—the abolition of 12 national currencies in Europe in favor of the euro on January 1, 1999—is very revealing.

Within Euroland, private euro-denominated bond issues grew explosively after that date. Overall euro bond issues in the first half of 1999 were 80 percent higher than a tabulation of all bond issues in the old legacy currencies for the first six months of 1998. Most strikingly, issues of euro-denominated *corporate* bonds were almost four times as high in 1999 as compared to 1998. Why the startling difference?

In the pre-euro regime, the German mark was king, the central or safe-haven European currency for the group. In effect, Europe was on a common monetary standard based on a key currency where other European countries tried, with some uncertainty, to maintain exchange rate stability against the mark. Thus, private corporations in European countries on Germany's financial periphery—such as Italy, Portugal, and Spain, which mainly issued bonds in lire, escudos, and pesetas, respectively—suffered currency risk relative to German issuers of mark-denominated bonds. The resulting risk premiums—higher interest rates, particularly at the longer term in these countries—kept finance short-term and largely bank-based. For example, in the early to mid-1990s, interest rates on bonds denominated in Italian lire were as much as 5 percentage points higher than those on bonds denominated in German marks.

After January 1, 1999, the extinction of these risky peripheral currencies allowed previously hobbled Italian, Portuguese, Spanish (and even French?) firms to lengthen the term structure of their debts by issuing euro-denominated bonds at much lower interest rates, now close to those paid by German firms, while escaping from the clutches of their bankers. European banks, in turn, are madly consolidating, although unfortunately only at the national level. Even highly indebted governments, albeit under the constraint of the Maastricht Agreement, can roll over their large government debts (now denominated in euros) at interest rates within half a percentage point or so of those paid by the German federal government.

The *demand* for longer-term euro-denominated bonds also increased. European insurance companies and pension funds as well as banks had been confined to keeping the bulk of their assets denominated in the home or domestic currency in order to match their domestic currency liabilities. But with the move to a common and, for the formerly peripheral countries, a stronger currency, these financial institutions became free to diversify and acquire euro-denominated assets on a Western Europe–wide basis from foreigners who are willing to sell euro-denominated bonds in the newly created market. Thus the term structure of corporate finance in Western Europe is being lengthened with the lower interest rates reflecting lowered overall portfolio risk.

In summary, in encouraging risk sharing through portfolio diversification in international bond markets, preliminary evidence from the Western European experiment suggests that on both the demand and supply sides a common currency may be considerably better than a common monetary standard based on a key currency. In middle and eastern Europe, countries now use the euro itself as a key currency for securing exchange stability. Although the greater price level stability and mutual exchange rate security from such a policy are still substantial, the full benefits of international bond-market diversification will have to wait until these countries accede to the EU and then to the euro.

Stock Markets and Home Bias

An enduring empirical puzzle in the finance literature is why owners of common stock appear to diversify much less internationally than what a proper risk-return trade-off based on the capital-asset pricing model (CAPM) would predict. Karen Lewis (1999) nicely reviews this empirical literature. But what is striking, at least to me, is how little emphasis has been given to currency risk per se in explaining home bias.

In computing historical means, variances, and covariances of returns to holding foreign stocks in comparison to U.S. stocks, authors typically translate everything into dollar terms at the exchange rate prevailing during the period over which the foreign returns were calculated. In these econometric studies (often quite elaborate), industry risks are thereby completely melded with exchange rate risks. However, this melding, although almost universal in the literature, is a mistake.

Absent currency risk *within* a country like the United States, the stock market ideally distributes capital across industries according to their expected returns and risks vis-à-vis the general market. Highly paid analysts specialize in particular industries to estimate the future risk and return of industry X against the general market and then disaggregate further to pick winning firms within that industry. In the absence of stock market bubbles and crashes, all this is well and good for increasing industrial efficiency.

Now take such a group of domestic industry specialists and broaden their range to study the same industries in a foreign country, with its own monetary regime, as well as those at home. In picking winners abroad compared to at home, exchange rate risk now tends to reduce the effective expertise of industry analysts. Noise is introduced into the information set within which they normally work because their profit projections have to be translated back into dollars through the uncertain exchange rate.

And this noise problem is not easily resolved by hiring foreign exchange specialists to project the future course of the exchange rate. Because a floating exchange rate between any pair of industrial economies approximates a random walk in the short and medium terms, the rate can't be predicted with any accuracy.

The upshot is that expert industry analysts and portfolio managers tend to be cautious and recommend, for any one industry, lesser holdings of those common stocks denominated in foreign currencies than in the domestic currency. In the aggregate across all industries, therefore, holdings of foreign stocks will be less than a purely mechanical application of an international CAPM model would project. This argument about loss of technical expertise is probably not the only reason for home bias in international equity holdings, but it is a leading candidate. It helps to explain why much of the investment in foreign stocks that does occur is in country funds: the Korea Fund, Thai Fund, India Fund, and so on. Instead of picking individual industry stocks, U.S. investors pick countries with more general (currency) risk characteristics. They show less concern for the character of individual stocks within the country fund in question.

Considering money, bonds, and equities together, what can we conclude about asset diversification to deal with asymmetric supply shocks across regions or countries? Clearly, under floating exchange rates, currency risk will undermine international risk sharing and diminish cross-holdings of all three financial assets. But even a credibly fixed exchange rate between any pair of countries will still leave a residual currency risk. Full asset diversification by risk-averse financial intermediaries with narrow profit margins will still be inhibited. Only a common money will convince financial intermediaries to diversify as freely across national boundaries as they do across regions in the same country—as seems to be implicit in Mundell II.

7.5   Aggregate Demand Shocks: A Further Taxonomy

Mundell I focused on asymmetric demand shocks and the need for countercyclical macroeconomic policies: "Suppose demand shifts from the products of country B to the products of country A ... with the need to allow an appreciation of B's currency to restrain aggregate demand in B—and a depreciation of A's currency to stimulate it in A" (Mundell 1961, 511). But under what circumstances are such asymmetrical demand shocks likely to occur?

Diversified Industrial Economies

Suppose A and B were highly diversified industrial economies, say, Germany and France, each producing thousands of goods with a huge overlap in product lines. Could consumer preferences suddenly shift in the way Mundell I implies? It is difficult to imagine that consumer preferences would suddenly shift en masse away from thousands of French goods in favor of thousands of German goods. The law of large numbers in product diversification would be overturned. One could, perhaps, imagine a narrower demand shift away from autos toward motorcycles, but this would not be particularly country-specific. Thus, for diversified economies, the need for exchange rate flexibility to offset volatility in consumer preferences is negligible.

Apart from pure shifts in consumer preferences, there is another kind of "demand" shock that economists, e.g., Harry Johnson (1972), used to believe would warrant an exchange rate adjustment. Suppose country A began to inflate aggregate demand so as to create incipient (or actual) inflation. An ongoing depreciation of A's currency could accommodate this to avoid a loss in A's international competitiveness while obviating the need for domestic disinflation and a possible rise in unemployment. But with the death of the Philips curve, we now know that such accommodation would violate the principle of time consistency in policymaking and simply lead to further instability. Unless the country in question has a chronic need for revenue from the inflation tax, better that it be forced to disinflate to maintain the exchange rate.

This dilemma, to disinflate or not to disinflate to maintain economic competitiveness with one's trading partners, only arises because countries have separate monetary regimes. Under a common currency, differential rates of inflation could not persist.

Undiversified Economies

Particularly for primary products producers with unstable terms of trade, the argument is often made (Kenen 1969) that countries retain exchange rate flexibility—to devalue when the terms of trade turn against the country—in order to ameliorate the resulting income fluctuations. But this view has several problems.

First, as described, tying the exchange rate to the fortunes of one or two primary products undermines private portfolio diversification and international risk sharing. Foreigners would not want to hold financial claims on the domestic economy if they knew the exchange rate was volatile. And this reluctance would make it difficult for domestic nationals to hold financial claims on foreigners without the economy as a whole running (an expensive) current account surplus, that is, allowing net capital flight.

Second, the liquidity value of the domestic money itself could be impaired. If only one product were produced domestically, say, coffee, and the purchasing power of domestic money were tied to the price of coffee, people would opt to hold foreign currencies for domestic transacting. In an economy producing one or two exports but importing a broad basket of goods of all kinds, the natural way of satisfying the stable money axiom is to peg the currency to that of a highly diversified trading partner. Otherwise workers would be reluctant to accept wages specified in term of domestic rather than foreign money.

The Endogeneity of the OCA Criteria

The presence of asynchronous demand shocks, or asynchronous income fluctuations more generally, could well diminish as trade integration increases. Of course, under a common currency, asynchronous demand shocks would be quite minor because of the disappearance of separate national monetary policies. As Jeffrey Frankel (1999, 24) puts it for nascent monetary unions, "The OCA criterion might be satisfied ex post even if not ex ante."

But short of adopting the rather draconian solution of forming a monetary union, as Frankel and Rose (1998) show, trade integration itself reduces the extent to which income fluctuations are uncorrelated, or asynchronous. For 21 industrial countries from 1959 to 1993, they first computed correlations of income changes between every pair of countries. They then regressed these correlation coefficients on a measure of trade integration for each pair. Across their 21 countries, higher trade linkages are associated with higher correlations in income fluctuations.

Asymmetric demand shocks across countries of the kind that so concerned Mundell I seem to be diminishing as globalization proceeds. But even with an efficient international capital market under fixed exchange rates, as envisaged in Mundell II, problems of macroeconomic control would still remain. In normal times, having portfolio diversification across countries would smooth consumption in the face of (regional) output shocks, and monetary union is a big boost to financial market integration so that financial flows within the union are normally stabilizing.

However, even a fairly efficient international capital market would not rule out local booms and busts, as in California's Silicon Valley boom from 1995 to 2000 and subsequent bust, or within Euroland as with Ireland's boom and (mini) bust. Indeed, as Paul De Grauwe (2003) points out, being hooked up to a larger capital market could exaggerate regional bubbles if capital markets were not fully efficient. Even here, however, *returning to separate currency regimes as under Mundell 1 would not solve this problem*. In the absence of capital controls, problems of moral hazard in capital flows crossing international currency boundaries leading to overborrowing can be more acute (see chapter 6) than if countries shared a common currency. This undue incentive to build up debts in foreign currencies was only too obvious in the East Asian boom before the great crisis of 1997–1998. Then, once the crash occurred, the resulting wave of domestic bankruptcies was exacerbated because most of the debts were denominated in foreign monies.

7.6   A Negative Summing Up

There are only two good reasons for any country *not* to be on a common currency regime or a common monetary standard with its trading partners. A common monetary standard is one of highly credible fixed exchange rates but where national monies remain in circulation. The late nineteenth-century gold standard is a good example.

First, a country could not participate in either a common currency regime or a common monetary standard if its own public finances were too weak. If its government needed to retain control over issuing its own currency in order to extract more monetary seigniorage from the financial system, possibly through inflation, than a common currency regime would permit, then no fixed exchange rate regime would be feasible or advisable. More subtly, by owning its own central bank, the government becomes the preferred borrower in the national capital markets. Because the government alone owns the means settlement on interest-bearing debt denominated in the domestic currency, it can float public debt at the lowest interest rates in the domestic capital market (McKinnon 1997). This preferred access to the domestic bond market also allows the national central bank to act as a lender-of-last-resort for domestic commercial banks.

For example, several Eastern and Middle European countries do not yet have sufficient fiscal and financial control domestically to allow them to give up their national central banks in order to join a broader monetary union. And, as Mario Nuti (2000) suggests, adopting a currency board may not be a satisfactory halfway house: the country loses control over its national central bank without gaining access to the discount window of the central bank for the broader monetary union.

Second, no sufficiently stable monetary standard exists in the rest of the world. Natural trading partners, by the OCA criteria, are themselves not stable in a monetary sense. The members of Euroland took several decades of intense bargaining over economic integration and mutual fiscal constraints before the stage was set for the European Central Bank to credibly issue a common currency. However, because the euro is now firmly established as a stable European monetary standard, the much smaller Eastern and Middle European countries now have more incentive to join it.

At the present time, the political will for full-scale economic and monetary integration with neighboring countries simply doesn't exist elsewhere. However, a less politically demanding common monetary standard based on a key currency might achieve much, although certainly not all, of the benefits of a common currency (McKinnon 1996). A successful common monetary standard requires two key interrelated conditions:

• A credible anchoring mechanism so that countries that attach themselves to the standard succeed in stabilizing the purchasing powers of their national monies.

• Close trading partners attach themselves convincingly to the same standard.

The gold standard's great advantage was that it was international. By the late 1870s most economies that were significant international traders had adopted it. Moreover, it provided a credible anchoring mechanism for national price levels until interrupted by World War I, in August 1914. This lack of persistent inflation and the gold standard's universality meant that exchange rates were credibly fixed and capital markets—particularly bond markets—were remarkably well integrated from the 1870s to 1914. The gold standard's great drawback, of course, was recurrent liquidity crises from runs on gold, and this was a principal reason for the Great Depression of the 1930s.

In the modern period, the U.S. dollar serves as a (quasi) monetary anchor for most countries outside of Europe. It has the great advantage over the nineteenth-century gold standard of being a fiat-managed currency and, in the modern period, not itself subject to runs or liquidity crises. However, the dollar standard has major drawbacks.

First, although informal pegging to the dollar is widespread in Asia, the Americas, and much of Africa in the short run (Calvo and Reinhart 2002), these exchange rate pegs are soft and lack credibility, particularly over the long term. In contrast, gold mint parities in the nineteenth century were highly credible on a long-term basis, although occasional short-term suspensions could occur. But it is the long-term credibility in exchange rate parities that was the key to the remarkable integration of capital (mainly bond) markets in the late nineteenth century (see chapter 8).

Second, the modern dollar standard is not universal enough in securing stable exchange rates. In the 1990s, when Argentina pegged strongly to the dollar, the other members of Mercosur did not. So even if one considered Mercosur to be an OCA, Argentina was upset by Brazil's large discrete devaluations and by Chile's allowing its currency to float downward. Similarly, in the increasingly integrated East Asian economies before the 1997 crisis, all countries except Japan had been informally pegged to the dollar. However, because of weak or nonexistent commitments to maintain their dollar exchange rates in the long run, they were all vulnerable to inadvertent beggar-thy-neighbor devaluations by the five crisis economies or by Japan itself. But the desire for a common monetary standard in East Asia remains strong. After the 1997–1998 crisis most East Asian countries resumed informal dollar pegging (McKinnon 2001a; and see chapter 1). Nevertheless, positive or negative risk premiums, resulting in large interest differentials, can only be eliminated by lengthening the terms to maturity over which these exchange rates are stable.

In conclusion, outside of Euroland and the drive for "euro-ization" in Middle and Eastern Europe, the best interim hope for a natural OCA such as East Asia is to recognize the inevitability of dollar predominance and work toward rationalizing the rules of the dollar standard game (McKinnon 1996, 2004). And to this issue we now turn in chapter 8.

8

Rationalizing the Dollar Standard in East Asia: Living with Conflicted Virtue

Chapters 1 through 7 identified the ways in which foreign exchange risk threatens the financial stability of the increasingly integrated East Asian economy. Without a common East Asian money, the problems associated with actual *and potential* exchange rate fluctuations become more acute as the integration of trade in goods and services proceeds. Because of the central role of the U.S. dollar in the world economy in general and in East Asia in particular, much of this exchange risk is measured by fluctuations of each Asian currency against the dollar.

Before the crisis of 1997–1998 five of the East Asian economies—Indonesia, Korea, Malaysia, Philippines, and Thailand—had borrowed heavily at short term in foreign currencies (largely dollars) and, without capital controls, were vulnerable to capital flight and contagious devaluations. As memories of the crash dim, a similar euphoric boom based on foreign borrowing is not outside the realm of possibility. For example, a populist government could once more dismantle prudential financial regulations and lean on banks to become more expansionary. An excessive buildup of foreign exchange *liabilities* could again be triggered—the overborrowing syndrome described in chapter 6. Alternatively, foreign lenders could again become too exuberant; in 2003, private capital flows into emerging markets generally were sharply higher (*Wall Street Journal*, January 23, 2004).

8.1 Conflicted Virtue Again

Today, however, East Asia's most pressing problem is the converse of the one in 1997–1998, as shown for Japan and China in chapters 4 and 5, respectively: an excess buildup of foreign exchange *assets*, resulting in conflicted virtue. Japan, Singapore, and Taiwan have had current account surpluses for more than two decades. Since 1995, China has had more modest current account surpluses, but the rapid internal buildup of a liquid dollar overhang has been compounded by huge inflows of foreign direct investment. Even the five former crisis economies are becoming creditors, at least at the margin. Since 1997 they have run with trade surpluses.

Table 8.1 shows the evolution from 1990 to 2003 of the current account surpluses of ten East Asian countries measured as shares of their respective GNPs. The upper panel shows Japan, Singapore, and Taiwan to be chronic surplus economies over the whole time frame. Even before the 1997–1998 crisis they had surpluses in part because they were net lenders to the others. The middle panel shows the crisis economies, Indonesia, Korea, Malaysia, Philippines, and Thailand, having large current account deficits before 1997, when they were borrowing heavily in world markets, and the shaded area shows their remarkable postcrash recovery and move to surpluses as they repaid their debts and accumulated liquid dollar assets. The third panel shows China with more variable current account surpluses, with a deficit in 1993 but no tendency toward larger surpluses (as a share of GNP) in recent years.

Finally, at the bottom of table 8.1, the *sum* in U.S. dollar terms of the ten countries' current account surpluses is shown. For comparison, the current account deficits of the United States from 1990 to 2003 are on the last line of the table. In 2003 surplus national savings in the East Asian economies of about $270 billion, as represented by the sum of their current accounts, now covers about half of the huge U.S. current account and saving deficit of $542 billion. And because of the well-known gap in the international accounts, where the sum of the world's current account deficits exceeds that of its surpluses, the extent of this coverage could well be underestimated.

Table 8.2 shows the rise in official foreign exchange reserves (overwhelmingly in U.S. dollars) of the ten East Asian countries from 1990 to 2003. As shown in the shaded area, the only significant pause in reserve accumulation occurred in 1997 in the five crisis economies, with echo effects of the crisis in Japan, Singapore, and Taiwan. But from 1998 to 2003 all countries increased their dollar reserves, with particularly sharp increases in Japan, Taiwan, Korea, and China.

In what sense has this accumulation of official exchange reserves been excessive? In both private and official portfolios, the East Asian economies are now acquiring large stocks of dollar assets, most of them in highly liquid form. In chapters 4 and 5 we made rough esti-

Table 8.1
Comparison of East East and U.S. Current Account Surpluses, 1990–2003

	1990	1991	1992	1993	1994	1995	1996	1997	1998	1999	2000	2001	2002	Preliminary 2003
Percent of GDP														
Japan	1.44	1.96	2.96	3.01	2.71	2.10	1.40	2.24	3.01	2.55	2.51	2.12	2.82	3.05
Singapore	8.45	11.32	11.87	7.24	16.17	17.67	15.16	15.58	22.59	18.60	14.48	19.00	21.50	27.74
Taiwan	6.96	7.11	4.14	3.14	2.66	2.07	3.91	2.43	1.29	2.91	2.88	6.37	9.11	9.76
Indonesia	-2.61	-3.32	-2.00	-1.33	-1.58	-3.18	-3.37	-2.27	4.29	4.13	5.25	4.75	4.18	3.97
Korea	-0.79	-2.82	-1.25	0.29	-0.96	-1.74	-4.42	-1.71	12.73	6.03	2.65	1.93	1.28	1.89
Malaysia	-1.97	-8.51	-3.67	-4.46	-6.06	-9.71	-4.43	-5.92	13.19	15.92	9.41	8.28	7.58	12.11
Philippines	-6.08	-2.28	-1.89	-5.55	-4.60	-2.67	-4.77	-5.28	2.37	9.48	8.24	1.84	5.38	4.42
Thailand	-8.53	-7.71	-5.66	-5.09	-5.60	-8.07	-8.07	-2.00	12.73	10.13	7.60	5.40	6.05	5.78
China	3.13	3.32	1.36	-1.94	1.28	0.23	0.88	4.09	3.30	2.11	1.90	1.46	2.86	1.89
Hong Kong	—	—	—	—	—	—	—	—	2.68	7.50	5.51	7.54	10.82	9.93
Billions of U.S. Dollars														
Total East Asia current account surplus[a]	54.28	73.46	117.25	117.79	132.85	93.82	44.16	129.37	246.41	233.84	215.76	181.51	242.31	269.94
U.S. current account surplus	-78.96	3.69	-48.03	-81.95	-117.71	-105.19	-117.16	-127.68	-204.67	-290.87	-411.46	-393.74	-480.86	-541.70

Sources: International Monetary Fund, *International Financial Statistics*; Republic of China, Taiwan District, financial statistics, October 1994 and August 2000; International Institute of Finance, Inc., online database; *The Economist*, January 16 and January 23, 2004.
Notes: Shaded area shows recovery of crisis economies after 1997.
a. Current account surplus of Hong Kong is not included in the sum of East Asian countries between 1990 and 1997.

Table 8.2
Official Foreign Exchange Reserves in East Asia, 1990–2003 (billions of U.S. dollars)

	1990	1991	1992	1993	1994	1995	1996	1997	1998	1999	2000	2001	2002	Preliminary 2003
Japan	69.49	61.76	61.89	88.72	115.15	172.44	207.34	207.87	203.22	277.71	347.21	387.73	451.46	673.53
Singapore	27.53	33.93	39.66	48.07	57.89	68.35	76.49	70.88	74.42	76.30	79.69	74.85	81.37	96.30
Taiwan	72.44	82.41	82.31	83.57	92.45	90.31	88.04	83.50	90.34	106.20	106.74	122.21	161.66	206.60
Indonesia	7.35	9.15	10.18	10.99	11.82	13.31	17.82	16.09	22.40	26.25	28.28	27.05	30.75	33.80
Korea	14.46	13.31	16.64	19.70	25.03	31.93	33.24	19.71	51.96	73.70	95.86	102.49	120.81	150.30
Malaysia	9.33	10.42	16.78	26.81	24.89	22.95	26.16	20.01	24.73	29.67	28.63	29.59	33.28	44.00
Philippines	0.87	3.19	4.28	4.55	5.87	6.24	9.90	7.15	9.10	13.10	12.94	13.32	13.02	13.40
Thailand	13.25	17.29	20.01	24.08	28.88	35.46	37.19	25.70	28.43	33.80	31.93	32.35	38.04	40.20
China	28.59	42.66	19.44	21.20	51.62	73.58	105.03	139.89	144.96	154.68	165.57	212.17	286.41	403.25
Hong Kong	24.57	28.81	35.17	42.99	49.25	55.40	63.81	92.80	89.61	96.24	107.54	111.16	111.90	118.40
Total	267.88	302.92	306.37	370.67	462.85	569.96	665.01	683.60	739.17	887.65	1004.39	1112.90	1328.68	1779.78

Sources: International Monetary Fund, *International Financial Statistics*; Republic of China, Taiwan District, financial statistics, October 1994 and August 2000; *The Economist*, January 16 and January 23, 2004.
Note: Shaded area shows pause in reserve accumulation during the 1997 crisis.

mates of the total liquid dollar assets held privately and officially in Japan and China, respectively. But in 2002 and 2003 private stocks seem to be declining in most or all of these countries. Because of the clamor from foreigners for East Asian countries (now particularly China) to appreciate their currencies or let them float upward, nervous private holders are dishoarding their dollar assets in order to get back into the domestic currency. Worried about a possible loss in mercantile competitiveness and possible deflation from exchange appreciation (the syndrome of conflicted virtue), their governments then step in to buy these privately held dollar assets and add them to their official exchange reserves. So, in 2003 there was an explosive increase in official exchange reserves in excess of current account surpluses (table 8.3).

For Japan, China, Taiwan, and Korea, but not necessarily all East Asian countries, this table provides indirect evidence of the great shift in private portfolio preferences. From the end of 2002 to the end of 2003 the accumulation of official dollar reserves *exceeded* the current account surplus by about $90 billion in Japan, $90 billion in China, $16 billion in Taiwan, and $20 billion in Korea. Although conflicted virtue is now a potential problem within all the East Asian economies, it is more immediate in these four countries. Is there any way of relieving the upward pressure on the exchange rate to appreciate while still providing a sustainable flow of finance for an ongoing current account surplus?

The Singapore Solution

A fifth country, Singapore, is a seeming anomaly in dealing with conflicted virtue. A glance at table 8.1 indicates that this small island economy has had persistent current account surpluses that are much larger as a share of its GDP than any other country in the table. Since 1990 these current surpluses average about 15 percent of GDP and go to an amazing 21.5 percent in 2002 and 27–28 percent in 2003. Nevertheless, there has been no obvious excess reserve accumulation since 1990 or earlier. In comparison, growth in the official reserves held by the Monetary Authority of Singapore (MAS) have been quite modest. Table 8.3 shows that in 2002 the current account surplus was U.S.$18.7 billion while reserve accumulation was just U.S.$6.5 billion; in 2003 the surplus was U.S.$25.6 billion while official reserves increased by U.S.$14.9 billion. Unlike China and Japan, Singapore shows little evidence of domestic nationals rushing to unload their private U.S. dollar

Table 8.3
East Asia Current Account Surpluses and Changes in Official Reserves, 1991–2003 (billions of U.S. dollars)

	1991	1992	1993	1994	1995	1996	1997	1998	1999	2000	2001	2002	Preliminary 2003
Total East Asia[a]													
Reserve changes	35.04	3.46	64.30	92.18	107.11	95.05	18.59	55.57	148.48	116.74	108.51	215.79	451.10
Current account	73.46	117.25	117.79	132.85	93.82	44.16	129.37	246.41	233.84	215.76	181.51	242.31	269.94
Japan													
Reserve changes	−7.73	0.13	26.83	26.43	57.30	34.89	0.53	−4.65	74.49	69.50	40.52	63.73	222.07
Current account	68.20	112.57	131.64	130.26	111.04	65.79	96.81	118.75	114.60	119.66	87.80	112.45	132.00
China													
Reserve changes	14.07	−23.22	1.76	30.42	21.96	31.45	34.86	5.07	9.72	10.90	46.59	74.24	116.84
Current account	13.27	6.40	−11.61	6.91	1.62	7.24	36.96	31.47	21.12	20.52	17.40	35.42	25.54
Taiwan													
Reserve changes	9.96	−0.10	1.27	8.88	−2.14	−2.27	−4.54	6.84	15.86	0.54	15.47	39.45	44.94
Current account	12.47	8.55	7.04	6.50	5.47	10.92	7.05	3.44	8.38	8.91	17.92	25.68	28.80

Korea

Reserve changes	-1.15	3.33	3.06	5.33	6.90	1.31	-13.53	32.25	21.74	22.15	6.63	18.32	29.49
Current account	-8.32	-3.94	0.99	-3.87	-8.51	-23.01	-8.17	40.36	24.48	12.24	8.24	6.09	9.80

Singapore

Reserve changes	6.40	5.73	8.41	9.82	10.46	8.14	-5.61	3.53	1.89	3.38	-4.83	6.52	14.93
Current account	4.88	5.91	4.21	11.40	14.80	13.98	14.91	18.54	15.18	13.28	16.14	18.70	25.60

Sources: International Monetary Fund, *International Financial Statistics*; Republic of China, Taiwan District, financial statistics, October 1994 and August 2000; *The Economist*, January 16 and January 23, 2004.

Notes: Shaded area shows excess accumulation relative to current account surplus.

a. Current account surplus of Hong Kong is not included in the sum of East Asian countries between 1990 and 1997.

holdings in favor of Singapore dollars. The MAS has no trouble targeting its exchange rate against the U.S. dollar.

What makes Singapore different? In effect, the government national-
izes most of the flow of domestic private saving and controls the part
of it that is invested in claims on foreigners. All Singapore residents
have a high proportion of their wages or salaries, about 30 percent
over the years, deducted at the source into a defined contribution
pension scheme, the Provident Fund. People build up interest-bearing
claims within the fund denominated in Singapore dollars, but the government decides where and how the funds will be invested. A high
proportion is invested within the economy in residential building and
commercial enterprises, including the government-owned holding
company Temasek, which has a controlling interest in most Singapore
companies. Another substantial proportion is transferred to a government investment corporation, the GIC, for investing overseas. The GIC
then invests in a variety of different countries in fairly illiquid stocks
of equities, bonds, and commercial real estate. This is most unlike the
MAS's official exchange reserves, which are generally held in liquid
dollar assets such as U.S. Treasury bonds.

A second channel through which Singapore invests overseas is when
Temasek leans on Singapore companies to set up overseas subsidiaries
or plants—in effect outward foreign direct investment (FDI). Unlike
the GIC, these companies retain a controlling interest in their foreign
operations.

If the GIC's and Temasek companies' ordinary large outflow of overseas investment is insufficient to finance all of Singapore's enormous
current account surplus, then (incipient) upward pressure on the Singapore dollar could appear. The MAS would then intervene to buy
U.S. dollars, showing an increase in official reserves. But any untoward
or unusual buildup of official reserves by the MAS is then simply
transferred to the GIC to make further investments abroad. Consequently, the accounts of the MAS itself never show a large buildup of
official reserves that could be getting out of hand, and nervousness in
the foreign exchange markets regarding a forced or accidental appreciation of the Singapore dollar is minimized. Fortunately, Singapore's
economy is so small that foreign mercantilists are prepared to ignore
its proportionately huge current account surpluses. The U.S. Secretary
of the Treasury is unlikely to bother making a special point of Singapore's "unfair" trading practices while trying to talk the Singapore dollar up—ostensibly, but incorrectly—to reduce its trade surplus.

In summary, Singapore has avoided the worst of the syndrome of conflicted virtue by simply avoiding the buildup of a liquid dollar overhang in *private* hands. Instead, mainly illiquid overseas investments remain in government hands. That said, Singapore still has been unable to avoid running current account surpluses that could be too large, that is, too much saving is transferred abroad, for its long-run well-being. However, this may well reflect a pull from the United States as much as a push from Singapore.

But could other East Asian economies follow Singapore's lead in nationalizing, that is, having the government intermediate, the whole flow of international finance associated with their current account surpluses? The problem is the starting point for collecting domestic saving. Other governments don't generally have anything like a provident fund that forcibly collects most of domestic saving, which the government then directly allocates into foreign investments that it controls. Instead, the others are more normal market economies where most domestic financial saving is voluntary and flows through financial intermediaries, such as banks and insurance companies, whose allocation decisions are not controlled by the government. It is these private domestic intermediaries, as well as individuals and firms, that build up the overhang of liquid dollar claims on foreigners.

Moreover, these other economies don't have the advantage of being small. If a large economy like Japan or China were to set up a government-run overseas investment corporation for inducing a capital outflow that roughly matched the balance-of-payments surpluses from the rest of the accounts, such an institution would be highly visible. When such a public corporation bought substantial properties abroad, people would complain (possibly justifiably) that it was not being governed by the market and was subsidizing Japanese or Chinese mercantile interests. Thus most governments hold their official foreign exchange reserves in U.S. Treasury bonds or similar liquid instruments because of the general perception that such investments are market-neutral and do not impinge on the ordinary ebb and flow of private commerce. Perhaps it is no accident that Singapore's GIC is a very secretive organization: outsiders have little or no idea of the geographic scope of its investments or the forms they take. Also unclear is how much the Singapore government leans on Temasek-controlled companies to invest abroad.

That said for Singapore, governments in several of the other East Asian economies may well wind up *inadvertently* nationalizing much of the flow of international finance. That is, suppose nervousness regarding a potential exchange appreciation continues, with large conversions of privately held dollar assets into their domestic currencies, as shown so vividly in 2003 for Japan, China, Taiwan, and Korea in the last column of table 8.3. The endgame is that domestic private holders of dollar assets completely dishoard existing *stocks*, and official exchange reserves rise commensurately as governments intervene to prevent their currencies from appreciating. But there is still a *flow* problem. Ongoing current account surpluses, adjusted for inflows or outflows of foreign direct investment (see chapter 5), will require governments to buy dollar assets continually.

Notice that this last assessment of the endgame is relatively optimistic. It assumes that there are no further inflows of hot money from foreigners speculating on currency appreciation. Even with effective controls on new capital inflows, the financing of the current account surplus will devolve completely onto each national government with continuing large buildups of official reserves.

Is floating the exchange rate a solution? Unfortunately, a country with a chronic current account surplus and the inability to lend in its own currency cannot meaningfully float its currency, even in the absence of capital controls. Because of the reticence of private wealth owners to buy and hold claims in foreign currencies (conflicted virtue), any attempt to float would lead to an indefinite upward spiral in the exchange rate. In order to prevent deflation, the government would eventually be forced back into the market to buy dollars and stabilize the exchange rate. Notice that the exchange rate appreciation itself will have no predictable effect on the current account surplus (McKinnon and Ohno 1997). Then, through its buildup of official exchange reserves, the government once more would find itself to be the sole international financial intermediary for the current account surplus.

Jettisoning the Dollar?

Could this excess accumulation of official dollar reserves, a seemingly low-yield investment, be somehow resolved by jettisoning the U.S. dollar as the de facto key currency in the region? To secure mutual exchange rate stability, or at least avoid inadvertent beggar-thy-neighbor devaluations, or appreciations putting upward pressure on others to appreciate, could East Asian countries negotiate a dollar-free agreement among themselves? A common East Asian currency comes immediately to mind. However, full monetary and fiscal integration in the European style, leading to an Asian version of the euro, is not feasible politically. Although East Asia is potentially an optimum currency area (see chapter 7), it has no supernational government equivalent to the European Union (EU) to harmonize fiscal and commercial rules.

But is some looser arrangement for mutual exchange rate stabilization, where all East Asian countries are treated symmetrically and separate national monies continue to circulate, still possible? Chapter 7 investigated the pros and cons of such arrangements and concluded that having a symmetrical agreement to stabilize exchange rates, however desirable politically, is simply not feasible economically. I propounded an *impossibility theorem*: without first defining a common anchor for national price levels, viable exchange rate agreements—whether bilateral or multilateral—are impossible to sustain because they would leave the common price level indeterminate. In the absence of some commodity standard such as gold or silver (palm oil?), one national currency must be selected as the unambiguous anchor. Then, if the remaining members all subordinate their monetary policies to support interventions to keep their exchange rates stable against this anchor currency, a measure of mutual exchange stability can be achieved.

Of course, the country chosen as the anchor must have a track record of keeping its own price level stable. And given the inherent asymmetry of the situation, where only the anchor country could conduct an independent monetary policy, the other members would need to be confident that the center country would continue to maintain price stability in the future. Before the advent of the euro, when various European countries attempted to set mutual parities for exchange rates, Germany with its hard mark naturally played this central anchoring role. But these asymmetrical exchange rate arrangements in Europe were uncomfortably accident-prone. Like the world dollar standard today, the old European Monetary System (EMS) of the 1980s into the mid-1990s had a strong central money with a financially fragile periphery: countries like Italy, Spain, Portugal, and Greece. Currency attacks took the form of a rush out of lire, pesetas, escudos, drachmas, and so on, into German marks.

Unfortunately, East Asia has no natural anchor country. Japan, with the region's largest economy, is mired in deflation with its zero-interest-rate trap. As described in chapters 3 and 4, Japanese domestic monetary policy is essentially broken, and Japan itself is in need of an outside anchor against ongoing deflationary expectations. The yen is surprisingly little used as a currency of invoice in East Asian trade (see chapter 1). China is still a developing country with immature domestic financial markets and residual capital controls that make the renminbi impractical as an international reserve currency. And the other East Asian countries are simply too small for the anchor position. In short, agreeing on any one country to be the anchor would be difficult to negotiate, and the resulting political and economic asymmetries would be hard for the peripheral countries to accept.

Another approach to reducing the region's dependence on the U.S. dollar is to introduce basket pegging, where smaller East Asian governments give more weight to the yen and euro in setting their exchange rates (Williamson 2000) or to have a more elaborate regional basket currency arrangement (Ogawa and Ito 2002). At the microeconomic level, chapter 1 showed how basket pegging would introduce more uncertainty for private traders trying to construct their own hedges by forward contracting. Here, at the macroeconomic level, it suffices to note that all these trade-weighted baskets aim to stabilize relative "real" exchange rates among trading partners but leave open the question of how the nominal price level in each country (or the group) would be determined. The issue of a common nominal anchor is not discussed or incorporated.

So willy-nilly, we come back to the institutional reality of the dollar standard with its common nominal anchor (see chapter 1). However, can new rules for the dollar standard game, with old ones better understood, reduce foreign exchange risk? To overcome financial fragility, what should be the key objectives of a reformed East Asian dollar standard?

8.2   Reform Objectives

In sketching new rules for individual East Asian countries, note that such rules may only be desirable, or even feasible, if other trading partners in East Asia are on the same foreign exchange regime. For example, it could be dangerous for any one small East Asian country to commit to a long-run dollar parity for its exchange rate if its close trading partners did not also do so. Thus, in interpreting the feasibility and desirability of the reform objectives sketched here, the maintained hypothesis is that all the major players in the increasingly close-knit East Asian economies have the same overall objectives and agree to abide by a common set of rules. But first consider the reform's overall objectives:

• Greater *long-run* exchange rate security in dollar exchange rates among all East Asian economies including Japan

• A common and highly credible monetary anchor against the risk of devaluation and *inflation* in debtor economies, and against the risk of appreciation and *deflation* in Japan, China, and other emerging creditor countries

• Mutual understanding of more appropriate policies for regulating banks and international capital flows

A more formal collective agreement to stabilize mutual exchange rates by pegging to the dollar would help Japan overcome its prolonged economic slump and relieve pressure on China to appreciate the renminbi. The expectation of ongoing deflation in Japan is now so ingrained that a major international program for ending the threat of yen appreciation and ongoing internal deflation must be seriously considered, perhaps with the explicit cooperation of the United States (McKinnon and Ohno 1997; and see chapter 3). A fixed yen/dollar parity has greater stabilizing power as a nominal anchor if the effective dollar area is larger rather than smaller. And tethering the yen would make it easier for China and the smaller East Asian economies to resist appreciation. The long-term threat of repeated appreciations of the renminbi could force China down a deflationary path similar to Japan's of the 1980s and 1990s.

A second, incidental, consequence would be a better alignment of interest rates—smaller interest differentials between debtors and creditors within East Asia. In particular, if Japan's zero-interest-rate liquidity trap is sprung by eliminating the negative risk premium in Japanese interest rates (see chapter 4), speculative hedge funds would no longer be attracted to the yen carry trade. The need for draconian regulation of banks and other financial institutions to prevent undue foreign exchange exposure, either overborrowing or overlending, would be lessened. The "margin of temptation" for borrowers (see chapter 6) —banks and firms in debtor economies—to build up unhedged, and perhaps unhedgeable, foreign currency liabilities would be reduced. However, to prevent undue financial risk taking in some emerging-market countries, capital controls (as in China) might still be necessary.

A third consequence would be the dampening or elimination of the intra–East Asian business cycle generated from fluctuations in the yen/dollar rate (see chapter 2). However, even a reformed East Asian dollar standard would remain vulnerable to worldwide financial disturbances, particularly those associated with the United States itself.

A fourth consequence would be to help lengthen the term structure of domestic finance within the developing countries of East Asia, that is, to reduce original sin in the sense discussed in the introduction and in chapter 1. A credible lengthening of the term to maturity of exchange rate commitments would help with the development of a longer-term domestic bond market.

The Restoration Rule and Regressive Expectations

In comparing "good fixes" for floating to "bad fixes" for exchange rates in chapter 6, our short-run analysis proceeded without specifying the term structure of interest rates and exchange rate expectations into the more distant future. In common with the literature on the subject, we focused on the incentives to overborrow *before* any speculative attack. Moreover, also in common with the literature, the exchange rate obligations of the authorities *after* a (successful) attack were not specified. In a model that had only one term to maturity, we defined a good fix ex ante to be one where any peripheral country maintained nominal exchange rate stability and purchasing power parity against the center country's currency.

However, implicit in the ideal of a good fix is that it is sustainable in the more distant future. Even if a surprise speculative attack upsets the fixed-rate system in the short run, the macroeconomic fundamentals—fiscal strength, the size of the domestic financial system, and the determination of the authorities—would still allow the economy to recover its nominal exchange rate and price level equilibrium in the long run. If such a favorable long-run expectation could be sustained, the fundamental loss of confidence in their currencies that the five Asian countries experienced in late 1997 and early 1998 could have been limited.

The behavior of countries operating under the international gold standard before 1914 is instructive. In the face of a liquidity crisis, a country would sometimes resort to gold devices: it would raise the buying price for gold or interfere with its exportation. This amounted to a minor, albeit temporary, suspension of its traditional gold parity. In more major crises, including wars, a few outright suspensions for some months or years occurred. After any suspension and devaluation, however, the gold standard generally succeeded in having countries return to their traditional mint parities. The resulting long-run stability in exchange rates helped anchor the common price level and long-term interest rates. In early 1914, exchange rates, wholesale prices, and interest rates in the industrial countries were virtually the same as they had been in the late 1870s.

This gave the pre-1914 gold standard great long-run resilience. After any short-run crisis that forced the partial or complete suspension of a gold parity, the country in question was obliged to return to its traditional parity as soon as practicable (Bordo and Kydland 1995). I have dubbed this unwritten obligation of the classical gold standard "the restoration rule" (McKinnon 1996, ch. 2). Even when a currency crisis undermined the government's ability to sustain convertibility in the near term, exchange rate expectations remained regressive with respect to the country's traditional gold parity. Because of the restoration rule, long-term interest rates showed little volatility by modern standards (McKinnon and Ohno 1997), and, without significant financial risk, their levels also remained low: about 3 percent in the United Kingdom and 4 percent in the United States. The international long-term bond market was large and vigorous, and was the main vehicle for transferring capital to what were then developing countries.

For the pre-1914 gold standard, Charles Goodhart and P. J. R. Delargy (1998) studied how high-growth debtor countries on the periphery of Britain responded to speculative attacks. Their sample included Austria, Argentina, Australia, Italy, and the United States (which experienced several attacks). They conclude,

The onset and initial context of the Asian crisis, involving an interaction between a toppling investment boom and a febrile banking system, should not have been surprising. From an historical point of view, it was depressingly familiar. Moreover, it will happen again and again. Much of the pattern is, probably, an inherent feature of development.

What, however, differed from our pre-1914 crises and the Asian crisis was the international monetary regime and the consequential implications for post-crisis monetary conditions in the affected countries. Confidence in the maintenance of the gold standard, pre-1914, led to stabilizing mean-reverting expectations, and hence a rapid restoration of gold reserves, liquidity, and low interest rates alongside the maintenance of continued price stability. In the main case in our pre-1914 sample where there was no such confidence (Argentina), pressures on the exchange rate were eased by a (debt) moratorium, allowing a sharply improving trade balance to bring about the needed monetary expansion. (298)

The parallel for a restored East Asian dollar standard is quite clear. Each central bank sets its long-run monetary policy to be consistent with maintaining a "traditional" exchange rate against the dollar, which amounts to having the same long-run rate of price inflation (optimally zero) in its producer price index as in the United States and in the other dollar bloc countries of East Asia. In the short run, the exchange rate need not stay precisely at its parity rate. Depending on each country's situation, some kind of band with harder or softer edges is appropriate.

Traditionally, the advantages of a restoration rule have been discussed in the context of a country suffering a liquidity crisis with (temporary) capital flight into an external foreign exchange asset—into gold in the nineteenth century in all countries, but it could apply to emerging-market debtors with capital flight into dollars in the twentieth and twenty-first centuries. Although the government is forced to suspend temporarily its dollar parity as exchange reserves are depleted after an attack, such a rule would inform the market what its future exchange rate policy will be. For a debtor economy in crisis, this forward-looking information on the intent to return to its traditional parity would limit increases in domestic interest rates *and* the short-run depreciation of its currency, either or both of which could bankrupt many domestic firms and financial institutions. After the attack, the regressive expectation of gradual exchange appreciation attracts foreign capital back into the domestic currency at lower short-term interest rates; this could leave longer rates relatively undisturbed because foreign creditors have more assurance that private foreign debts could eventually be repaid.

While all this is well and good and still valid for many debtor economies, the new millennium is shaping up quite differently. As huge U.S. current account deficits continue to flood the world with dollar liquidity (table 8.1), more and more countries must tend toward current account surpluses and the buildup of potentially excess liquid dollar assets: the problem of conflicted virtue. Table 8.1 shows that all ten East Asian economies have had current account surpluses since 1997, but such surpluses are beginning to show up in such unlikely places as India and Brazil, poor emerging markets that one would first think should be absorbing capital net rather than being net lenders. So, as more countries become international creditors that cannot lend in their own currencies, currency crises will increasingly take the form of a run *into* their domestic currencies rather than out of them.

However, for these potentially crisis-prone creditor countries, the restoration rule can still be very useful. Suppose an East Asian country starts with an exchange rate close to purchasing power parity with the United States and with its neighboring dollar bloc countries. Now suppose a currency "attack" that takes the form of a run into the domestic currency, as in the case of Japan (see chapters 3 and 4) and China (see chapter 5). To prevent deflation, maintaining a constant exchange rate is the first-best strategy, as China has managed from 1994 to 2004 with 8.28 yuan/dollar.

But if the pressure is great enough and capital controls are weak or absent, the government may become unwilling to keep expanding the domestic money supply or keep reducing domestic interest rates sufficiently to avoid appreciation. Then, in such unusual circumstances, the embattled government could suspend its dollar parity and let its currency jump, that is, float discretely upward. But the other side of the restoration rule would then come into play. The promise would be to gradually drive the exchange rate back down to its old parity when the dust settles. Again, regressive expectations would take hold, but this time the market would expect the currency to depreciate gradually back to parity.

Nudging the exchange rate gradually down toward its traditional parity would have the great advantages of keeping domestic short-term interest rates higher (from the principle of open interest parity) and limiting the deflationary pressure from what turns out to be just a temporary appreciation. Postattack, domestic nationals would stop dishoarding and become willing to reaccumulate dollar assets, thus taking the pressure off increases in official exchange reserves. In contrast, if the government were to lose control altogether and allow its currency to appreciate unidirectionally—whether by floating or continually repegging—with no restoration, domestic interest rates would be bid down toward zero with no private holding of dollar assets. The result would be the liquidity trap in the context of a falling domestic price level, as Japan has experienced (see chapters 3 and 4).

However, the credibility of any commitment to an exchange parity in the long term, and the restoration rule that goes with it, is less if that nation alone adopts it. When a group of countries closely integrated in foreign trade, as in East Asia, agree to this gold standard convention, the credibility of any one country adhering to it increases. Then if country A comes under attack and is forced to temporarily suspend its parity exchange rate, any currency appreciation (depreciation) is more likely to be seen as temporary. Contagion with neighboring countries will be limited because markets will know that countries B, C, and D will not suspend just because A was inadvertently forced to. With an unchanging bloc of neighbors with fixed exchange rates, country A can then more easily retrieve its precrisis exchange rate—another virtuous circle. But the virtuous circle could be strengthened further if the International Monetary Fund, rather than pushing countries into unrestricted floating, were to recognize the positive neighborhood effects from a postattack restoration rule.

8.3   The United States: Is Benign Neglect Enough?

So far, this book has focused on what the East Asian economies themselves should, or should not, do. But East Asia, and much of the rest of the world, uses the U.S. dollar as an outside key currency. For a common dollar-based monetary standard in East Asia to work satisfactorily, is it sufficient for the United States to passively ignore what is going on?

The classic international facilitating role of a key currency country (McKinnon 1993b; 1996) can be summarized by the following three rules:

1. Leave the domestic U.S. capital market open so that foreigners, whether private or government, are free to hold liquid dollar assets or borrow in dollars without restraint.

2. Do not target the dollar's exchange rate against other national monies. Stay passive as foreign governments freely choose their exchange rates against the dollar—and thus, incidentally, determine a consistent set of cross exchange rates with each other.

3. Conduct an independent national monetary policy so as to stabilize the purchasing power of the dollar over a broad basket of internationally tradable goods and services.

Rules 1 and 2 facilitate the dollar's central role as a vehicle currency for clearing international payments among commercial banks while allowing foreign central banks to intervene freely to target their exchange rates against the dollar and thus establish a consistent set of cross exchange rates with each other. On the other hand, if the U.S. government has foreign exchange objectives of its own, this consistency is lost and conflict in official exchange rate objectives becomes possible. Because foreigners can transact freely in dollar assets against their own currencies or those of third parties, privately held dollar balances and official dollar exchange reserves—largely U.S. Treasury bonds—are a vital source of international liquidity.

But this international facilitating role of the dollar only works well if the dollar's purchasing power over a broad basket of internationally tradable goods is expected to remain stable, as per rule 3. Then the international demand for liquid but stable-valued dollar assets is high and grows naturally with the growth of the world economy.

However, rule 3 means much more. The dollar becomes a natural nominal anchor for the price levels of other countries that peg to the dollar, as the East Asian dollar bloc does (see chapter 1). Then, countries with trade surpluses become reluctant for their currencies to appreciate against the dollar because of the internal deflationary threat, as illustrated in tables 8.2 and 8.3, by the huge buildup from 1990 to 2003 of dollar exchange reserves in East Asia.

So far, nothing I have said indicates that the United States is misbehaving. Insofar as it follows rules 1, 2, and 3, the United States has played the dollar standard game passively and correctly, with its valuable facilitating role in the world economy. Indeed, these three rules define the classic role of benign neglect (of the rest of the world) by the center country. Against this, however, aberrant U.S. behavior has worsened the syndrome of conflicted virtue in East Asia in two important respects.

First, by pressuring Japan from the 1980s into the mid-1990s to appreciate the yen (see chapter 3), and then in the new millennium suggesting that China should become more "flexible" and let the renminbi float upward (see chapter 5), the United States clearly violates rule 2. The effect is to destabilize portfolio preferences within these two large economies and make runs out of dollars into their currencies more likely; then contagious runs in the other smaller East Asian economies are possible. That said, U.S. policy improved after April 1995, when the then U.S. Secretary of the Treasury, Robert Rubin, announced a new strong dollar policy and forswore continual efforts to talk the dollar down against the yen or other currencies with the attendant threat of trade sanctions. Worryingly, this strong dollar policy has frayed with the current concern over China's huge bilateral trade surpluses with the United States.

Second, the United States has reversed the normal role of a key currency country from being a dominant international creditor into being the dominant international debtor. Historically, a national money gets established because a large trading country's open national capital markets become a vehicle for investing funds abroad. After the Napoleonic wars, Britain in the nineteenth century evolved into an international creditor simultaneously with the City of London's developing first the institutions of discounting commercial bills, then an international bond market at longer term, followed by facilities for floating new equity issues. By the end of the nineteenth century almost half of British national saving was being invested abroad, and sterling had become the world's key currency. In addition to borrowing, foreigners deposited or bought bonds in London, making the sterling-gold–based capital market the most important international financial intermediary.

After World War II all other industrial countries had exchange controls on making international payments. Unscathed by the war, the United States alone had a broad and deep national capital market and a saving surplus. The dollar quickly became the international money, and the United States ran large current account surpluses until the end of the 1960s. It became the great international creditor by lending at long term to the rest of the world.

But in the 1950s and 1960s, when the United States was not running a current account deficit, how was international dollar liquidity provided to the rest of the world? How could foreign governments rebuild their official dollar exchange reserves and private foreigners rebuild their stocks of liquid dollar assets? Under the Bretton Woods regime of (fairly) safely fixed exchange rates, huge long-term capital outflows—including foreign direct investment, official foreign aid, and U.S. purchases of a wide variety of other relatively illiquid foreign assets—exceeded the U.S. current account surplus. This gap was then mainly covered by a flow of fairly short-term capital into the United States: foreigners built up their stocks of dollar bank accounts in New York, U.S. Treasury bills and bonds, and so on. The United States acted as a giant international financial intermediary by lending long, in excess of its current account surplus, and borrowing short. This allowed foreigners to build up their stocks' dollar liquidity in line with their rapid postwar economic growth (Despres, Kindleberger, and Salant 1966).

But the last two and half decades have told a different story. While still a net international creditor, the United States began to run large current account and fiscal deficits in the 1980s and very large current account deficits from the mid-1990s to the present. In 2004, U.S. net debts to foreigners approach $4 trillion, or about one-third of America's huge GNP. So far, however, this has not undermined the key currency role of the dollar in the international economy in general or in the East Asian economy in particular. Apparently, the economies of scale and positive network effects of having a single international money have become so strong that they preempt displacement. Over the past decade, the success of the U.S. Federal Reserve Bank in keeping the U.S. price level stable, combined with the expectation that it will remain stable (as reflected in low interest rates), has quelled uneasiness about rising fiscal and trade deficits. Because of its status as the world's central money, the United States alone can go deeply into debt in terms of its own currency, thus being immune to a currency attack in the mode of less developed debtor economies with original sin (see chapter 1). Without inflating, the United States alone can cover its large fiscal deficits by virtually unlimited foreign borrowing, a "virtuous" circle of a sort.

However, this historically very unusual current account deficit of the key currency country is forcing other countries to run increasingly large current account surpluses, at least collectively. This is most evident in East Asia where, in 2004, all ten countries are running surpluses on current account. But it is hardly a sensible free choice for countries that are still developing, and whose per capita incomes are quite low relative to those of the United States, to be net lenders to the United States at the low rates of interest available on U.S. Treasury bonds. In this brave new world, the underlying U.S. failure to save, together with its current account deficit, seems to be the forcing variable.

The current degenerate form of the dollar standard has trapped the East Asian countries into running large current account surpluses, with the attendant syndrome of conflicted virtue. There is pressure on them to appreciate their exchange rates against the dollar, but any appreciation (dollar devaluation) won't correct either the U.S. saving deficiency or East Asian current account surpluses. However, sharp appreciation could throw the foreign creditors of the United States in East Asia and elsewhere into deflationary spirals. They are indeed trapped.

Agreeing to mutually fixed exchange rates with the dollar, and thus with each other, seems at this juncture to be the least uncomfortable way of living within the trap. This won't change current East Asian current account surpluses, but it will avoid deflation and a slowdown in economic growth. If done with some fanfare through a collective East Asian agreement that makes the fixed exchange rate regime more credible, portfolio preferences could be better stabilized. Short of going to the Singapore solution of nationalizing the main flow of domestic saving and overseas investment, private financial and nonfinancial firms as well as individuals could become more willing to accumulate dollar balances as the counterpart of East Asia's current account surpluses.

However, springing the trap itself depends on a sea change in U.S. behavior rather than on anything the East Asians might do. To end its current account deficits, the United States needs both to encourage greater domestic private saving and to end the lack of saving by the federal government. Because of their unduly easy access to international credit over the course of several decades, U.S. households and the federal government have learned to live in a financially profligate manner. Weaning them away from this financial profligacy will be difficult.

But one aspect of the current "equilibrium" in international trade and financial flows that makes most Americans, including even some in the federal government, very uneasy, is the industrial consequences of the trade deficit. Transferring foreign saving to the United States in real terms means that U.S. exports of goods and services must contract as imports increase. So far, the contraction in U.S. manufacturing employment has borne the brunt of this adjustment. But now that more and more service activities have become internationally tradable, outsourcing of service jobs, even some relatively high-end ones, is becoming commonplace.

In contrast, if U.S. domestic saving and investment are brought into balance so that the current account deficit goes to zero, there would be no net loss of high-tech jobs, and U.S. technological leadership would be more easily maintained. True, the rise of new industrial competitors like China in the new millennium, as with Japan earlier, would always create problems of industrial adjustment in the United States. Some tradables industries would prosper while others would fall into decline. But there needs to be no net decline in the manufacturing base.

Instead, by having a net saving deficiency in the U.S. economy covered by heavy foreign borrowing, the resulting large current account deficit forces a net contraction in U.S. tradable activities and a much more wrenching hollowing out of U.S. manufacturing and tradables service industries.

The conceptual problem here, however, is to get the American people and politicians to connect deindustrialization with their saving deficiency. It is all too easy politically to associate the large net influx of imports with foreigners' manipulating their exchange rates and otherwise engaging in unfair trading practices. But neither exchange rate changes nor U.S. protectionism will correct the net trade deficit and the saving deficit that lies behind it.

However, if the United States does see the light—that it is in its own best long-run interest to save more privately and that the federal government should run with fiscal surpluses rather than deficits with a better balance in foreign trade—then the East Asian countries would be incidental beneficiaries. As their current account surpluses declined, their problems with conflicted virtue would be greatly mitigated.

Notes

Introduction

1. The renminbi ("people's currency") is the official currency of the People's Republic of China. It is issued by the monetary authority People's Bank of China. The base unit of the renminbi is the yuan. The currency name *reminbi* should not be confused with the base unit name *yuan*.

Chapter 1

1. Before the 1990s, China's official exchange rate against the dollar was often changed, and different rates existed for commercial transactions. Only the official exchange rate is reported in figure 1.1, but the foreign exchange market has been unified since 1994.

2. The difference between the price level for traded and nontraded goods (the Balassa-Samuelson effect) is only significant for Hong Kong and Korea.

3. In developing countries fiscal and monetary discipline are closely linked because the domestic bond markets are underdeveloped. With restricted access to domestic and international bond markets, printing money is the common means to finance public expenditure unless revenue from traditional taxes is substantial. A fixed exchange rate deprives the government of the inflation tax as revenue because undue monetary expansion would depreciate the domestic currency. Fiscal discipline is the only way to ensure the exchange rate's stability (Chin and Miller 1998).

4. As the leading currency of the European currency system, representing the euro since January 1, 1999.

5. It can be argued that the Swiss franc is not an arbitrary numéraire with respect to the German mark because the exchange rates of both currencies move in parallel to the U.S. dollar (Hernández and Montiel 2003, 37–39). However, since the German mark does not play a significant role in the currency basket of the East Asian countries and since the Swiss franc moves more independently of the yen and the dollar, we can neglect this point.

6. Previous tests did not yield any evidence of a cointegrating vector between the four exchange rates.

7. A more comprehensive model, which aggregates the three subperiods into one model and distinguishes the three subperiods by dummy variables, leads by and large to the

same results. We report the results for the three isolated subperiods because the respective R^2 give additional information about the goodness-of-fit for every single subperiod.

8. In the comprehensive model, which distinguishes the precrisis and postcrisis period by dummy variables, the coefficients diverge only slightly from the results for the three independent regressions as reported in tables 1.3, 1.4, and 1.5.

9. These countries are free floaters against the U.S. dollar, but not necessarily against other currencies. For instance, before January 1999, Germany was a member of the European Monetary System, which implied a stabilization of its exchange rate against other EMU currencies. Also, Switzerland might tend to reduce exchange rate volatility against the euro (Schnabl 2003).

Chapter 2

1. ROW trade is dominated by the European countries.

2. External financing is assumed to be more expensive than internal financing because external creditors face higher costs to obtain profits. While the domestic enterprise knows the profit of an FDI project, the outside creditor faces higher costs to acquire the information about the "true" return.

3. The EA_1 real growth rate (y_{EA_1}) is calculated as the weighted average of the real growth rates of eight ($k = 8$) smaller East Asian countries by the formula

$$y_{EA_{1t}} = \sum_{i=1}^{8} y_{it} \frac{Y_{it}}{\sum_{i=1}^{8} Y_{it}}$$

Y_i is the nominal GDP of country i in terms of the U.S. dollar, and y_i is the real GDP growth rate of country i.

4. For most countries the Augmented Dickey-Fuller test does not reject the null hypothesis of a unit root. Yet we view this acceptance as due to the low power of the test for our very short sample period.

5. The coefficients of the current and previous periods are added to get a long-run exchange rate multiplier, which is more fully explained later.

6. In reality, Japanese growth is not exogenous but strongly dependent on EA_1 growth. But because the main goal of this chapter is to describe the EA_1 business cycle, we treat Japanese growth as exogenous.

7. Although not captured in our sample (1980–2001), the downturn in U.S. high tech industries in 2001–2002 did strongly affect the smaller East Asian economies, particularly Korea, Taiwan, and Singapore.

8. We don't have any reasonable explanation for the significantly negative impact of Chinese real growth on Philippine real growth.

Chapter 3

We thank Rishi Goyal of Stanford University for his research assistance. Akiyoshi Horiuchi of the University of Tokyo, and Kunio Okina and Hiroshi Fujuki of the Bank of Japan, made helpful comments, although they may not agree with our main argument.

1. *OECD Economic Outlook*, December 1999, 226.

2. *New York Times*, July 30, 1998.

3. Because of a strong Balassa-Samuelson effect since the early 1950s, Japan's consumer price index has risen strongly relative to its wholesale price index. Nevertheless, in computing PPP exchange rates that balance international competitiveness at the factory gate, we believe that comparing wholesale price indexes (the producer price index in the United States) between the two countries is appropriate.

4. When applied to financially open industrial economies that would otherwise be stable, this elasticities approach for correcting a trade imbalance is misplaced (Komiya 1994; McKinnon and Ohno 1997, ch. 6). Instead, the persistent current account imbalance between the two countries reflects Japan's saving surplus on the one hand and abnormally low U.S. saving on the other.

5. In episodes of particularly sharp yen appreciations, the Bank of Japan typically responds by cutting short-term interest rates in order to dampen the yen's upward momentum. When Japan's short rates are already close to zero, this avenue may be pretty limited. In general, when researchers fit short-run reaction functions of the Bank of Japan for setting its discount rate, short-run exchange rate smoothing is an important objective (Cargill, Hutchison, and Ito 1997; Ueda 1992; 1995; Yoshino and Yoshimura 1995).

6. This new agreement could encompass several major currencies, including the euro (McKinnon 1996). But including the euro is not a pressing need: there is no "syndrome of an ever-higher euro." Moreover, Euroland is a huge, semiautonomous monetary area that is not greatly affected by fluctuations in the euro/U.S. dollar exchange rate.

7. Further calls for inflation beyond this (Itoh 1998; Krugman 1998; Meltzer 1998, etc.) are unwarranted.

Chapter 4

We are grateful to Andrew Coleman, Dale Henderson, and the participants of the symposium on Japan's Lost Decade: Origins, Consequences and Prospects for Recovery, held at the University of Michigan in March 2002, for helpful comments. The International Centre for the Study of East Asian Development, Kitakyushu, Japan, provided generous financial support.

1. Structural reforms are needed to raise Japan's long-term trend growth rate and its real return on capital. However, our argument is that such reforms are not central to addressing the current problems of deflation and macroeconomic instability in the economy.

2. This fear of an ever-higher yen was central in the earlier work of McKinnon and Ohno (1997; 2001).

3. Critics of the Bank of Japan argue that it is able to reinflate the economy even at zero short rates. But their formal models, such as the ones discussed in Krugman (1998) and Svensson (2001), do not show how the Bank of Japan would be able to reinflate the economy (or depreciate the exchange rate) when short-term interest rates are trapped at zero.

4. Note that φ must depend upon the existence of ongoing exchange rate volatility or on the possibility of a change in the exchange rate. If neither is present, there is no foreign exchange risk.

5. See Lane and Milesi-Ferretti (2001, fig. 11).

6. They assume that, on average or in steady state, $q = 0$, where q is the (log of) real exchange rate.

7. According to the International Monetary Fund's financial survey, domestic credit amounted to nearly $15 trillion in 2000.

8. See Goyal (2001).

9. See Bank of Japan, *Economic Statistics Annual*.

10. Japan ran a current account surplus in 1999, so a fall in its net foreign asset position in 1999 may appear puzzling. The fall is explained by a sharp increase in portfolio liabilities in 1999 associated with an inflow of foreign funds into the Japanese stock market and an increase in stock prices.

11. Average interest rates on new loans and discounts have fallen from more than 3.5 percent before 1995 to less than 2 percent since 1996.

12. See Bank of Japan (2001) for an explanation of how the composition of profit margin (the sum of the lending spread and the fund-raising spread) has changed after deregulation.

13. Data source: Bank of Japan, *Financial and Economic Statistics Monthly*.

Chapter 5

We thank Winnie Choi, Marcio Garcia, Nicholas Hope, Lawrence Lau, Michael Kurtz, Hong Qiao, Mark Spiegel, and Geng Xiao.

1. After one of McKinnon's seminars on Japan's problems, Marcio Garcia of the Pontifico Catholic University in Rio de Janeiro suggested that this creditor syndrome be called constructed virtue. We changed his terminology somewhat to conflicted virtue, which connotes more of a dilemma or impasse.

2. Notice that conflicted virtue would not arise in international creditor countries whose money is internationally accepted. Britain was the world's dominant creditor country in the nineteenth century, but sterling was used to denominate most British claims on foreigners, sometimes with gold clauses. Similarly, for two and half decades after World War II, the United States had large trade surpluses and was the world's biggest creditor country, but its claims on foreigners were largely in dollars.

3. We are grateful to Professor Lawrence Lau of Stanford University for this suggestion.

Chapter 6

1. However, a country risk premium could be introduced if there were expectations that effective capital controls (that could prevent exploitation of this arbitrage opportunity through administrative restrictions) would be imposed (Dooley and Isard 1980).

2. This "predictable" component will be covered in order for the bank to operate as an ongoing business, as it would otherwise not be able to cover its foreign currency liabil-

ities while the initial boom phase of the overborrowing syndrome was in progress and therefore enjoy the profits created for the banking sector during this period.

3. But the determinants of this margin of bank profitability in hedged and unhedged settings are worthy of separate investigation.

4. This chapter focuses on international overborrowing on the liabilities side of banks' balance sheets without looking at the parallel shift by households and firms of their non-interest-bearing domestic money into foreign exchange. Under a "bad fix" with ongoing inflation, this two-way flow of capital, where some entities deposit abroad while others overborrow, has been analyzed in McKinnon (1993a, ch. 9).

Chapter 7

Thanks to Paul De Grauwe and Klaus Desmet for helpful comments.

References

Asher, David L., and Robert H. Dugger. 2000. Could Japan's Financial Mount Fuji Blow Its Top? MIT Japan Program. Working Paper Series 00-01.

Bank of Japan. 2001. Developments in Profits and Balance Sheets of Japanese Banks in Fiscal 2000 and Banks' Management Tasks. *Bank of Japan Quarterly Bulletin*, November. ⟨http://www.boj.or.jp/en/ronbun/01/ron0108a.htm⟩.

———. 2002. Locational International Banking Statistics. ⟨http://www.boj.or.jp/en/⟩.

Bernanke, Ben. 2000. Japanese Monetary Policy: A Case of Self-Induced Paralysis? In *Japan's Financial Crisis and Its Parallels to U.S. Experience*, ed. Ryoichi Mikitani and Adam S. Posen, 149–166. Washington, D.C.: Institute for International Economics.

Bernanke, Ben, and Mark Gertler. 1989. Agency Costs, Net Worth, and Business Fluctuations. *American Economic Review* 79: 14–31.

Bordo, Michael, and Finn Kydland. 1995. The Gold Standard as a Rule: An Essay in Exploration. *Explorations in Economic History* 32: 423–464.

Buiter, Willem H. 1999. Optimal Currency Areas: Why Does the Exchange Rate Regime Matter? Scottish Economic Society Annual Lecture. Edinburgh. October.

Callen, Timothy, and Warwick J. McKibbin. 2001. Policies and Prospects in Japan and the Implications for the Asia-Pacific Region. International Monetary Fund Working Paper 01-131.

Calvo, Guillermo, and Carmen Reinhart. 2002. Fear of Floating. *Quarterly Journal of Economics* 117: 379–408.

Cargill, Thomas, Michael M. Hutchison, and Takatoshi Ito. 1997. *The Political Economy of Japanese Monetary Policy*. Cambridge, Mass.: MIT Press.

Chin, Daniel, and Preston Miller. 1998. Fixed Versus Floating Exchange Rates: A Dynamic General Equilibrium Analysis. *European Economic Review* 42: 1221–1249.

Ching, Stephen, and Michael B. Devereux. 2000a. Risk Sharing and the Theory of Optimal Currency Areas: A Re-examination of Mundell 1973. Hong Kong Institute for Monetary Research Working Paper 8-2000.

———. 2000b. Mundell Revisited: A Simple Approach to the Costs and Benefits of a Single Currency Area. Hong Kong Institute for Monetary Research Working Paper 9-2000.

Conley, John P., and William F. Maloney. 1995. Optimal Sequencing of Credible Reforms with Uncertain Outcomes. *Journal of Development Economics* 48 (October): 151–166.

De Grauwe, Paul. 2003. The Challenge of the Enlargement of Euroland. In *The Economics of EU Enlargement*, ed. F. Prausello. Milan: Franco Angelli.

Despres, Emile, Charles Kindleberger, and Walter Salant. 1966. The Dollar and World Liquidity: A Minority View. *The Economist*, February 5. Reprinted in Charles Kindleberger, *International Money: A Collection of Essays*, 42–52. London: Allen and Unwin.

Dominguez, Kathryn M., and Jeffrey A. Frankel. 1993. *Does Foreign Exchange Intervention Work?* Washington, D.C.: Institute for International Economics.

Dooley, Michael, and Peter Isard. 1980. Capital Controls, Political Risk and Deviations from Interest Parity. *Journal of Political Economy* 88 (2): 370–384.

Dornbusch, Rudiger, and Alejandro Werner. 1994. Mexico: Stabilization, Reform and No Growth. *Brookings Papers on Economic Activity* 1: 255–315.

The Economist. 2002. Koizumi's Depreciation Tour. January 17.

Eichengreen, Barry. 1992. *Should the Maastricht Treaty Be Saved?* Princeton Studies in International Finance 92-74. Princeton, N.J.: Princeton University Press.

———. 1997. *European Monetary Unification: Theory, Practice, and Analysis.* Cambridge, Mass.: MIT Press.

Eichengreen, Barry, and Tamim Bayoumi. 1993. Shocking Aspects of European Monetary Unification. In *Adjustment and Growth in the European Monetary Union*, ed. Francisco Torres and Francesco Giavazzi. New York: Cambridge University Press. Also in *European Monetary Unification: Theory, Practice, and Analysis*, ed. B. Eichengreen (1997).

Eichengreen, Barry, and Ricardo Hausmann. 1999. Exchange Rates and Financial Fragility. National Bureau of Economic Research Working Paper 7418.

Feldstein, Martin. 2000. Europe Can't Handle the Euro. *Wall Street Journal*, February 8.

Fidler, Stephen. 2001. Beijing Rules out Devaluation to Spur Exports. *Financial Times*, November 19.

Fischer, Stanley. 1999. On the Need for a Lender of Last Resort. Address to the American Economic Association, January 3.

———. 2001. Exchange Rate Regimes: Is the Bipolar View Correct? *Journal of Economic Perspectives* 15: 3–24.

Frankel, Jeffrey A. 1992. Measuring International Capital Mobility: A Review. *American Economic Review* 82 (2): 197–202.

———. 1999. *No Single Currency Regime Is Right for All Countries or at All Times.* Princeton Studies in International Finance 99-215. Princeton, N.J.: Princeton University Press.

Frankel, Jeffrey A., and Andrew K. Rose. 1998. The Endogeneity of the Optimum Currency Area Criteria. *Economic Journal* 108: 1009–1025.

Frankel, Jeffrey A., and Shang-Jin Wei. 1994. Yen Bloc or Dollar Bloc? Exchange Rate Policies in East Asian Economies. In *Macroeconomic Linkage: Savings, Exchange Rates, and Capital Flows*, ed. Takatoshi Ito and Anne Krueger, 295–329. Chicago: University of Chicago Press.

Frenkel, Jacob, and Michael Mussa. 1980. The Efficiency of the Foreign Exchange Market and Measures of Turbulence. *American Economic Review* 70 (2): 374–381.

Friedman, Milton. 1953. The Case for Flexible Exchange Rates. In *Essays in Positive Economics*, 157–203. Chicago: University of Chicago Press.

Froot, Kenneth A., and Jeremy C. Stein. 1991. Exchange Rates and Foreign Direct Investment: An Imperfect Capital Market Approach? *Quarterly Journal of Economics* 106: 1191–1217.

Fukao, Mitsuhiro. 2002. Japan's Lost Decade and Weaknesses in Its Corporate Governance Structure. Paper presented at the symposium Japan's Lost Decade: Origins, Consequences and Prospects for Recovery. University of Michigan. March.

Garber, Peter, and Mark P. Taylor. 1995. Sand in the Wheels of Foreign Exchange Markets: A Sceptical Note. *Economic Journal* 105 (428): 173–180.

Goodhart, Charles, and P. J. R. Delargy. 1998. Financial Crises: Plus ça change, plus c'est la même chose. *International Finance* 1 (2): 261–288.

Goyal, Rishi. 2001. Foreign Exchange Risk and Japan's Liquidity Trap. Ph.D. diss., Stanford University, Stanford, California.

Goyal, Rishi, and Ronald I. McKinnon. 2002. Japan's Negative Risk Premium in Interest Rates: The Liquidity Trap and the Fall in Bank Lending. *The World Economy* 26 (March): 339–363.

Hernández, Leonardo, and Peter Montiel. 2003. Post-Crisis Exchange Rate Policy in Five Asian Countries: Filling in the "Hollow Middle"? *Journal of the Japanese and International Economies* 17: 336–369.

Hicks, John R. 1937. Mr. Keynes and the Classics. *Econometrica* 5 (April).

Hillebrand, Eric, and Günther Schnabl. 2003. The Effects of Japanese Foreign Exchange Intervention GARCH Estimation and Change Point Detection. Japan Bank for International Cooperation Institute Working Paper 6.

Hoshi, Takeo. 1998. Expansionary Monetary Policy Is Precisely the Right Prescription. *Toyo Keizai* (journal). September.

International Monetary Fund. 2000. *Staff Report for the 2000 Article IV Consultation, Japan.* Washington, D.C.

———. 2001. *Staff Report for the 2001 Article IV Consultation, Japan.* Washington, D.C.

———. Various years. *International Financial Statistics.* CD-ROM.

Ito, Takatoshi, and Motoshige Itoh. 1998. Can Targeted 3–4% Inflation Be Achieved by Quantitative Easing? *Toyo Keizai* (journal). September.

Itoh, Motoshige. 1998. Inflation Policy Is Also an Option. *Nihon Kezai Shimbun*, June 25.

Jen, Stephen L. 2000. On the World's Largest Foreign Reserve Holdings. In *FX Pulse* (Morgan Stanley), April 13, 6–7.

Johnson, Harry. 1972. The Case for Flexible Exchange Rates, 1969. In *Further Essays in Monetary Economics*, 198–222. Winchester, U.K.: Allen and Unwin.

Kaminsky, Graciela L., and Carmen M. Reinhart. 1999. The Twin Crises: The Causes of Banking and Balance-of-Payments Problems. *American Economic Review* 89 (3): 473–500.

Kawai, Masahiro. 2002. Exchange Rate Arrangements in East Asia: Lessons from the 1997–1998 Currency Crisis. Bank of Japan Institute for Monetary and Economic Studies Discussion Paper 2002-E-17.

Kawai, Masahiro, and Shigeru Akiyama. 2000. *Implications of the Currency Crisis for Exchange Rate Arrangements in Emerging East Asia.* Washington, D.C.: World Bank East Asia Department.

Kenen, Peter. 1969. The Theory of Optimum Currency Areas: An Eclectic View. In *Monetary Problems of the International Economy,* ed. Robert A. Mundell and Alexander K. Swoboda, 41–60. Chicago: University of Chicago Press.

Keynes, John Maynard. 1936. *The General Theory of Employment, Interest, and Money.* London: Macmillan.

Komiya, Ryutaro. 1994. *Economics of Trade Surpluses and Deficits: Absurdity of Japan-U.S. Friction.* Tokyo: Toyo Keizai Shimpo Sha.

Krugman, Paul. 1993. Lessons of Massachusetts for EMU. In *Adjustment and Growth in the European Monetary Union,* ed. Francisco Torres and Francesco Giavazzi, 241–261. New York: Cambridge University Press.

———. 1998. It's Baaack: Japan's Slump and the Return of the Liquidity Trap. *Brookings Papers on Economic Activity* 2: 137–205.

Kurz, Mordecai. 1994. On the Structure and Diversity of Rational Beliefs. *Economic Theory* 4: 877–900.

Kwan, C. H. 2001. *Yen Bloc: Toward Economic Integration in Asia.* Washington, D.C.: Brookings Institution.

Lane, Philip, and Gian Maria Milesi-Ferretti. 2001. Long-Term Capital Movements. *NBER Macroeconomics Annual 2001.*

Lewis, Karen K. 1999. Trying to Explain Home Bias in Equities and Consumption. *Journal of Economic Literature* 37 (2): 571–608.

McCallum, Bennett. 2000. Theoretical Analysis Regarding a Zero Lower Bound on Nominal Interest Rates. *Journal of Money and Banking* 32 (4): 870–904.

McKinnon, Ronald I. 1963. Optimum Currency Areas. *American Economic Review* 53 (September): 717–724.

———. 1973. *Money and Capital in Economic Development.* Washington, D.C.: Brookings Institution.

———. 1979. *Money in International Exchange: The Convertible Currency System.* New York: Oxford University Press.

———. 1993a. *The Order of Economic Liberalization: Financial Control in the Transition to a Market Economy.* 2d ed. Baltimore: Johns Hopkins Press.

———. 1993b. The Rules of the Game: International Money in Historical Perspective. *Journal of Economic Literature* 31 (1): 1–44.

———. 1996. *The Rules of the Game: International Money and Exchange Rates.* Cambridge, Mass.: MIT Press.

———. 1997. Market-Preserving Fiscal Federalism in the American Monetary Union. In *Macroeconomic Dimensions of Public Finance: Essays in Honour of Vito Tanzi*, ed. Mario I. Blejer and Teresa Ter-Minassian, 73–93. London: Routledge.

———. 2000. The East Asian Dollar Standard: Life after Death? *Economic Notes* [by Banca Monte dei Paschi di Siena] 29: 31–82.

———. 2001a. After the Crisis, the East Asian Dollar Standard Resurrected: An Interpretation of High Frequency Exchange Rate Pegging. In *Rethinking the East Asian Miracle*, ed. Joseph E. Stiglitz and Shahid Yusuf, 197–246. New York: Oxford University Press.

———. 2001b. The International Dollar Standard and the Sustainability of the U.S. Current Account Deficit. *Brookings Papers on Economic Activity* 1: 217–226.

———. 2002. Optimum Currency Areas and the European Experience. *The Economics of Transition* 10 (2): 343–364.

———. 2003. Why Is It a Good Thing for Japan's Economy to Fix the Exchange Rate at 1 dollar = 120 yen? *The Weekly Economist*, Mainichi Press (in Japanese).

———. 2004. The World Dollar Standard and Globalization: New Rules for the Game? In *Exchange Rates, Economic Integration, and the International Economy*, ed. Leo Michaelis and Mark Lovewell, 3–28. Toronto: APF Press.

McKinnon, Ronald I., and Kenichi Ohno. 1997. *Dollar and Yen: Resolving Economic Conflict between the United States and Japan*. Cambridge, Mass.: MIT Press.

———. 2001. The Foreign Exchange Origins of Japan's Economic Slump and Low Interest Liquidity Trap. *The World Economy* 24 (3): 279–315.

McKinnon, Ronald I., and Huw Pill. 1996. Credible Liberalizations and International Capital Flows: The Overborrowing Syndrome. In *Financial Deregulation and Integration in East Asia*, ed. Takatoshi Ito and Anne O. Krueger, 7–42. Chicago: University of Chicago Press.

———. 1999. Exchange Rate Regimes for Emerging Markets: Moral Hazard and International Overborrowing. *Oxford Review of Economic Policy* 15 (Autumn): 19–38.

McKinnon, Ronald I., and Günther Schnabl. 2003. Synchronized Business Cycles in East Asia: Fluctuations in the Yen/Dollar Exchange Rate. *The World Economy* 26 (August): 1067–1088.

Meade, James. 1955. The Case for Variable Exchange Rates. *Three Banks Review* 27 (September): 3–27. Reprinted in *Readings in Money, National Income, and Stabilization Policy*, ed. W. L. Smith and R. L. Teigen. Chicago: Irwin, 1970.

Meltzer, Allan. 1998. Time to Print Money. *Financial Times*, July 17.

———. 1999. Comments: What More Can the Bank of Japan Do? *Bank of Japan Monetary and Economic Studies* 17 (3): 189–191.

Mundell, Robert A. 1961. A Theory of Optimum Currency Areas. *American Economic Review* 51 (November): 509–517.

———. 1963. Capital Mobility and Stabilization Policy under Fixed and Flexible Exchange Rates. *Canadian Journal of Economics and Political Science* 29: 475–485.

———. 1968. *International Economics*. New York: Macmillan.

———. 1973a. Uncommon Arguments for Common Currencies. In *The Economics of Common Currencies*, ed. Harry G. Johnson and Alexander K. Swoboda, 114–132. London: Allen and Unwin.

———. 1973b. A Plan for a European Currency. In *The Economics of Common Currencies*, ed. Harry G. Johnson and Alexander K. Swoboda, 143–172. London: Allen and Unwin.

Mussa, Michael, Paul Masson, Alexander Swoboda, Esteban Jadresic, Paolo Mauro, and Andy Berg. 2000. Exchange Rate Regimes in an Increasingly Integrated World Economy. International Monetary Fund Occasional Paper 193.

New York Federal Reserve Bank. 1998. Treasury and Federal Reserve Operations. April–June.

Nuti, D. Mario. 2000. The Costs and Benefits of Euroisation in Central-Eastern Europe before or instead of EMU Membership. William Davidson Institute Working Paper 340. Ann Arbor: University of Michigan.

Obstfeld, Maurice. 1998. The Global Capital Market: Benefactor or Menace? National Bureau of Economic Research Working Paper 6559.

Ogawa, Eiji, and Takatoshi Ito. 2002. On the Desirability of a Regional Basket Currency Arrangement. *Journal of the Japanese and International Economies* 16: 317–334.

Okina, Kunio. 1999. Monetary Policy under Zero Inflation: A Response to Criticisms and Questions Regarding Monetary Policy. Bank of Japan Institute for Monetary and Economic Studies Discussion Paper 99-E-28.

People's Daily Online. 2003. Japan Wants to Have Renminbi "Demonized": Analysis. March 12. ⟨http://english.peopledaily.com.cn/200303/12/eng20030312_113183.shtml⟩.

Pill, Huw. 1995. Financial Liberalization and Macroeconomic Management in an Open Economy. Ph.D. diss., Stanford University, Stanford, California.

———. 1996. A Simple Model of the Over-Borrowing Syndrome. Harvard Business School Working Paper.

Posen, Adam. 1998. *Restoring Japan's Economic Growth*. Washington, D.C.: Institute for International Economics.

Rajan, Ramkishen. 2002. Exchange Rate Policy Options for Postcrisis Southeast Asia. *The World Economy* 25: 137–163.

Reinhart, Carmen. 2000. The Mirage of Floating Exchange Rates. *American Economic Review* 90: 65–70.

Rhoads, Christopher. 2004. An Emerging Market Bubble? *Wall Street Journal*, January 23, C20.

Rodrik, Dani, Scott Bradford, and Robert Z. Lawrence. 1998. *Has Globalization Gone Too Far?* Washington, D.C.: Institute for International Economics.

Sakaguchi, Chikara. 2000. Japan Has Run Out of Options to Help Boost Fragile Economy. *Financial Times*, May 5, 4.

Sato, Kiyotaka. 1999. The International Use of the Japanese Yen: The Case of Japan's Trade with East Asia. *The World Economy* 22: 547–584.

Schnabl, Günther. 2003. *De jure versus De facto Exchange Rate Stabilization in Central and Eastern Europe.* Tübinger Diskussionsbeitrag No. 269.

Shirakawa, Masaaki. 2001. Monetary Policy under the Zero Interest Rate Constraint and Balance Sheet Adjustment. *International Finance* 4 (3).

Slavov, Slavi. 2002. Should Small Open Economies Keep All Their Eggs in One Basket? The Role of Balance Sheet Effects. Unpublished manuscript.

Smithers, Andrew. 2000. *Japan as a Laboratory for Economic Theory.* Report No. 140. London: Smithers and Co.

Svensson, Lars. 2000. The Zero Bound in an Open Economy: A Foolproof Way of Escaping from a Liquidity Trap. *Bank of Japan Monetary and Economic Studies* 19: 277–306.

Ueda, Kazuo. 1992. *Monetary Policy under Balance-of-Payment Disequilibrium.* Tokyo: Toyo Keizai Shimpo Sha.

———. 1995. Japanese Monetary Policy: Rules or Discretion? Bank of Japan's Seventh International Conference, October 26–27.

Urata, Shujiro. 2001. Emergence of an FDI-Trade Nexus and Economic Growth in East Asia. In *Rethinking the East Asian Miracle*, ed. Joseph E. Stiglitz and Shahid Yusuf, 409–459. New York: Oxford University Press.

Wall Street Journal. 2003. Illicit Inflows Help Chinese Payments Balance. May 13, A12.

Williamson, John. 1994. Estimates of FEERS. In *Estimating Equilibrium Exchange Rates.* Washington, D.C.: Institute for International Economics.

———. 2000. *Exchange Rate Regimes for Emerging Markets: Reviving the Intermediate Option.* Washington, D.C.: Institute for International Economics.

World Bank. 1993. *The East Asian Miracle: Economic Growth and Public Policy.* Oxford: Oxford University Press.

Wren-Lewis, Simon, Rebecca L. Driver, John Williamson, and Molly Mahar. 1998. *Real Exchange Rates for the Year 2000.* Washington, D.C.: Institute for International Economics.

Yoshikawa, Hiroshi. 1990. On the Equilibrium Yen-Dollar Rate. *American Economic Review* 80 (3): 576–583.

Yoshino, Naoyuki, and Masaharu Yoshimura. 1995. The Exogeneity Test of Monetary Policy: Instrumental Targets and Money Supply. Bank of Japan Monetary Research Institute (in Japanese).

Index